An Econometric Approach to a Marketing Decision Model

The MIT Press, Cambridge, Massachusetts, and London, England

An Econometric Approach to a Marketing Decision Model

Ronald E. Frank and William F. Massy

Set in Monotype Baskerville by Viscom International
Printed and bound in the United States of America
by The Colonial Press Inc.

ISBN 0 262 06037 X (hardcover)

Library of Congress catalog card number: 73-122256

ISBN 0 262 56189 1 (paperback)

To Iris and June

Preface

Six years ago the president of a nationally known manufacturing corporation asked the firm's research director to determine the feasibility of developing a model that could serve as an "artificial" test market. If such an artificial test market could be developed, it could serve as a tool for experimenting with a wide range of alternative marketing programs quickly as well as at relatively low cost and risk (in comparison with real-world experiments or tests).

That seemingly simple request led to the development and implementation of the model reported in this monograph.

Though the model is far from the "ultimate" solution to the problem posed by the president (it is continually being modified), the version reported in this book is sufficiently advanced relative to current practice to justify its dissemination in this form. We have also tried to document the several stages of model development, as well as the reasoning that went into our decisions at each stage, in considerable detail. We hope this will provide future model builders with useful insights and suggestions.

In the course of working on a problem of this scale and complexity, many persons play an important role. The most important single contribution to the success of the project was (and still is), in our opinion, the willing cooperation of not only the president but all the senior executives of the corporation that supported the project. They have taken innumerable hours out of their busy schedule to work with us in an effort to achieve the objective. To our knowledge it is still rare in practice for a marketing research department in a corporation, let alone for two consultants, to receive this form of support from top management over a prolonged period. In addition, we are deeply indebted to the firm's research director and his staff. They fully deserve coauthorship, but both they and the sponsoring firm have chosen to remain anonymous.

We should also note that the work reported in this book was substantially completed before the end of 1967, and the manuscript prepared during 1968. In a field that is moving as rapidly as that of marketing models, new developments are to be expected during a three-year period. We have made no attempt to incorporate such developments or references but rather present our work in its original form.

A special word of thanks is due Mollie Horowits and Famah Andrew, who spent many patient hours translating our handwritten hieroglyphics into typed copy.

R. E. F.

W. F. M.

An Econometric Approach to a Marketing Decision Model

1 Objectives and Strategy

Within the short span of sixty years organized systematic inquiry in the field of marketing has shifted from questions concerned primarily with description to those directly related to the needs of decision makers. For instance, in addition to counting the number of objects that fall in a particular category, many current studies focus on the interrelationships between an increasingly broad range of variables. It is no longer uncommon to find household demand studies that simultaneously take into account the relationships of fifteen or twenty household characteristics to the demand for a particular product. In addition to studies aimed at describing marketing phenomena, increasing attention is being addressed to the problem of prescribing which of several alternative courses of action is most appropriate in a given circumstance.

Models that simultaneously take into account the interrelationships between rather sizable numbers of variables and are at the same time primarily designed to serve as tools for evaluating alternative courses of action represent a new type of intellectual effort—an offspring of modern computer and statistical technology.

As this generation of "models of marketing systems" has begun to develop, the concept of a test market in a computer, once regarded as unlikely as a test tube baby, increasingly is becoming more of an objective than a joke.

1.1 Our Objective and Its Context

The purpose of this monograph is to report the creation of a computer model that is designed to serve as an artificial test market that contains sufficient realism to permit it to be used as a tool for evaluating alternative short-run, tactical promotional programs for a manufacturer of a branded, frequently purchased food product.

The product involved is purchased by the vast majority of households in the United States. It is bought on the average at a rate of several packages per month. It is sold predominantly through supermarkets and receives a significant amount of promotion at both manufacturer and retailer levels.

1.2 The Product's Marketing System

Figure 1.1 presents an overview of the product's marketing system. The product predominantly flows from manufacturers to retailers and from retailers to consumers. If a model is to serve as a useful tool for evaluating short-run promotional activities for a given manufacturer, it must include the following characterizations:

1. The response of retailers to manufacturer allowance programs.

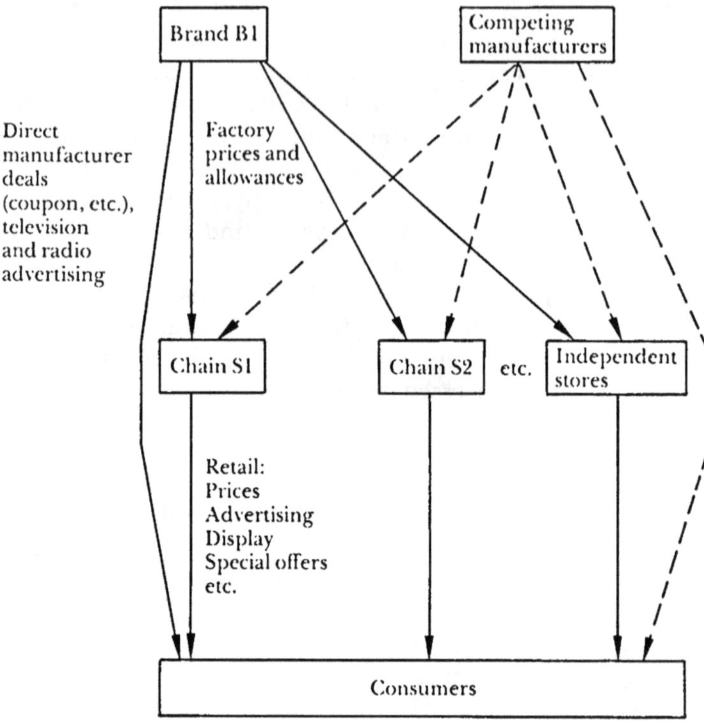

Figure 1.1 The product's marketing system.

2. The response of consumers to retailer promotions in terms of volume changes.
3. The transformation of volume movement figures for the brand into estimates of profit.

If a model fails to characterize adequately either the manufacturer-retailer interface or that for the retailer-consumer, it will be severely limited in its usefulness as an evaluative tool. For example, suppose one wants to know what the expected volume and profit would be by package size if the producer of a brand offered (1) an allowance of $9.26 to retailers for each case of the medium-sized package purchased during a specified six-week period, provided that they advertised the brand at least once; and (2) an additional allowance of $2.38 a case if the retailer would put up a special display for the brand's small-sized package in at least 20 percent of the stores in his chain.

In order to "answer" this question, one first must forecast likely retailer response to such an offer (i.e., how many retailers will accept it? Of those who do, how many will comply with the offer's requirements? Of those who comply, how long will they leave up their displays? and so forth).

Given retailer response, one must forecast, in turn, what will happen to consumer purchases of each size of the product (the promotion might result in the substitution of purchases of one size of the brand for those of another).

In addition to these problems, the model should also make provision for estimating the likely actions of competing brands and their impact on retailers and, ultimately, on consumers.

1.3 Our Model-Building Strategy

The empirical work reported in this monograph provides much of the underpinning for a simulation model designed to serve as a tool for evaluating alternative short-run manufacturer promotional efforts. The model predicts the rates of activity of the principal forms of retailer promotions, such as price discounts, newspaper advertising, displays, signs and banners, special offers, and premiums, as a function of the allowance offerings of the several manufacturers active in the market. (This is the manufacturer-retailer interface discussed in Section 1.2.) Then the simulation program uses these variables as inputs into a consumer demand model that predicts the retail sales of the various brands and sizes. Finally, the model provides summary predictions for sales and market share by class of retail store, the gross margin generated by these sales, and (after costing out the various allowances) the contribution to profit generated by the promotional package of a given manufacturer.

In summary, the simulation model provides a mechanism for relating manufacturer allowance offers to retailer promotional activity to consumer demand (volume movement) for each brand-size combination of the product, and volume movement to the cost of marketing and production and thus to profit. The model is designed to permit the evaluation of a wide range of alternative manufacturer allowance packages. It takes advantage of modern time-sharing computation facilities so as to permit virtually instantaneous assessment of alternatives. Furthermore, it is designed not only to permit, but to encourage, the combining of executive judgments as to the present state of market conditions and probable retailer responses with historical data.

The economic analysis simulation is what has been termed a "data-rich" model, in the sense that its components are based on actual historical data for the market in question. These data have been subject to considerable analysis prior to incorporation in the simulation, particularly in the case of the retailer–consumer demand interface. The advantage of using data-rich rather than hypothetical or "armchair" simulation models should be obvious; only in this way can the researcher —and more importantly, the managers who must use the model for decision-making purposes—be confident that the predictions generated by the model will bear a meaningful relation to market outcomes.[1]

The primary emphasis of this monograph is based on the development of an econometric model relating consumer demand for the various brands and sizes of the product under study to a wide range of retailer promotion variables. (The simulation built around these results will be described in the last chapter of the book.) This work is a logical extension of some of our previously published reports, although the product-market context and sources of data are quite different.

The relation between consumer brand share and retail price and dealing activity was explored by Frank and Massy (1965) and Massy and Frank (1965). These two papers also discussed some of the differences in the estimated parameters among classes of retail stores, package sizes, and consumers who exhibited a tendency to be loyal to the brand in question versus those who spread their purchases among many brands. This model-building effort was extended by Frank and Massy (1967) to include retailer-generated newspaper advertising. That report also included an analysis of response differences by groups of consumers in various socioeconomic and demographic categories. An analysis of the relations between manufacturer allowance offers and retailer advertising activity is reported by Massy and Frank (1966). (This is the only empirical study of the manufacturer-retailer interface for frequently purchased products known to the authors.)

The previous studies all make use of what is called "single-equation" analysis. That is, the demand (in these cases represented by market share) for each brand and size is analyzed one at a time. Although the independent variables in each equation may include measures of the advertising and promotion for other brands and sizes (as is the case when relative price ratios are used, for example), no attempt is made to examine the interrelations between the demands for all brands and sizes simultaneously.

The present study makes use of "multiple-equation" techniques. A model linking the demand for a given brand and size to the demands for all other brands and sizes (or, equivalently, to the promotional activities for each brand and size)

[1]See Massy (1967) for a discussion of some relationships between degree of confidence in marketing decision models and prospects for their implementation.

is postulated. Special statistical methods are required to estimate the parameters of a multiple-equation model; these are developed and discussed where appropriate in the context of this report.

The use of multiple-equation models is relatively new in marketing, although these techniques have been familiar to econometricians for the past twenty years or so. The only other applications to marketing problems known to the authors are those of Farley (1967) and Bass (1967). The former built and tested a model of the distribution and demand structure for personal hygiene products in Jamaica. (Some interesting methodological findings are also discussed in the Farley paper.) The latter reports the development and testing of a model of the relationship between annual cigarette advertising expenditures and sales. It is our opinion that multiple-equation models and estimation methods provide powerful tools for the analysis of marketing phenomena and that their use will increase markedly during the next few years.

1.4 The Need for Coding

Because of the competitively sensitive nature of much of our empirical data and the models built from them, it is necessary for us to code the product-brand information as well as the geographic areas included in the investigation. In addition, the regression coefficients and their standard errors that comprise the results of the multiple-equation model have also been scaled in such a fashion as to preclude a comparison of the relative effects of certain subsets of promotional variables. A more detailed description of the coding procedures used is given in Appendix A. In our opinion, the coding required is a small price to pay for the support required to develop this model as well as for the privilege of being able to make it a part of the professional literature of marketing.

1.5 Organization of the Study

Figure 1.2 presents the steps that were taken in order to develop the model. The study is organized around these steps as follows.

Chapter 2 presents the data collection and checking procedures that were required to generate the data base that was ultimately used to estimate the parameters of our consumer-demand models. This chapter also reports the definitions of demand and promotional variables that were used at the initiation of our model-building efforts.

Chapters 3 to 5 report the steps taken to develop estimates of the effect of retailer promotional behavior on demand.

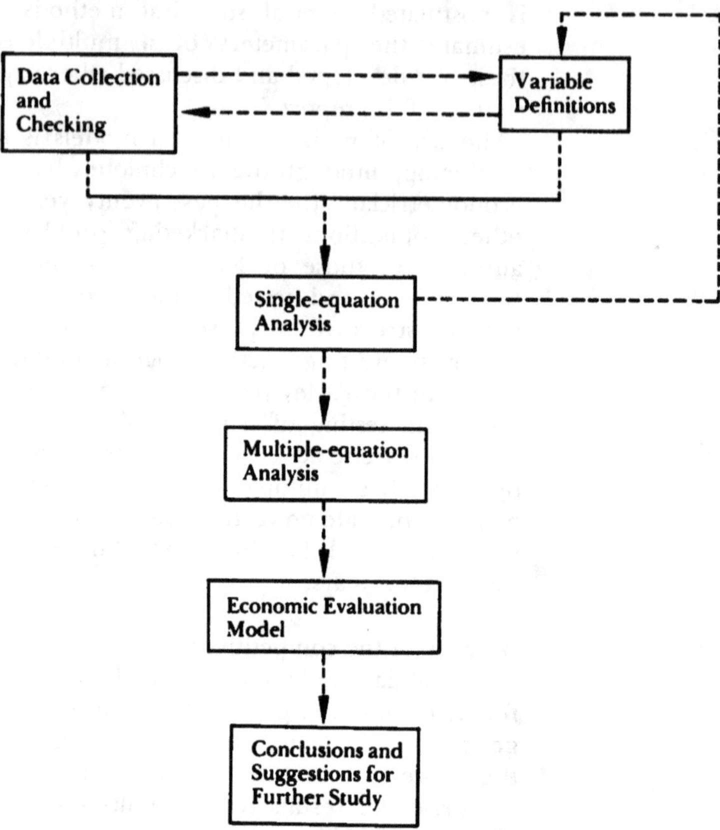

Figure 1.2 Steps in the development of the marketing decision model.

Two classes of statistical procedures are used: single-equation analysis (Chapter 3) and multiple equation analysis (Chapters 4 to 6). Single-equation analysis is used as the basis for performing the first round of model testing and development that we report in Chapter 3. This is followed by a chapter on the theory of the measurement and estimation procedure that underlies the multiple-equation model that we developed. This, in turn, is followed by Chapter 5, reporting a second round of experiments that led to further modifications of the model developed on the basis of single-equation analysis. Next, in Chapters 6 and 7, we report the results of our final analysis of the retailer-consumer interface, based on the final multiple-equation model.

Chapter 8 describes the structure of the "Economic Analysis Simulation Model." Examples of the interaction between man and machine made possible by the model are presented. Comparisons between selected test-allowance packages are reported. Chapter 8 concludes with a discussion of probable future directions for research both in the context of our work and with respect to the larger issue, that is, the development of complex market models.

2 The Data

2.1 Introduction

The objectives of this chapter are (1) to describe the audit that generated the data that serve as the bases for our analysis, and (2) to define the set of variables that were used during the first phase of the investigation, which is reported in the next chapter.

2.2 The Audit

A weekly audit of thirty stores was conducted over a sixty-three-week period in one of the country's largest metropolitan areas. The audit was conducted by a commercial marketing research corporation that specializes in this type of data collection activity. In each week for each of the thirty stores in the panel a detailed record was made of the sales and promotional activity for every existing brand-size combination of the product under investigation.

In addition to the store panel, a separate audit of weekly retail newspaper advertising activity for each of the stores in the panel was conducted by the company sponsoring the study. For every store-brand-size combination in the market a weekly time series of retail advertising activity was generated to match those created from the store audit.

The following sections provide a brief description of the design and content of the two audits.

2.2.1 Time Unit of Observation

A week was chosen as the unit of observation. It is the time unit used by most supermarkets as the basis for the design of their promotional programs. Most stores in this market area initiate their promotion on a Monday (a few on Wednesday or Thursday) and continue them up to and including the following Saturday.

Although a week is the unit of observation, in fact the audit procedure required two visits per week to each store. The weekly audit procedure began with counting in-store inventory (both on the shelf and in the back room) of all sizes and brands and then recording receipts from the warehouse in the past seven days. A condition of permission to audit in many stores was to perform the work on Monday, when business was at its lowest rate. This condition posed no problem as far as auditing sales was concerned, but it was distinctly unfavorable to maintaining a record of in-store merchandising. A typical Monday presented the auditor with empty or depleted shelves and displays and merchandising signs connected with the major sales activity of the previous four to seven days damaged or missing. The record of in-store merchandising activity was therefore made on either Thursday or Friday of each week.

2.2.2
Geographic Area

Three criteria were used to guide the choice of the geographic area that served as the basis for the development of the model:

1. The rate of feature advertisement (those involving unusually large price reductions) for the product under investigation must be above average, so that the area chosen would tend to be similar to a larger set of market areas that are characterized by exceptionally intensive advertised-price promotions. Two years of retail advertising activity were monitored in thirty market areas. These data served as the basis for analyzing the areas in terms of their rate of feature activity.
2. Each of the major national (or near national) brands must be represented in the market, although no one of them dominates it.
3. Seven-day features predominate, as these were typical of a broad range of other market areas.

2.2.3
Store Selection Criteria

Address lists of retail grocers in the market area were obtained from company sources, from some chain grocers, from newspaper advertisements, and from the classified phone directories. These lists were combined with the following types of information:

1. Shipments for each account.
2. Whether or not each account was a house account and/or one of the ten top nonhouse accounts in each company sales territory within the metropolitan area.
3. Frequency of advertising and feature (major) promotions by the 100 most active independent accounts and all chain accounts for the year just prior to the beginning of the audit.

This information enabled us to cull from the list those stores whose volume of business ranked them in the "Ma and Pa" group, and whose lack of promotional activity eliminated them from a study designed to measure the relation of such practices to product sales.

Approximately 350 stores were personally inspected by Market Research Department personnel to obtain the following information as a base for deciding whether to include the store in the sample:

1. Did it have three or more check-out counters?
2. Did it have a product section larger than a specified minimum size?
3. Did it stock the four major brands in the small and medium package sizes as well as any size of one other brand of secondary importance in the market area?
4. Was feature pricing in effect for seven days?

In addition, an attempt was made to include some subsets of the total of thirty stores that were geographically contiguous to one another. One of the principal reasons that a grocer cuts price on a product is the belief that it increases his share of the market. Our desire to measure the effects of such price leading caused us to cluster-sample some of the thirty stores—a cluster being several stores within a mile radius which gave the appearance of competing with one another for the available business. Eighteen of the stores in the panel were located in one of six geographic clusters, while the other twelve were not located close to other stores included in the audit.

2.2.4 Measurements

In addition to the inventory and purchases for every store-brand-size combination, weekly measurements were made of virtually every retail promotional variable that might have an influence on a brand-size's demand, including both in-store promotion and retail advertising activity. These variables included the following:

1. The amount of space devoted to retail newspaper advertisements, together with the price offered in the ad and whether or not a retail coupon was included or trading stamps or some other form of special promotion were offered.
2. The size of a display, if any, as well as its location in the store.
3. The presence or absence of a sign on the display (if a display is present), together with information as to the content of the sign, such as whether it contains only a brand name or a price plus a brand name.
4. Whether or not a shelf marker is present and, if so, what information it contains.
5. Whether or not signs are used in the windows in the store and, if so, what information they contain.
6. The number of shelf facings as well as the height of the shelf and the brands that are to the left and right of the one being measured.
7. The presence and absence as well as the rating of any special offers, such as in-pack or on-pack premiums, reuse packages, coupons toward later purchase, retailer coupons, and combination offers with other products.

In addition to the normal checking procedures followed by the research firm, hundreds of hours were spent by company personnel checking and double-checking the accuracy of the information throughout the entire sixty-three-week period during which the panel was run. Over the entire sixty-three-week period approximately 125,000 store-brand-size-week specific records were generated. Computer programs were written which preprocessed the raw data and outputed the initial set of variables that were used at the start of our analysis.

2.3 Coding Procedures and Initial Variable Definitions

The brands present in the market during the period of the investigation were coded into eight categories: B1 to B6 plus "Store's Major Private" and "Other." The categories B1 to B6 represent the six leading brands in the market, although they are *not* coded in the order of their market shares. There are three package size categories, which are hereafter referred to as small, medium, and large.

In the sections that follow, operational definitions are reported for both demand and promotional variables.

2.3.1 Sales Measures

Sales in units (based on weight) for the product were calculated for each store-brand-size-week combination as the sum of beginning inventory plus receipts minus ending inventory. Two problems arose that necessitated modifying this definition of weekly sales (demand) for the purpose of our analysis. In Sections 2.3.1.1 and 2.3.1.2 each of these problems will be discussed, together with the changes that resulted in our definition of sales.

2.3.1.1 Phase Adjustment

Analysis of early data revealed that on occasion there were very large sales of a store-brand-size combination during unpromoted weeks. In a study of these instances we found that such large sales were occurring immediately before or after a promoted week during which there were smaller sales than might be expected. It was logical to assume that the large sales in the week following a promotion were most likely made during the week of the promotion and simply were inaccurately time-recorded by the store. Inaccurate reporting of high sales during unpromoted weeks even in only a relatively few instances can seriously bias downwards the estimated effects of promotional activity.

To correct this error, a program was written that examined all weekly sales in excess of a specified breakpoint. If there was no promotion during a week with exceptionally high sales, the week before and the week after were checked for promotion. Sales in excess of the breakpoint were then moved one week forward or one week back, depending upon when the promotion was. If no promotion was adjacent, the sales were allowed to stand as recorded. The amount of the breakpoint was chosen so that it would err on the conservative side (i.e., it would result in fewer units of demand being reallocated from one week to another than in fact should be the case).

2.3.1.2
Final Definition of Demand

The study had been designed with the intent that observations from different stores would be pooled together for various analyses. A population of weekly sales observations (after phase adjustment) for a given brand-size combination for, say, all thirty stores, can be thought of as having two principal sources of variation: (1) *between*-stores variation in the level of sales; and (2) *within*-store variation in week-to-week sales. The objective of our study primarily was to determine the effect of promotional activity on week-to-week variation in *within*-store demand and not to explain differences in sales volume *between* stores. We therefore sought a way to adjust the weekly sales figures for each brand-size so as to remove the *between*-store variation in their magnitude. This was done by the following means:

1. Calculating separately for each store-brand-size (720 combinations) the average sales (after phase adjustment) in those weeks during which there was no promotion in that store for the brand-size under consideration (what hereafter we will refer to as "normal" sales for that store-brand-size combination).
2. Dividing the weekly series of actual sales (after phase adjustment) for the store-brand-size being analyzed by its "normal" sales figures.

The resulting quotient is the proportionate increase attributable to promotional activity. By using this transformation it was possible to combine stores that could not otherwise be grouped for the purposes of subsequent analysis. The mnemonic YR_t was adopted to represent our operational definition of demand in week t as the ratio of actual demand (sales) in week t to normal demand.

2.3.2
Promotional Variable Definitions

The following subsections contain mnemonic titles for each of the promotional variables, together with their operational definitions.

2.3.2.1
Advertised-Price Variables

Eight variables were used as a basis for describing the retail advertisement, if any, for a given store-week-brand-size combination. Six of the variables served to categorize a store's retail advertisement for a brand-size combination in a particular week in terms of the amount of discount, if any, represented by an "actual" price at which the brand-size was offered versus the "normal" price for that brand-size in that particular store. (The terms *normal* and *actual* will be defined later in this subsection.) The variables are defined as follows:

1. AD0. Number of square inches devoted to advertisements in which the discount (actual − normal price) for the brand-size is zero.

2. AD1. Number of square inches of ads in which the discount is equal to or less than k (k = actual − normal).

3. AD2. Same as AD1 except for discounts equal to or less than $2k$.

4. AD3. Same as AD1 except for discounts equal to or less than $3k$.

5. AD4. Same as AD1 except for discounts equal to or less than $4k$.

6. AD5. Same as AD1 except for discounts equal to or greater than $5k$.

In addition, two other variables served as measures of the content of advertising, as follows:

7. ILLD. Whether or not the advertisement contained an illustration of the product (1 if yes, 0 if no). This type of coding convention is referred to as a dummy variable. All variables coded in this fashion have a mnemonic title ending with a *D*.

8. COUPD. Whether or not the advertising contains a coupon offering a cents-off cash refund at the time of purchase.

Normal Price: In order to calculate the amount of an advertised-price discount, it was necessary to establish a normal price for each brand-size-store week. References to this normal price use the abbreviation NPL, or Normal Price Level.

Our concept of a normal price was one that changed only when there was a real downward or upward adjustment in the nonpromoted price of the brand, and not one that changed because of tactical price changes by the store or one whose changes were basically errors caused by failure of the store to coordinate the various sources for indicating price—price stamps, shelf markers, shelf signs, display signs and store signs. To effect this concept of real changes, the following rules were established. In a given brand-size-store, if the price for weeks t, $t-1$, and $t-2$ were nonadvertised and were different from $t-3$, the NPL would be recalculated by adding to week t half of the difference between it and week $t-3$. In week $t+1$ the actual price and normal price would be identical. This rule always considered four weeks, t through $t-3$, and operated from the third week of the audit through the sixty-second.

Actual Price: There were six sources of price information: (1) window sign; (2) in-store sign; (3) display sign; (4) price marked on majority of stock; (5) price on the shelf marker; and (6) price shown in the ad. These sources occasionally differed as to price. For these instances, we created a program that examined the price in question with the sales for the current week (t) and the prior week ($t-1$). If there was no promotion in $t-1$, the lowest price was allowed to stand. If there was a promotion in $t-1$, the questionable low price was rejected and the next lowest price from the six sources was taken.

The price discount used to categorize retail ads for the AD0 to AD5 variable specification was simply the difference between the aforementioned normal price and actual price.

2.3.2.2
Unadvertised Price Discounts

There were occasions when the grocer reduced the price of the product but did not advertise it. These in-store price reductions are referred to as UAPs—unadvertised price discounts.

9. UAP. NPL minus actual price for weeks without advertisements. A second unadvertised cents-off type of activity was also recorded as follows:

10. CEOP. Cents-off printed on the package, if any.

2.3.2.3
Displays

11. UODN. Number of units on display.

12. LODD. Location of display (coded 1 if adjacent to the shelf area devoted to the product and 2 if outside this area).

13. SODD. Presence or absence of a sign on display.

14. SODBD. Presence or absence if a sign on display mentioned both brand and price.

15. SODOD. Presence or absence if a sign on display mentioned either the price or brand but not both and/or mentioning information other than price or brand, such as some form of a special offer.

The purpose of variables 14 and 15 was to divide signs into separate categories according to the nature of their content. In practice it amounts to distinguishing between standard-type signs (SODBD) and those involving some form of deviation from normal practice (SODOD).

2.3.2.4
Window Signs

16. SIWD. Any sign in the store window—visible either from inside or out of the store. Marquee-type signs were included in this variable.

17. SIWBD. Sign in window stating brand only and no other information. Of course, SIWD must be active for this variable to occur.

18. SIWOD. All other types of window signs excluding those described in SIWBD (e.g., signs stating price or some form of special offer).

2.3.2.5 In-Store Signs

19. SISD. Any sign in the store.
20. SISBD. Any sign in the store mentioning brand only.
21. SISOD. Any other sign in the store.

2.3.2.6 Shelf Markers

22. SFMD. Any shelf marker.
23. SFMPD. Any shelf marker containing a price.
24. SFMOD. All other shelf markers not included in SFMPD, such as those mentioning brand only or the brand and a special offer.

2.3.2.7 Special Offers

25. SPOD. Any special offer.
26. SPOPD. A special offer employing an in- or on-pack premium.
27. SPORD. A special offer involving a reusable package.
28. SPOCD. A special offer utilizing a retailer coupon.
29. SPOOD. All other special offers, such as a coupon for later purchase or a combination price with another product.

2.3.2.8 Shelf Position

30. TOFN. Total number of facings.
31. SLFD. Whether or not the shelf on which the particular brand-size combination was stocked was at least two shelves from the floor.

2.3.2.9 Competing Promotions, Same Store

32. ZFM. Whether or not another of the top four brands in the market was on promotion in the week under consideration in the same store.

2.3.2.10 Competing Promotions, Other Stores

Four variables were used as measures of the magnitude of competing store advertised-price promotions and their coverage. Two of them served as measures of the magnitude of the price discount offered by competing stores and two as measures of the number of stores offering advertised-price promotions. They were as follows:
33. CPE. Maximum competitive price discount for the "same brand-size combination" in a competing store. By the same brand-size combination we mean the same one for which the variable appears as a predictor. For example, if an equation were developed for B1 medium-sized packages, then this variable would be the maximum price difference between the store whose demand is being predicted and stores that are its principal competitors. For example, this variable was

equal to 80 in store A for medium-size B1 if (1) store B advertised medium-size B1 for 80¢ off regular price in the same week, and (2) store B was the competing store offering the lowest price for medium-sized packages of B1.

34. CNE. Number of competitive stores advertising the same brand and size in the same week. For example, this variable was equal to 5 if 5 competing stores advertised at a discount medium-size B1 in the same week.

35. CPM. Maximum competitive price discount for another major brand in a competing store. For example, this variable was equal to $2.60 for B1 in store A if store B advertised B2 at $2.60 off and that store offer was the greatest discount below A's prices for medium-sized packages for brands other than B1.

36. CNM. Number of competitive stores advertising a major brand in the same size-week. For example, the variable would equal 5 if 5 competing stores advertised at a discount any brand other than B1.

2.3.2.11 Carry-Over Effects of Promotional Variables

Our previous modeling activity (Frank and Massy, 1967) in markets of this type led us to believe that the effect of a promotion conducted in week *t* would probably "carry over" into subsequent time periods. The carry-over could be either positive or negative in magnitude. Positive carry-over effects might be incurred if a promotion caused a basic change in customer preferences that lasted beyond the actual time of the promotion, whereas a negative carry-over effect would be found if customers tended to stock up (i.e., if all the promotion was doing was shifting the time distribution of demand and not increasing total demand). Our past experience led us to believe that the stronger of these two forces would be the stocking-up effects. Two variables were included in the initial formulation of our analysis in order to measure the direction and magnitude of any carry-over effects. They were as follows:

37. YR_{t-1}
38. YR_{t-2} The ratio of actual sales (after phase adjustment) to normal sales one week prior to the current week $(t-1)$ and two weeks prior to the current week $(t-2)$.

Equations that incorporate these terms are derived from a model that assumes that the effect of each variable dies away to zero according to an exponential decay law. The model was first introduced by Koyck (1954) and will be discussed in more detail in Chapter 3.

2.4 Summary

The aforementioned variables served as the basis for initiating the analysis that led ultimately to the development of a multiple-equation model. In the chapter that follows we will report the initial experiments that led to the formulation of the market model.

3
Single-Equation Analysis
3.1 Introduction

In order to build a multiple-equation model that would provide a useful representation of the market under investigation, questions such as the following must be answered:

1. Of the promotional variables that we originally intended to include in our analysis, are there any that are active so infrequently as to make their inclusion in the final model of little use?
2. What is the degree of multicollinearity among the independent variables? That is, are there two or more variables whose nominal definitions are different, but which in fact seem to measure the same type of promotional behavior? To the extent that this occurs, the number of variables in the analysis can be reduced with little or no loss of information; conversely, to include all such variables invites statistical instability.
3. Are the effects of certain variables, such as advertising, linear, or does some nonlinear transformation (such as the square of the advertising variables) constitute a more appropriate working hypothesis?
4. Are the stores in the panel reasonably homogeneous as to the response of demand to changes in promotional variables? To the extent that responses to promotional variables differ from one type of store to another (e.g., high-volume versus low-volume stores—with respect to this product's sales—or one chain versus another), then separate multiple-equation runs should be made for each store category.
5. To what extent do the effects of certain promotional variables interact with the level of others? For example, does the effect of an SIWD depend on the extent, if any, of a UAP? If interactions such as these are important, the multiple equation model should be specified so as to take them into account.

The resolution of issues such as these required the execution of an extensive set of analyses. Although it would have been desirable to use the same statistical procedure for conducting them as was to be used for the final analysis, three factors led us to go in a different direction:

1. To our knowledge, no statistical program existed at the time we initiated the study that would be capable of doing the type of analysis we anticipated.
2. We were operating under a time constraint that would not leave us enough time to write and debug such a program and then start the analysis.
3. We estimated that the probable running time for the statistical package we envisioned, even on an IBM 7094, would make it too expensive a tool to use as a basis for conducting the initial exploration required to develop the final model.

We therefore decided to use single-equation analysis for the explorations. This procedure is not as satisfactory as the multiple-equation analysis as it does not take into account the interrelations between the demand and promotional activities for a given package size for different brands, let alone those associated with the eight brand categories for different package sizes.

3.2 Logical flow of the Analysis

Figure 3.1 reports the steps taken in the single-equation analysis. There are three stages to the analysis, each of which is represented by one of the three rows of boxes in the figure. The first stage consists of the steps taken to arrive at the initial formulation of the single-equation model; next is the differential response analysis (i.e., the study of whether or not responses to policy variables vary by store type); and last is a series of experiments that led to a further reformulation of the model. Section 3.4 discusses the initial formulation of the model. Sections 3.5 and 3.6 report the results of the differential response analysis, and Section 3.7 presents the experiments aimed at reformulating the model. (The rationale for evaluating the analysis represented by each box in the flow diagram is presented along with the report of the respective results.)

The results reported in Section 3.4 are based on a fifteen-week data period—namely, weeks 9 to 23 of the store audit. We chose to avoid the first eight weeks, as the error rate in the data was originally higher than we desired. At the time that this phase of the work was initiated, the data for the first five weeks (during which most of the recording errors occurred) were still being corrected. The findings in Sections 3.5 to 3.7 are based both on the fifteen-week data and on a thirty seven-week period (weeks 1 to 37).

3.3 A Methodological Comment on the Single-Equation Variable Specifications

For the single-equation analysis, regression runs are specific to a given brand and size. The dependent variable is the sales ratio for store and week (or the square root of the sales ratio —see Section 3.4.3). The independent variables are measures of the absolute magnitude of promotional activity for the brand-size combination under study, together with lagged values of the sales ratio.

Normally for a market such as this, one would express a brand's promotional activity in *relative* as opposed to absolute terms. For example, one might specify AD5 activity as a ratio of the AD5 activity of the brand-size under investigation to an average of the AD5 activity for competing brands. The single-equation analysis that we shall report did not specify promotional variables in this fashion. Instead, the *absolute* amount of

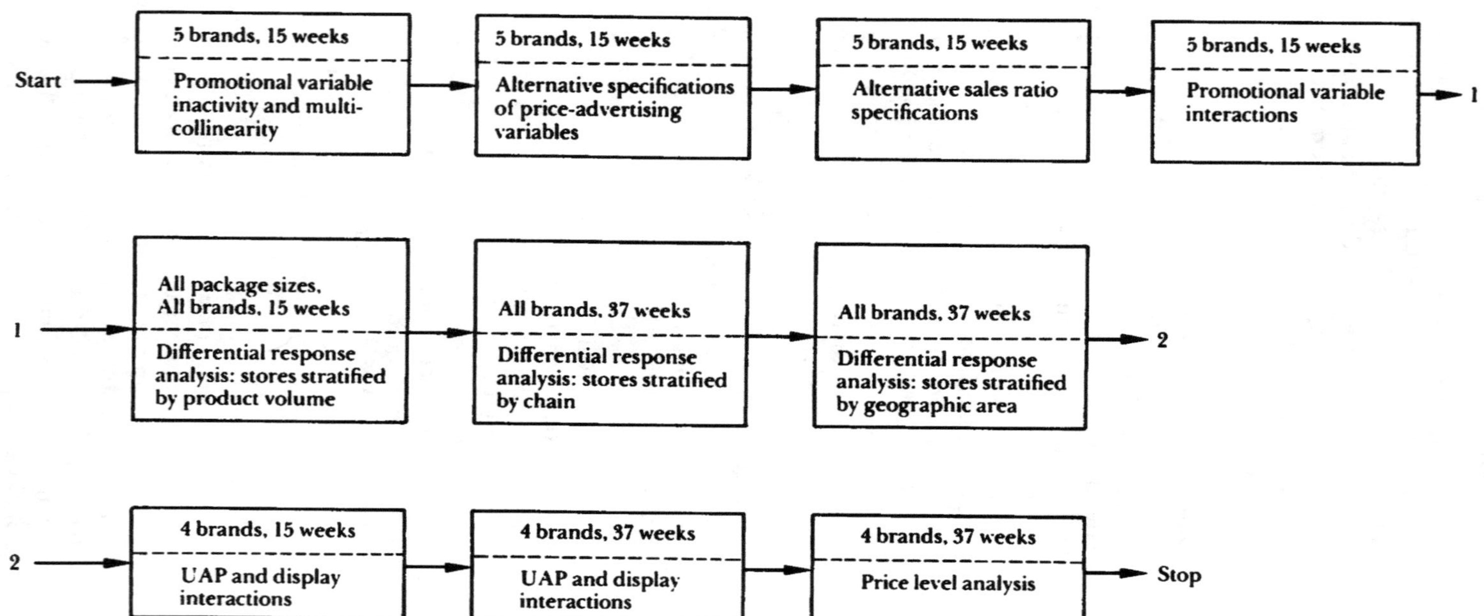

Figure 3.1 Steps in single-equation analysis.

*Except where indicated, the analysis is based on the medium-size package market segment, which is the most heavily promoted of the three package size categories.

an AD5 for the brand-size under study is used as a measure of this type of promotional activity. In a similar fashion, absolute quantities are used as measures of the other components of a given brand-size promotional program.

While these specifications are probably not optimal for a single-equation analysis, they are designed to correspond as closely as possible to those that are appropriate for the multiple-equation model. A multiple-equation model takes into account the relative promotional activity of brands in a market in a different fashion than does a single-equation model. This will be discussed in detail in Chapter 4.

Although we did not use relative measures of promotional activity in the single-equation analysis, it is quite likely that our results corresponded closely to what would be obtained if they had been used. If we computed the simple correlation between the absolute measure that we used and a measure of relative promotion for a given brand-size, the correlation would be relatively high. In other words, the absolute variable specifications can be thought of as surrogates for the relatives. The reasoning behind this conclusion is as follows:

1. It is exceedingly rare that a given store promotes more than one brand in a size category at a time.
2. This means that if relatives are used, they would tend to have a value of zero (no promotion for the brand under study and some for one or more competing brands), an infinite value (some promotional activity for the brand under study and none for competing brands), or a value of one when there was no promotional activity for any of the brands in a given size category. This product, especially the medium-size container, is promoted quite frequently by most stores, and therefore the most frequent values of a relative measure of promotion would be zero or infinity.
3. If a relative measure is zero in a given week, an absolute measure of activity would also be zero. If a relative measure is infinity, an absolute measure of activity would be a nonzero value. (For most of the variables in the model it would be one as they are dummy variables.)
4. Therefore, the absolute and relative measures tend to be highly correlated. The only important difference between the two is that when the absolute measure is zero the relative measure can be either zero or one. This qualification is less important for medium-size packages than it is for the small and large sizes. However, the medium size is the focus of most of the promotional activity in this market.

3.4 Initial Formulation of the Model

The initial formulation of the single-equation model consisted of the following four steps: (1) deletion of inactive and collinear variables; (2) analysis of nonlinear effects; (3) study of the stability (homoscedasticity) of the variance about the regression surface; and (4) analysis of selected interactions between promotional variables.

3.4.1 Variable Deletion

At the start of our analysis, the extent of activity and collinearity were checked for each variable listed in Section 2.3 in order to determine which, if any, of the promotional variables would have to be deleted from the study. Of the thirty-six promotional variables, fifteen were deleted. Three of these were virtually inactive, eight were collinear with one or more of the other variables, and six were deleted for other reasons.

3.4.1.1 Inactive Variables

The following dummy variables were eliminated from the analysis because their rates of activity were so modest that they precluded our assessing their effects:

1. SODBD. This is an indicator of the presence or absence of a sign containing brand name as well as price and/or cents-off information on a display. This variable had a zero rate of activity for all brands.
2. SIWBD. This variable is a measure of whether a sign promoting the product, appearing in the window of a store, included only the brand name. It is also inactive for all brands.
3. SISBD. This variable indicates whether or not an in-store sign promoting the product contains the name of a specific brand. It is completely inactive for all brands except B5, where it is active only 0.9 percent of the time.

3.4.1.2 Collinear Variables

The bulk of the collinearity analysis is based on results for brands B1, B2, and B5. Some of the work also involves B4. As a result, the following variables have been eliminated:

1. SODOD. Its simple correlation with SODD is 1.0 for B1, B2, and B5.
2. SIWOD. It also has a simple correlation of 1.0 with SIWD for all three brands.
3. SISOD. Its simple correlation with SISD is 1.0 for both B1 and B2 and .84 for B5.
4. CNM. Its simple correlation with CPM by brand is as follows: B1, .80; B2, .80; B4, .82; and B5, .79.
5. CNE. Its simple correlation with CPE by brand is as follows: B1, .86; B2, .89; B4, .89; and B5, .92.

The variables CPM and CPE (which were not deleted) measure the "scale of competing store promotions" for the same brand and size, as well as for other brands in the same size as the one being studied. The scale of competitive action, in this context, can be thought of as having two dimensions: the level of advertised price associated with competitive promotion (CPM and CPE), and the number of competing stores engaged in competitive promotion (CNE and CNM).

Five measures of special offer activity are listed in Section 2.3.2.7: (1) whether or not any form of a special offer is made (SPOD); (2) in- or on-pack premium (SPOPD); (3) reuse pack (SPORD); (4) a retailer coupon (SPOCD); and (5) all other types of special offers (SPOOD). For all the brands, the dominant forms of special offer activity are either SPOPD or SPORD. By definition they are going to be highly correlated with SPOD. Thus SPOD was deleted rather than SPOPD and SPORD so as to be able to evaluate separately the effects of each of the two types of special offers.

The collinearity that leads to the deletion of the first three variables reflects the fact that when a sign appears promoting a brand (whether it is on a display, a window, or some other place in a store), it virtually always contains more information about the offer than just the name of the brand.

3.4.1.3 Miscellaneous Deletions

Six variables were deleted for reasons other than their inactivity or collinearity. They are as follows:

1. SPOOD. The content of this variable is so heterogeneous as to make its interpretation meaningless.[1]

2. TOFN. This variable is eliminated from the single-equation analysis because the number of rows and shelf positions for major brands simply does not vary from week to week.

3. SFMD is not eliminated because of misunderstanding of its definition during this phase of work. It appears in the results for the differential response analysis in Sections 3.5 to 3.7, but is deleted from the multiple-equation runs reported in Chapter 6. Fortunately, this variable is virtually uncorrelated with both the dependent variable and the other independent variables and therefore does not seriously bias any of the results that are reported.

4. SFMPD and SFMOD. These variables are deleted for two reasons: (1) Shelf markers carried information other than just price in fewer than 1 percent of the weeks for all but one of the brands. The only exception is for B5, for which fewer than 3 percent of the shelf markers contain information in addition to price. (2) Several of the first regressions that were

[1]This variable is included in the differential response analysis for small package size, where we thought it might be of some importance.

run to check on multicollinearity produced results that supported the contention that the presence or absence of a shelf marker is important and that variations in content are not.

5. ILLD and COUPD. Neither ILLD or COUPD is included in the first four steps in the initial formulation of the model, as they were unavailable at that time. They are not included, therefore, in the reporting of single-equation results. They did become available after the differential response analysis was completed. Regression analysis for each of the eight brands involving the remaining twenty-one variables (Section 3.4.1.4), together with ILLD and COUPD, was run on all package sizes. The ILLD added virtually nothing to either predictive efficacy or structural insight, whereas the COUPD variable was highly collinear with SPOCD. We did not redo the portion of the differential response analysis that had been completed. The variables are deleted from further consideration in the study.

3.4.1.4 Summary of Remaining Variables

Fifteen variables were deleted from the original list of thirty-six appearing in Section 2.3.2. The remaining twenty-one variables serve as the basis for virtually all the single-equation analysis to be reported in this chapter. The twenty-one variables are as follows:

1. AD0	8. CEOP	15. SPOPD
2. AD1	9. UODN	16. SPORD
3. AD2	10. LODD	17. SPOCD
4. AD3	11. SODD	18. SLFD
5. AD4	12. SIWD	19. ZFM
6. AD5	13. SISD	20. CPE
7. UAP	14. SFMD	21. CPM

In addition YR_{t-1} and YR_{t-2} are included in these regressions to allow for possible carry-over effects.[2]

3.4.2 Nonlinear Effects

Using the set of twenty-one variables reported in the previous section, two alternative hypotheses were examined as to the nature of the effect of the advertising-price variables on demand (YR_t) for a given package size of a brand. The first hypothesis is that demand increases as a linear function of the amount of retailer advertising space devoted to it in a given

[2]The exact number of variables in a given equation varied somewhat from one result to the next. The variables that were deleted up to this point could not be salvaged for inclusion in the regression runs for any of the brand-size combinations. Of the list of twenty-one variables, some of them were completely inactive or highly collinear in the case of one brand-size combination as opposed to another and therefore do not appear in all the equations.

week. The alternative hypothesis is that demand depends on the presence or absence of an advertisement and not on its size.

Advertising variables AD0 and AD2 through AD5[3] were included in a linear regression, together with the other fourteen promotional variables, to serve as the basis for evaluating the first hypothesis. In order to examine the second hypothesis, the advertising price variables were transformed to dummy variables (i.e., zero if no advertising and one if an ad occurred).

The two aforementioned regressions were run for each of five brands for the medium-size packages. The resulting coefficients of determination (R^2's) are reported in Table 3.1. In the case of three of the brands, B2, B4, and B5, the dummy variable transformation (i.e., the alternative hypothesis) resulted in a marked increase in predictive efficacy. For one brand, B4, the R^2 increased by only one percentage point. The only brand for which the dummy variable transformation resulted in a lower R^2 is B3, which went from an R^2 of .73 before transformation to .64.

In spite of the contradictory evidence associated with the B3 results, we decided to adopt the dummy variable specifications for AD0 through AD5. We discounted the B3 results for two reasons:

1. It is not as important a brand in terms of its effect on promotional practices in the area as are the other four brands.
2. Its average rate of AD0–AD5 activity for the medium package size is considerably less (by about two-thirds) than that for the other four brands. Three of the advertising variables are completely inactive (AD0, AD1, and AD2), while the other three are active an average of only 1.2 weeks out of 100. Comparable weeks out of 100 for the other four brands are B1, 3.8; B2, 4.0; B4, 2.5; and B5, 3.8. We felt that B3's results should be discounted due to the relatively low rate of experience associated with the presence of advertising-price promotional activity.

3.4.3. Homoscedasticity Transformation

An analysis of the residuals associated with the regressions used for checking collinearity revealed that the variance of the error in estimating YR increases roughly as a linear function of the forecasted value of YR (i.e., the error is heteroscedastic). The standard linear regression model assumes that the error term is constant (homoscedastic). In order to stabilize the variance, we experimented with a square root transformation of YR_t. (YR_{t-1} and YR_{t-2} are also subjected to

[3]AD1 is excluded because of its low level of activity.

Table 3.1 Coefficients of Determination for Raw Variable and Dummy Variable Specifications of Price-Advertising Variables for Five Major Brands (medium-size packages)

Brand	Raw Variable	Dummy Variable
B1	.66	.67
B2	.40	.58
B3	.73	.64
B4	.62	.70
B5	.51	.62

the square root transformation to maintain consistency with YR_t.)

Our evaluation of this square root transformation is based on contrasting the result of two alternative regression runs for each of five brands (B1 to B5).

The variables included in the regressions are listed as follows:

AD0	UODN	SLFD
AD2	SODD	LFM
AD3	SISD	CPE
AD4	SFMD	CPM
AD5	SPOPD	YR_{t-1}
UAP	SPORD	YR_{t-2}
CEOP	SPOCD	

The advertising-price variables are transformed to dummy variables. The only difference between the two models is that in one the YR terms are transformed by taking their square root and in the other no transformation is performed.

The results provided support for the use of the square root transformation. With the exception of B3 the coefficient of determination increased as a result of the square root transformation. In addition, the t-ratios for the advertising-price variables (which are the major determinants of demand) also increased. The coefficients of determination for each brand are as follows:

	YR	
	Raw	Square Root
B1	.67	.74
B2	.58	.74
B3	.67	.65
B4	.70	.74
B5	.62	.69

The low rate of retail advertising activity for B3 probably accounts for its deviation from the pattern established by the other four brands. The error variance for B3 is more stable before transformation than for the other brands. The extreme expected values of YR for which the conditional variance tended to be the highest occurred less often for B3 than for the other brands. They are primarily associated with retail advertising activity. Hence the transformation may be somewhat less appropriate for that brand than the others.

The findings with respect to the t-ratios are essentially the same as those for B5, except in the case of B3.

Based on these results, the square root transformation of the YR variable was incorporated into our model.

3.4.4 Interactions

An interaction is defined as the existence of a relationship between the *effect* of one independent variable and the *level* of another. For example, suppose that we are interested in evaluating the effects of an unadvertised price discount (UAP) and the amount of any cents-off offer printed on a package (CEOP). One hypothesis is that the effects of both variables are linear and independent of each other. This hypothesis can be written in the form of a regression equation, as follows:

$$\mathrm{YR}_t = a + b_1\mathrm{UAP}_t + b_2\mathrm{CEOP}_t.$$

According to this model, the effect of UAP, b_1, in no way depends on the magnitude of CEOP. An alternative hypothesis is that the effect of a UAP would be greater when associated with a cents-off offer on a package. One way to evaluate this hypothesis is to contrast the result associated with the previous model with the following one:

$$\mathrm{YR}_t = a + b_1\mathrm{UAP}_t + b_2\mathrm{UAPCEOP}_t,$$

where $\mathrm{UAPCEOP}_t$ is the cross-product of UAP_t and CEOP_t. This equation can be rewritten as follows:

$$\mathrm{YR}_t = a + b^*\mathrm{UAP}_t,$$

where

$$b^* = b_1 + b_2\mathrm{CEOP}_t.$$

The magnitude of the coefficient of UAP, b^*, now is a linear function of the magnitude of CEOP_t.

In addition to this interaction hypothesis, the following five additional hypotheses were investigated.[4]

1. SIWUAP. The effect of SIWD is positively correlated with the level of UAP.
2. NSIUAP. The effect of a sign either in-store or on the window is positively correlated with the magnitude of UAP.
3. UODNLO. The effect of a product display outside the product's section is increased by the presence of a sign in the window or in the store.
4. UODNP. The effect of a display is increased if it is accompanied by a relatively large UAP (i.e., a UAP that is greater than the maximum price discount for an AD2 advertisement).
5. UODNO. The effect of a display is increased if it is accompanied by either an AD0 or an AD1 type advertisement.

The aforementioned interactions were tested for each of the five brands listed in Table 3.2. For each brand, four sets of seven regressions were run. Six of the regressions analyzed the effects of one of the interactions, while the seventh regression served as a "base model" against which the results of the interaction regressions could be compared. The base model consisted of the twenty-one promotional variables that remained after the inactivity and collinearity checks that were previously reported. The advertising variables in the base model are dummy variables. Included in the base model are the square root of YR_{t-1} and YR_{t-2}. The dependent variable is the square root of YR_t. Each interaction regression differed from the base model in a fashion analogous to the previously discussed UAPCEOP example. That is, the interaction term was added and one of the independent variables that comprised it was deleted.

One set of seven regressions is based on the entire thirty-store, fifteen-week data base. The other three sets were based on ten large, medium, and small stores, respectively. (A store's size is measured in terms of its sales of the product category being studied.)

Table 3.2 reports the coefficients of determination for each of the regressions. Of the 140 regressions that were run, only 73 yielded results. The remainder either had a zero rate of

[4]We had hoped to conduct three other interaction analyses. They would have evaluated the following hypotheses: (1) that the effect of an in-store sign is positively correlated with the magnitude of UAP; (2) that the effect of a display in the product section is increased if it is accompanied by a window or in-store sign; (3) that the effect of a display is increased if it is associated with no price discount or a modest one (AD0 or AD1 type advertising). Unfortunately, the promotional combination defined by each interaction term occurred too infrequently to permit any analysis.

Table 3.2 Coefficients of Determination for Base Model and Base Model Plus Each of Six Interaction Terms by Brand and Store-Volume Category

Interaction	Brands				
	B1	B2	B3	B4	B5
All Stores					
Base Model	.74	.67	.64	.74	.69
UAPCEOP	.74	*	.64	*	.69
SIWUAP	.74	.67	—	.74	—
NSIUAP	.77	.67	.64	.74	.69
UODNLO	.74	.67		—	.69
UODNP	.74	.67		—	.69
UODNO	.74	.67	—	—	—
Large Stores					
Base Model	.72	.86	.79	.79	.81
UAPCEOP	.72	.86	.79	.79	.81
SIWUAP	.72	*	—	—	—
NSIUAP	*	*	.79	.79	.81
UODNLO	.72	—		—	—
UODNP	*	—		—	.81
UODNO	.72	*	—	—	—
Medium Stores					
Base Model	.86	.70	.43	.81	.81
UAPCEOP	.86	.70	.43	.81	.81
SIWUAP	—	—	—	—	—
NSIUAP	.86	.70	.43	.81	.81
UODNLO	*	*	—	—	.81
UODNP	*	*	—		.81
UODNO		.71	—	—	—
Small Stores					
Base Model	.76	.77	.61	.81	.69
UAPCEOP	.76	*	.61	*	.69
SIWUAP	—	—	—	.81	—
NSIUAP	.76	.77	.61	.81	.69
UODNLO	—	—	—	—	—
UODNP		—	—	—	—
UODNO	—	—	—	—	—

— Interaction variable was zero across all observations.
*Computational failure due to complete collinearity of interaction terms with one or more other independent variables.

activity for the interaction term or else the degree of collinearity between the interaction term and the remaining variable was so great as to lead to a computational failure on the part of the regression program.

If our hypotheses represent important aspects of the market's actual behavior, one would expect the regressions with the interaction terms present to do a better job of predicting the YR series and/or cause changes in the effects of one or more of the variables previously included in the model (i.e., structural changes). A contrast of the predictive efficacy of the base model regression with each of the six interactions for each of the twenty sets of seven equations led to the conclusion that these interactions contributed nothing to the goal of prediction. In only one case is the coefficient of determination for an interaction greater than that for the base model, namely, the NSIUAP interaction for B1 based on the pooled data for all thirty stores.

In addition, the interaction terms failed to make an important positive contribution to our understanding of the structure.

3.4.5 Summary

As a result of the analysis reported in Section 3.4 the twenty-one variables listed in 3.4.1.4 were adopted as the basis of the "store differences in response" and the carry-over effects analysis reported in the following two sections. In addition, the dummy variable specification was adopted for AD0 through AD5, as was the square root transformation for YR variables.

3.5 Store Differences in Response

The primary objective of the differential response analysis for stores is to answer this question:

Are there differences in the response of demand to promotional activity between various market segments, such as: (1) Stores that do a "high, medium, or low volume" of business for the product category? (2) Stores that belong to one chain as opposed to another? (3) Stores that are located in one geographic area as opposed to another?

The answer is extremely important. To the extent that response differences do exist between stores, they must be taken into account in designing the multiple-equation model. For example, if high-volume stores show a considerably greater sensitivity to promotional activity than stores in the medium or low group, a separate set of estimates for the multiple-equation model should be used to describe them. In effect, the more differences observed in responses by type of store, the more complex is the final set of multiple equation models required to represent the market area adequately.

The analyses required to answer the differential response questions will also be used to answer one other question that must be faced prior to the multiple-equation runs, namely: Are the effects on demand in a given week due to promotional activities in *preceding* weeks of sufficient importance to necessitate provision for their measurement (i.e., is there a need to include the lagged YR values, the purpose of which was to measure carry-over effects of promotional activity)?

Our answers to both of these questions, together with supporting evidence, are presented in Sections 3.5.1 and 3.5.2.

3.5.1 Variation in the Activity and Effects of Promotional Variables by Store Group

Three alternative bases for store stratification are investigated, namely, (1) store volume, (2) the chain to which a store belongs, and (3) the geographic area in which it is located.

A more extensive analysis was conducted for stratification based on volume than for either of the other two alternatives. Within each of the three package size segments, regression runs were made by brand for all stores as well as for each of the three store volume categories in which the number of observations was greater than fifty.[5] The brand-size combinations included in the volume analysis are as follows: small size B1 to B5; medium size—B1, B2, B4, B5; large size—B2. All runs are based on fifteen-week data. The independent variables that are used in the differential response analysis are as follows:

AD0	UAP	SIWD	SPOPD	CPE
AD1[6]	CEOP	SISD	SPORD	CPM
AD2	UODN	SFMD	SPOCD[6]	YR_{t-2}
AD4	LODD	SILLD[7]	SLFD	YR_{t-3}
AD5	SODD	SCOUPD[7]	ZFM	YR_t

Both the chain and geographic analyses were run on the thirty-seven-week data base for medium-size packages only. These two analyses were run for brands B1, B2, B4, and B5.

The larger data base is required because of the number of chain and geographic categories for which we deemed it desirable to make separate regression runs for each of the brands. Nine chain categories (S1 to S8, plus an "other stores"

[5] There are ten stores in each volume category.

[6] These variables appear in some regression runs but not in others, due to variations in the degree of activity and collinearity from one store segment to another.

[7] These are included in the small- and large-size regressions but not the medium-size runs.

category) and seven geographic ones (G1 to G6, plus an "other areas" category) were included in the analysis.

Three sets of data are presented as a basis for our evaluation of variations in response by store segments: (1) the extent to which each store group made use of the different promotional variables; (2) differences in the effect of the promotional variables from group to group; and (3) differences in the extent to which each group's weekly demand is predicted by the single-equation model.

Table 3.3 reports summary statistics for each of the three approaches to store stratification. These results are averages from regression runs on the data for medium-size packages for the top four brands in the market. The first column gives the proportion of regression coefficients in a particular store segment that are greater than in their "base" group. The base groups are the "other" categories for both the store identity and geographic analysis and the "medium" category for the volume analysis. Variables that are active either in the category being compared or in its base category, but not in both, are excluded from the calculation.

These statistics are by far the most important ones in the table for the purpose of determining how to stratify our sample of stores. Ideally, one would like to group together stores that are similar in terms of their response to promotion. The closer one comes to achieving within-group similarity, the greater will be the between-group differences.

3.5.1.1 Store Versus Geographic Stratification

There is a greater degree of variation in response to the promotional variables between store identity categories than between geographic areas. The range and standard deviation for the store identity analysis are 40.8 and 12.5 percent, respectively, while the same statistics for the geographic grouping are 24.7 and 9.6 percent. On the basis of response to promotional variables, the store identity system of stratification is superior. However, this measure does not provide a complete picture. Store segments vary not only with respect to the response of *demand given a particular form of promotional activity* but also in terms of their mix of promotional activities.

Column (2) of Table 3.3 presents the average percentage of weeks that AD3, AD4, and AD5 promotions are used in each store segment, while column (3) reports the average percentage of UAP activity. These variables tend to be the most highly correlated with YR of any of the promotional variables.

The variation in AD3, AD4, and AD5 activity from one store segment to another is also greater for the store identity runs than for the geographic runs. However, the same is not the

Table 3.3 Summary of Differential Response Results (medium-size package)

Basis of Stratification	Percent of Coefficients Greater than Base (1)	Average Percent AD3–AD5 (2)	Percent UAP (3)	R^2 (4)	Number of Stores (5)
Store Identity					
S1	**54.8**	**2.6**	**21.4**	**.72**	**2**
S2	**29.0**	**0.3**	**24.7**	**.21**	**4**
S3	**41.5**	**5.8**	**17.3**	**.58**	**3**
S4	**56.1**	**6.1**	**9.3**	**.71**	**3**
S5	**28.6**	**0.0**	**22.3**	**.00**	**3**
S6	**69.4**	**4.5**	**5.0**	**.83**	**2**
S7	**52.6**	**5.4**	**20.8**	**.68**	**2**
S8	**29.8**	**1.7**	**18.2**	**.20**	**2**
Other	**Base**	**4.7**	**14.3**	**.63**	**10**
Standard Deviation	**12.5**	**2.2**	**6.1**	**.28**	
Range	**40.8**	**6.1**	**19.7**	**.83**	
Geographic Area					
G1	**51.2**	**3.0**	**13.9**	**.87**	**2**
G2	**42.4**	**2.3**	**17.6**	**.60**	**3**
G3	**54.4**	**5.4**	**15.6**	**.74**	**4**
G4	**29.7**	**3.4**	**15.5**	**.52**	**4**
G5	**34.3**	**2.8**	**37.7**	**.48**	**2**
G6	**53.5**	**5.5**	**16.0**	**.68**	**2**
Other	**Base**	**3.4**	**14.8**	**.62**	**14**
Standard Deviation	**9.6**	**1.2**	**7.8**	**.13**	
Range	**24.7**	**3.3**	**23.8**	**.39**	
Volume					
High	**67.5**	**3.8**	**13.9**	**.76**	**10**
Medium	**Base**	**2.6**	**9.1**	**.77**	**10**
Low	**51.2**	**4.2**	**3.4**	**.72**	**10**
Standard Deviation	**8.2**	**8.7**	**4.3**	**.02**	
Range	**16.3**	**1.6**	**10.5**	**.04**	

case for UAP activity, in which the range and standard deviation for the geographic runs are 23.8 and 7.8 percent, whereas for the store run they were 19.7 and 6.1 percent. Most of the variation in the geographic analysis is due to the fact that 37.7 percent of the observations for area G5 contain unadvertised price discounts. This extreme behavior is primarily due to the promotional activity of one store. It often engages in in-store promotion of brands without supporting retail advertising, as well as in the substitution of a brand not being advertised for one that is being promoted. If this category is ignored, the range of variation in geographic UAP activity drops from 23.8 to 3.7 percent.

The relative magnitude of the range and standard deviation of the coefficient of determination (R^2) of the store identity analysis with that for the geographic runs is consistent with the results for regression coefficients, AD3 to AD5, and UAP.

Whether one looks at the response to promotion or at the rate of activity of the principal promotional variables, the store identity segments exhibit a greater degree of idiosyncratic behavior than those based on geographic location. This finding is also consistent with our a priori judgment. Within the limited geographic area from which our data are generated, there are few indications that there are systematic geographic differences other than those that are bound up with store differences (as was the case for UAP activity in area G5). Based on these findings, we decided to delete geographic store stratification from the design of the multiple-equation model.

3.5.1.2 Store and Volume Stratification

A comparison between *the variation within* the store and volume strata appears to result in a conclusion similar to that for the store identity and geographic area strata; namely, that the stratification by store identity revealed more idiosyncratic behavior. However, there are only three store categories (with ten stores each) in the volume analysis, whereas there are nine categories in the store identity runs, with an average of only 3.4 stores per category. One would expect that by chance alone there would be more variation between categories containing a smaller number of stores. The volume analysis was done at a time when only fifteen weeks' data were available. This is too small a sample size to permit as many volume segments as there are for the store identity analysis that is based on thirty-seven weeks' data.

Fortunately, the issue is not a critical one, as there is a relatively high degree of correlation between a store's membership in a volume category and its identity, as can be seen in Table 3.4. The numbers in the body of the table refer to each store's rank in terms of volume.

Because of the high degree of association between a store's chain membership and its relative volume, we decided to design our stratification system for the multiple-equation model so that it would *tend* to group stores on both of these dimensions simultaneously.

3.5.1.3 Final Store Stratification for the Multiple-Equation Model

Our criterion for the final grouping of stores is the same as that discussed in Section 3.5.1, namely, similarity in the response to promotion and mix of promotional activities.

The most clear-cut decision was to group the S2, S5, and S8

Table 3.4 Cross-Classification of Individual Store Membership in Store Identity and Volume Analysis

	Volume		
Store Identity	High	Medium	Low
Chains			
S6	4, 5†		
S4		11, 13, 15	
S1	2, 3		
S8	7	14	
S2		17, 19, 20	27
S5		18	24, 30
S3			26, 28, 29
S7			23, 25
Other*			
S9	1		
S10	6		
S11	8		
S12	9		
S13	10		
S14		12	
S15		16	
S16			21, 22
S17			31

*S9 to S17 are the code numbers for the stores that comprised the "other" store category.

†Numbers refer to the store's rank (of 30 stores) in terms of total sales of the product under study.

stores into what we will call the "low response segment." These stores are all in the low-volume category and they all are characterized by relatively low response of demand to promotion, as well as below-average rates of advertised-price reduction activity and coefficients of determination. Their UAP activity is above average; however, UAP's tend to be less effective in influencing demand than are AD3's, AD4's, and AD5's. Therefore, despite the apparent inconsistency of their UAP activity with the other criteria, we decided to group them together.

The argument for grouping S1, S4, S6, and S7 is not quite as strong. Four of the eight store categories involved are in the high-volume category, two are the first and third stores within the medium-volume category, and two are in the low-volume category.

In spite of this fact, they share one important attribute: they all exhibited above-average response of demand to promotion (see the first column of Table 3.4). With the exception of S1, moreover, they have similar degrees of AD3 through AD5 activity and represent the four store categories with the highest degree of predictive efficacy (fourth column, Table

3.3). This group of stores is termed the "high response segment." For the purpose of constructing the multiple-equation model, we decided to add one other store to this group—, S9. It had the highest volume of any of the thirty stores, and high volume appears to be associated with above-average response to promotion. In addition, the similarity of the store's promotional practices to that of other members of the group supported this decision.

The grouping of the remaining twelve stores is based to a greater degree on judgment and company experience than on actual data. We observed that stores with extremely low response to promotion also tend to sell relatively less of the product than those exhibiting extremely high response to promotion. The "other" category in the store identity analysis is composed of four high-volume stores (excluding S9), two belonging to the medium category, and two small stores. On the basis of the working hypothesis that relative volume and response are associated (at least at the extremes), we decided to split the "other" group store members into two groups, one consisting of the six low- and medium-volume stores and the other of the two low-volume outlets. Finally, we combined the two low-volume stores with the S3 stores. The S3 stores are all small stores that exhibited an inconsistent pattern of below-average response to promotion and above-average AD3 to AD5 activity, together with coefficient of determination (.58) that is considerably closer in magnitude to that for the other category than to the previously defined low-response group of stores. These two groups are called the "mixed response high-volume and low-volume segments." The final grouping of stores is as follows:

A. High response (9)

1. S1 (2)
2. S4 (2)[8]
3. S6 (2)
4. S7 (2)
5. S9 (1)

B. Low response (9)

1. S2 (4)
2. S5 (3)[8]
3. S8 (2)

[8]One S5 store was added as a replacement for the S4 store. It was the second lowest volume store in the panel.

C. Mixed response, high volume (6)

1. S10 (1)
2. S11 (1)
3. S12 (1)
4. S13 (1)
5. S14 (1)
6. S15 (1)

D. Mixed response, low volume (6)

1. S3 (3)
2. S16 (2)
3. S17 (1)

3.5.2 Carry-over Effects

The model for the differential response analysis regression runs is a distributed lag model that assumes that the effect of each of the promotional variables decays at a constant rate over time. The coefficients of the lagged demand variable (YR_{t-1} and YR_{t-2}) are used to adjust the coefficients of the promotional variables for the degree to which there are carry-over effects, using the following formula:

$$\text{Cumulative effect of } X_i = b(1) + (\lambda_1) + (\lambda_1^2 + \lambda_2) + (\lambda_1^3 + 2\lambda_1\lambda_2) + (\lambda_1^4 + 3\lambda_1^2\lambda_2 + \lambda_2^2) + (\lambda_1^5 + 4\lambda_1^3\lambda_2 + 2\lambda_1\lambda_2^2) + (\lambda_1^6 + 5\lambda_1^4\lambda_2 + 5\lambda_1^2\lambda_2^2 + \lambda_2^3) + \ldots,$$

where b is the raw coefficient of the ith promotional variable and 1 and 2 are the coefficients of YR_{t-1} and YR_{t-2}, respectively. For example, if the values of λ_1 and λ_2 are $+.10$ and $+.05$, the adjusted coefficient of each promotional variable would be about 17 percent greater than its corresponding raw value. In general, when the λs are both small, the percentage of adjustment is slightly more than $\lambda_1 + \lambda_2$.

There are a total of 113 regression runs included in the differential response analysis. Given that there are two lagged demand variables in each regression run, a total of 226 coefficients for lagged variables were computed. Table 3.5 reports the lagged coefficients for a typical subset of these regressions, the small, medium, and large size, all-store runs by brand.

Nearly all the lagged variable coefficients are positive, which indicates that the direction of the carry-over effect, to the extent that it is important, is to increase the impact of the promotional variables.

We found no rationale to support the hypothesis that the lagged coefficients should vary significantly from brand to brand, or from one store segment to another. Moreover, the

Table No. 3.5 Regression Coefficients for Lagged Demand Variables (YR_{t-1} and YR_{t-2}) by Brand and Size of Container*

	YR_{t-1}			YR_{t-2}		
Brand	Small	Medium	Large	Small	Medium	Large
1. B1	−.017	.041	.056	.028	−.023	.046
2. B2	.075	.076	.296	−.028	.035	.102
3. B3	.223	.007	†	.068	.129	†
4. B4	.080	.132	−.009	−.000	.038	.030
5. B5	.060	.063	.004	.075	.007	.113
6. B6	.095	.100	†	.067	.035	†
7. Store Major Private	−.126	.067	†	−.085	.205	†
8. Other	.122	.248	†	.264	.060	†
Average for 8 brands	.082	.092	†	.049	.061	†
Average for first 6 brands	.082	.070	.087	.035	.031	.073

*These coefficients are uncoded.
†Sample size insufficient to run regression analysis.

t-ratios showed that most of these coefficients are not significantly different from zero, and certainly not different from one another. Therefore, the average magnitude of the coefficients is a better indicator of the actual degree of carry-over effects than the value of any specific pair of coefficients. The average coefficients that implied the greatest degree of carry-over effects are those for all eight brands for the medium package size runs. They imply more than a 15.3 percent adjustment in the raw value of each of the promotional variable coefficients.

However, this probably overstates the true value of the carry-over effects in that the last two brand categories consist of more than one brand. To the extent that there are differences in the average value of the YRs from one brand to another within a category, there would be an association between the lagged and current values of YR due to the heterogeneous mix of brands. The observed coefficient for these two categories then consists of two components, one caused by carry-over effects, and another caused by the heterogeneity of the brands with respect to their average YR value.

Using the average coefficients for medium-size packages only for the first six brand categories results in about an 11 percent increase in the coefficients of the raw promotional variables due to carry-over effects.

The magnitude of the lagged coefficient of the remaining regression runs in the differential response analysis is of about the same magnitude of those reported in Table 3.5. Of a total of 186 coefficients that are not reported in that table, only five are equal or greater than .183, with a maximum value of .580. (These extremes easily could have occured by chance.) In none of these five cases, nor in the case of less extreme values, is there evidence that an unusually high coefficient for YR_{t-2} is associated with an unusually high value for YR_{t-1}.

On theoretical grounds, we would expect that a large promotion for a given brand in one week would lead to negative carry-over effects. Households that tended to be loyal to that brand would be expected to adjust the timing of their purchases to take advantage of the promotion, and hence would be out of the market in succeeding weeks. However, the observed values of the carry-over effects tend to fall in the range of −5 to +15 percent, and there are no negative coefficients of any magnitude for the major brands.

This anomaly may well be due to errors in the phasing of the sales and promotional data from the store audit, rather than to the effects of promotions on the timing of consumer demand.

If some of the sales due to a promotion in a given week are misreported as occurring in the following week (as would happen if the auditor missed an invoice during the week of the promotion, for example), this would tend to inflate the coefficient of YR_{t-1}. Residual sales values left over from the phase adjustment procedure (see Section 2.3.1.1) have the same effect. Finally, sales made after the Monday audit of a promotion week would be incorrectly reported as occurring in the following week. If the carry-over effects of promotion on consumer demand are negative but of small magnitude, the positive effects of phase errors in the audit would probably dominate the lagged sales coefficients.

Because of the relatively small magnitude of the observed carry-over effects, and the chances of their overstatement due to phase errors in the audit, we decided not to include the lagged demand variable in the multiple-equation model.

3.6 Reformulating the Model

The results reported in Section 3.5 were generated over a period of about ten months. During this time we were continually screening possible alternative specifications for the final multiple-equation model. Two alternatives were important enough to justify further single-equation analysis. The first of these consists of several hypotheses as to the nature of the effects on demand of unadvertised price discounts and in-store display.

The need for the second analysis is created by a sharp drop in the price level for the product for all brands in the market that occurred in approximately the thirty-third week of the audit. Once the new price level was established, retailers no longer made as sharp a decrease in price when they featured a brand in their weekly promotions. As a result many advertisements that were classified as AD5's in the period prior to the price cut were coded as AD3's during the latter time period. This change in price level led to the formulation and evaluation of a series of hypotheses as to the nature of the effect of price on demand.

3.6.1 Unadvertised Price Discounts and In-Store Display

Our interpretation of the results of the differential response analysis revealed that two questions that were not adequately dealt with as the model was currently specified possibly could be answered by making a few simple changes in the existing set of variables.

1. Many UAP's were believed to be the result of substitutions of one brand for the same size units of another brand that was on promotion. For instance, if B2's medium-size package was advertised at a sharp price reduction in a given week and the store's stock of B2 ran low late in the week, B5 might be substituted for B2 at the B2 advertised price. This sequence of events would generate an AD5, perhaps, for B2 and a relatively large UAP for B5. We hypothesized that the effects of this kind of UAP might be less than those of a UAP that did not involve substitution. In order to answer this question, the UAP and ZFM variables were replaced by two new variables defined as follows:

(a) UAPZFM. This variable is defined as those UAP's that occur when another major brand is promoted (in the same size).

(b) UAPNFM. These are the UAP's that occur when no competing promotion is present.

This change in specifications created two UAP variables—one that fluctuates from week to week when no competing promotions are present and another that fluctuates when competing promotions occur.

2. Is the effect of the presence or absence of a display different when it is placed in the product's own section of a store as opposed to some other location? In order to answer this question, LODD and UODN were replaced by two new variables as follows:

(a) UODD1. This is a dummy variable whose magnitude in a given week is equal to $(\text{UODN}-\text{LODD})^{\cdot 1}$. It has a value of one when a display is out of the product's section and a value of zero when there is no display outside of it (although there might have been a display in the product's own section). (b) UODD2. This is also a dummy variable whose magnitude in a given week is equal to $(\text{UODN})^{.1} - \text{UODD1}$. It has a value of one when a display is in the product's section and zero when no display is present in the section.

Eight regression runs were made, one for each of the eight medium–package-size–brand categories. The variables included in the runs were as follows:

AD0	UAPZFM	SIWD
AD1	UAPNFM	SISD
AD2	UODD1	CPE
AD3	UODD2	CPM
AD4		YR_{t-1}
AD5		YR_{t-2}

The results were based on the fifteen-week data base. Results leading to the same conclusion were also obtained with the thirty-seven-week data base.

All the coefficients for the two UAP variables have a positive sign, with one exception—UAPZFM for B6, which is only −.001. Moreover, the coefficient of UAPZFM is less than that of UAPNFM for all major brands except B2; this differential is consistent with our hypothesis. As the insertion of two UAP variables did not lead to collinearity problems, we decided to adopt this modification of the model.

In contrast, the splitting apart of the display variable was associated with results that not only varied from brand to brand but also strongly conflicted with prior judgment about the nature of the effects of displays. For example, the coefficient for UODD1 was negative for both B2 and B1, as was the coefficient for UODD2 for B5. While one might expect a UODD1 to have a different effect than a UODD2, it was impossible to rationalize strong negative effects for these variables, let alone to rationalize the variations from brand to brand.

A number of the inconsistencies were probably an artifact of the low rate of activity associated with displays during the period of time covered by the panel. In the full sixty-three-week period there was a total of approximately thirty displays for all container sizes of the four major brands.

Because of the gross inconsistencies in our results and the sparsity of data, we made two decisions with respect to the specifications of displays in the multiple-equation model: (1) not to code separately displays in and out of the product section; and (2) to code only the presence or absence of a display and not the size of the display.

3.6.2 Price-Level Analysis

The change in market price level mentioned in Section 3.6 led us to experiment with three different formulations of the single-equation model, as follows:

1. The normal price level series (NPL) was included as an additional independent variable in the analysis.
2. The actual price variable (ACTP) was included as an additional independent variable.
3. A set of six interaction terms consisting of the cross-products of ACTP and each of the advertising-price variables (AD0 through AD5) was included in the analysis.

The price decline occurred at different points in time from brand to brand. In this respect, there is a distinct possibility that the brand whose price dropped earliest might experience sharply increased volume. If this occurred, then one of the price level variables should serve as a predictor of demand for one or more of the brands during the period of price adjustment. If the market response was immediate, ACTP might be the best predictor of the adjustment; however, if information about the adjustment spread slowly from customer to customer, then NPL might do a better job, because NPL series adjusted less rapidly to price changes than ACTP.

The interaction terms were designed to test the hypothesis that the effect of a particular advertising-price variable would be negatively correlated with the actual price level. This would happen if customers evaluated a price discount in terms of the percent off the normal price it represented as opposed to the absolute amount of the discount.

Our results were based on thirty-seven weeks' data for the top four brands for the medium-package-size category. All runs failed from the standpoint of our objectives. When the variables listed here were added to the base model, in every case they were so highly collinear with one or more of the independent variables already in the equation that they added nothing by way of increasing predictive efficacy or structural insight.

3.7 Concluding Comment

The outcome of the experiments reported in this chapter is summarized in Chapter 5, which will report still further experiments that led to the final market model. The experiments reported in Chapter 5 will be based on multiple-equation techniques in contrast to those reported in this chapter, which are based on single-equation analysis. Chapter 4 discusses the theory underlying the multiple-equation model.

4

Theory of the Multiple-Equation Model

4.1 Introduction

The results of Chapters 1 through 3 were based on regression analyses in which the data for each brand and package size were considered in isolation. This was tantamount to assuming that there was not interaction between the promotional activities of one brand and size and the sales of other brands and sizes—even other sizes of the same brand. However, our beliefs run counter to this assumption. There is every reason to believe that substitution interactions do exist.

The multiple-equation model used to obtain the results presented in the remainder of this monograph was developed to measure the direction and magnitude of these interbrand and intersize promotion interactions. In brief, the model assumes that the promotional activities of any given brand and size affect the sales of the various other brands and sizes to different degrees. The sign of the coefficient describing the effects of one brand's promotion on another brand's (or size's) sales is a measure of whether the relation between the two brands (or two sizes) is one of relative substitution or complementarity. If one brand's promotion leads to a decrease in the sales of the other brand (compared to the average of that brand's sales when it is not being promoted), the two are relative substitutes, whereas if the result is an increase in the other brand's sales compared to its average, the relation is one of complementarity. The magnitude of the relevant coefficient is a measure of the strength of the promotional interaction between the two brands or sizes. The incorporation of promotional interactions into the model represents a significant extension of the single-equation results previously reported. The general topic of multiple-equation systems, of which the model to be reported here is a special case, is discussed extensively in Goldberger (1964) and Johnson (1963).

The principles of promotional interaction will be discussed, with the aid of numerical examples, in Section 4.2. Then the multiple-equation model itself will be developed in Section 4.3. The belief that the sales of each brand and size both affect and are effected by the sales of all other brands and sizes leads to a somewhat more complicated set of model definitions than were employed in connection with the single equation results. The basic structure of the model will be given in Sections 4.3.1 and 4.3.2 and extended to cover the idiosyncrasies of the present data base in Section 4.3.3. While some degree of mathematical notation will be essential for describing the model, the more extensive mathematics required to prove its theoretical adequacy will be omitted or relegated to the two appendixes to Chapter 4. Use of the multiple-equation model also leads to certain problems of statistical estimation methodology that did not arise in single-equations work. These will be described in Section 4.4. (Empirical evidence relevant to the choice between competing estimation methods will be presented at the beginning of Chapter 5.) The reader who is concerned primarily with findings should review the basic definition of the model, given in Section 4.2 and Sections 4.3.1 and 4.3.2, and then skip directly to Chapter 6, where final results are reported.

4.2 Promotional Interaction

Before describing the multiple-equation model we should consider the nature of promotional interaction. The single-equation results reported in Chapters 1 through 3 provided abundant evidence that advertised price reductions move large amounts of the product under study, at least for the brand and size being promoted during the week in question. If one brand and size receives more or greater price discount promotions than another during a particular period of time, the more heavily promoted brand achieves the larger share of the market. If the divergences between the promotions for the two brands are large, the differences in market share are also large. One might say that in this hypothetical case the first brand was substituted for the second, and that the change in market share was due to some kind of *substitution effect*. We need to examine the exact nature of this substitution effect in order to understand the multiple-equation model, and indeed the single-equation results as well.

In order to do this, we consider a hypothetical market that consists of only three brands, A, B, and C, each available in a single container size. Except for the limitation in the number of brands and sizes, we assume a market identical to the one being studied empirically.

If we were to audit the promotional activities of the three brands, we would find some weeks in which brand A was promoted, some for B, and some for C. While there might be a few weeks in which none (or more than one) of the brands was promoted, we will ignore these possibilities when constructing the numerical examples.

We now define variables $\overline{Y}_A$, $\overline{Y}_B$, and $\overline{Y}_C$ to represent the mean sales in weeks without promotion for brands A, B, and C. For simplicity assume that $\overline{Y}_A = \overline{Y}_B = \overline{Y}_C$. The $\overline{Y}$ variables are the same as the "normal sales" variables used to normalize sales and calculate YR (see Section 2.3.1.2 for details). Thus, $YR_A = Y_A/\overline{Y}_A$, and so forth. (We will ignore the square root transformation for the purposes of this demonstration.) Several representative situations will now be considered.

4.2.1 The Case of No Interaction

The simplest case would be one in which, when one brand was being promoted, the YR's of the other two brands were both equal to one. This is illustrated by the hypothetical time series in Table 4.1. In this example, the market shares of the three brands are all equal to 33⅓ percent. Now suppose that for a short period of time (for example, two to three months), brand A was able to garner what otherwise would have been brand C's promotions. Then the time series of sales would look like Table 4.2. Brand A increased its share of promotions to 67 percent and its share of market to 52 percent. The change in market share was purely the result of the change in the promotional mix, not of any change in consumer preferences as they were indicated by $\bar{Y}_A$. Brand C's share declined because of the loss of its promotion. Brand B maintained its promotional share; its share of market was not affected by the trade-off of promotions between brands A and C.

We have illustrated the situation in which there was no interaction between the promotion of one brand and the sales of any other. Each brand obtained a sales ratio of 5.0 when it was promoted and a

Table 4.1 No Promotional Interaction: First Illustration

Week	Brand Being Promoted	Sales Ratio for Brand			
		A	B	C	Total
1	A	5.0	1.0	1.0	7.0
2	B	1.0	5.0	1.0	7.0
3	C	1.0	1.0	5.0	7.0
Total		7.0	7.0	7.0	21.0
Share of Market		33%	33%	33%	100%

Table 4.2 No Promotional Interaction: Second Illustration

Week	Brand Being Promoted	Sales Ratio for Brand			
		A	B	C	Total
1	A	5.0	1.0	1.0	7.0
2	B	1.0	5.0	1.0	7.0
3	A	5.0	1.0	1.0	7.0
Total		11.0	7.0	3.0	21.0
Share of Market		52%	33%	15%	100%

"normal" ratio of 1.0 when it was not promoted, regardless of what other brand was on special that week. If the real world were like this example, all information about the effects of promotional variables on sales could be obtained from single-equation regressions based on the time series of promotion and sales for each brand separately; there would be no need for a multiple-equation model.

What real-world conditions would tend to make demand behave like this illustration? The most likely possibility is to suppose that there is a large pool of consumers who are not committed to any particular brand but instead shop for specials. These consumers buy brand C when it is on sale but are just as happy to buy brand A when it is the weekly special. In contrast, a hard-core, loyal group of customers tend to stay with brand C even when it is not on sale. In the numerical example, the hard-core group produced an average weekly sales volume of $\bar{Y}$ for the particular brand, which led to a sales ratio of 1.0 for brand C even in the absence of promotions. The group of special price-seeking customers produced a sales volume of $4\bar{Y}$; when added to the loyal group, this yielded a sales ratio of $(1+4)=5$ when a brand was on promotion.

4.2.2 A Case with Interaction

Now suppose that there is some degree of relative brand preference even among members of the group of customers who habitually seek out price specials. That is, some consumers prefer brand B but buy brand A when the latter is on special, others prefer brand C but buy brand B when it is on special, and so on. This implies that responses to promotions will vary from brand to brand and that the sales ratios for brands that are not on promotion during a particular week will vary, depending on which of the other brands is currently being promoted. This can be illustrated as in Table 4.3. In this example, we assumed that total weekly sales for the store were the same no matter what brand was on promotion (this need not be the case in general) and that the "off-week" sales ratios for each brand averaged 1.0 (this is true by definition if $\bar{Y}$ is the average sales in weeks without promotion for the time period in question).

The ratios in Table 4.3 imply that sales of $0.8\bar{Y}$ are obtained from customers who are loyal to brand B in the face of brand A's promotion, while A gets only $0.5\bar{Y}$ in the face of brand B's promotion. In contrast, A obtained $1.5\bar{Y}$ and B got $1.2\bar{Y}$ when brand C was specialed. Given that total volume was the same no matter what brand was being promoted, these differences in drawing power were reflected in variations in promotional

Table 4.3. Promotional Interaction: First Illustration

Week	Brand Being Promoted	Sales Ratio for Brand A	B	C	Total
1	A	5.5	0.8	0.7	7.0
2	B	0.5	5.2	1.3	7.0
3	C	1.5	1.2	4.3	7.0
Total		7.5	7.2	6.3	21.0
Share of market		36%	34%	30%	100%

responses among the three brands, and hence in their market shares. On balance, A was the most popular brand in the market, followed by B, with C as a rather poor third in terms of market share—assuming, of course, that the number of promotions for the three brands was the same.

Now let us consider what would happen if brand A suddenly acquired all brand C's promotions. Then the time series would look like Table 4.4. Brand A increased its market share by 19 points, brand B lost 2 points, and brand C lost 17 points. In the first example, in which a group of price-motivated customers without brand preferences was assumed, the same change produced an increase of 19 points for brand A, no change for B, and a loss of 19 points for C. Moderation of the strict "no-preference" assumption cost brand B as much as 2 points in market share in this example, even though there was no change in the number of brand B promotions. This occurred because brand A's promotions hurt brand B more than did brand C's promotions.

Table 4.4 Promotional Interaction: Second Illustration

Week	Brand Being Promoted	Sales Ratio for Brand A	B	C	Total
1	A	5.5	0.8	0.7	7.0
2	B	0.5	5.2	1.3	7.0
3	A	5.5	0.8	0.7	7.0
Total		11.5	6.8	2.7	21.0
Share of Market		55%	32%	13%	100%

4.2.3
Summary

These examples illustrate two distinct types of substitution effects: substitution of *promotions* of one brand for those of another and substitution of *demand* for one brand by that for another, given a particular mix of promotional activity. In a real market, the former would be initiated and carried through by retailers, perhaps as the result of changes in the relative allowance offerings by manufacturers. The second type of substitution occurs at the level of the consumer, who changes his choice of brand as a result of the retailer's promotional activities.

The consumer demand model, which is the subject of this part of our monograph, is concerned exclusively with the effects of retailers' promotional activities on the sales of the various brands and sizes of the product under study. The mix of promotional activities by retailers is treated as a given factor so far as this model is concerned. (The economic analysis model described in Chapter 8 concerns itself in part with the response of retailers to the allowances offered by manufacturers.) While changes in the mix of promotional activities by retailers could and did lead to substantial changes in the market share positions of brands during the period covered by our data, this fact was irrelevant in regard to estimation of the demand response to particular promotions —when and if they occurred.

The two hypothetical cases discussed here differ in their assumptions about the nature of demand substitution. The first example uses the assumption that was implicitly adopted in the single-equation work reported in Chapter 3. That is, we specified a situation in which promotions by one brand affect all other brands (and sizes) equally. In the second example, we allowed the promotions of each brand to have different effects on sales of other brands and sizes. This is the assumption to be used in developing our multiple-equation model for consumer demand.

The substitution coefficients of the multiple-equation model (which will be defined later) are measures of the sales ratios in each row of Tables 4.1 through 4.4, whereas the single-equation model assumed that all off-diagonal terms were equal to 1.0. The multiple-equation model does not introduce the idea of substitutability as such, but instead relaxes the rigid and unrealistic assumption of *equal substitutability* required by the single-equation approach. This generalization is important for two reasons: (1) it may be important to understand the nature of the differences in the degree of substitutability of one brand for another brought to light by the multiple-equation model in order to assess the vulnerability of certain brands and sizes to promotions by other sizes and brands; and (2) the existence of differential substitutability may be a significant factor in our forecasts of future market shares and volumes conditional on anticipated changes in retailers' promotional mixes.

4.3 Definition of the Multiple-Equation System

The objective of the multiple-equation model was to obtain estimates of each of the demand response ratios given in the hypothetical time series presented in Sections 4.2.1 and 4.2.2. This included both the response of the sales of a brand to its own promotional efforts, which we will henceforth call *main effects*, and the effects of promotional activities of each other brand upon the given brand. These effects were represented by "nonpromotion" demand response ratios in Tables 4.1 through 4.4. We will call them *interaction effects* because they represent the interaction of one brand's promotion upon another brand's sales.

4.3.1 The Reduced Form System

The kind of result to be obtained from the multiple-equation model is best described in the notation of mathematical functions. Let $\mathbf{X}_{it}$ be the vector of promotional activities for brand i at time t, for a particular store, and let R_{it} be the square root of the demand response ratio for that brand and week.[1] According to the interaction assumptions outlined in Section 4.2.2, the demand response ratio for brand i is a function of the promotional activities of all the brands in the market. That is, the market can be described by the following system of equations:

$$
\begin{aligned}
R_{1t} &= f_1(\mathbf{X}_{1t}, \mathbf{X}_{2t}, \ldots, \mathbf{X}_{Nt}), \\
R_{2t} &= f_2(\mathbf{X}_{1t}, \mathbf{X}_{2t}, \ldots, \mathbf{X}_{Nt}), \\
&\cdots\cdots\cdots\cdots \\
R_{Nt} &= f_N(\mathbf{X}_{1t}, \mathbf{X}_{2t}, \ldots, \mathbf{X}_{Nt}).
\end{aligned}
\tag{4.1}
$$

There is one equation for each of the N brands in the market, and each equation depends on the promotional vectors for all

[1] A *vector* is a shorthand expression for an ordered list of numbers. For instance, the vector

$$\mathbf{X}_{it} = (\text{AD0}_{it}, \text{AD1}_{it}, \text{AD2}_{it}, \ldots, \text{CPM}_{it})$$

provides a convenient way of expressing the current values of all the promotional variables for brand i. This convenience of expression can be extended to two-dimensional tables of numbers, which are called *matrices*. In addition to their notational convenience, vectors and matrices form the basis for a powerful tool for the manipulation and solution of simultaneous linear equations, *matrix algebra*. Although vector notation is used in the text of this monograph to represent one-dimensional lists of numbers, matrix notation and matrix algebra are used only in the appendixes that provide proofs of the computations described in the text.

N brands.[2] Equation 4.1 is called the *reduced form system,* which is one part of the mutiple-equation model.

In the first equation the relation between $\mathbf{X}_{1t}$ and R_{1t} is the main effect mentioned earlier, while the relations between $\mathbf{X}_{2t}$ through $\mathbf{X}_{Nt}$ represent the interaction effects. In the single-equation model all the interaction effects were assumed to be zero, which reduced equation (4.1) to the following simplified system containing only main effects:

$$\begin{aligned} R_{1t} &= g_1(\mathbf{X}_{1t}), \\ R_{2t} &= g_2(\mathbf{X}_{2t}), \\ &\dots \\ R_{Nt} &= g_N(\mathbf{X}_{Nt}). \end{aligned} \tag{4.2}$$

Use of the function notation g in Equation 4.2 and f in Equation 4.1 emphasizes that the estimates of the main effects may well be different, depending on whether or not the interaction effects are taken into account.

The large number of brands and sizes (a total of twenty-four brand/size combinations) and the number of different promotional variables (a total of seventeen in some of the runs) present in the store audit data base preclude the estimation of the coefficients of Equation 4.1 directly by linear regression. If this were attempted, every promotional variable for every brand and size would have to be included in the regression relation corresponding to each equation in Equation 4.1. This would mean that each regression would contain $24 \times 17 = 408$ independent variables—which was obviously out of the question. Hence, an indirect approach to the estimation of Equation 4.1 was required.

4.3.2 A Simplified Explanation of the Structural System

We will develop the logic of the multiple-equation model using the *three*-brand, *one*-size hypothetical market discussed in Section 4.2. This is desirable in order to simplify the notation and avoid the use of matrix algebra. For the same reasons, we will assume that there was only one active promotional variable for each brand. The results to be developed here will be extended to apply to the full store audit data base in the next subsection.

The indirect method for estimating the coefficients of the

[2] The symbol f_i is that of a "mathematical function." The concept of a function means only that the variable on the left of the equal sign *depends upon* the variables enclosed within the parentheses to the right of the function symbol: for example, R_{1t} depends upon $\mathbf{X}_{1t}$ and $\mathbf{X}_{2t}$ and . . . $\mathbf{X}_{Nt}$. The symbol f_{it} does not itself describe the nature of the dependence; however, in this report we will be concerned exclusively with linear relations between variables and hence linear functions. The single-equation regressions described in Chapter 3 provide an example of a function where Y depends linearly on the X's.

linear functions in Equation 4.1 begins with the specification of the following *structural equation* system; (*Note*: γ represents the effect of a set of brand-size sales on the dependent variable R_{it}).

$$\begin{aligned}
&\text{(a)}\quad R_{1t} = \gamma_{12}R_{2t} + \gamma_{13}R_{3t} + b_{11}X_{1t},\\
&\text{(b)}\quad R_{2t} = \gamma_{21}R_{1t} + \gamma_{23}R_{3t} + b_{21}X_{2t},\\
&\text{(c)}\quad R_{3t} = \gamma_{31}R_{1t} + \gamma_{32}R_{2t} + b_{31}X_{3t}.
\end{aligned} \tag{4.3}$$

There is one structural equation for each brand (and size) included in the analysis, just as was the case for the reduced form system. The difference between the two systems is that whereas each equation in the reduced form system contained the promotional variables for all the brands but only the sales ratio for its own brand, each structural equation contains the sales ratios of all the brands but only the promotional variables for its own brand. In a sense, the set of structural equations is the reverse of the reduced form set. The individual equations of the structural equation set given by Equation 4.3 may contain fewer variables than the corresponding equations in the reduced form set—at least when the number of promotional variables is at all large. (The structural equations for the audit would at worst contain $23 + 17 = 40$ variables, compared to the 408 variables required for each equation in the reduced form system.[3]) Hence, the coefficients of the structural set are much easier to estimate than those of the reduced form system.

The γ and b coefficients in Equation 4.3 can be estimated from empirical data by applying ordinary regression methods to one equation at a time. (Other, potentially better, methods of estimation are also available; they will be discussed in Section 4.4.) The resulting b coefficients (the coefficients of the promotional variables) are more or less comparable to the single-equation coefficients reported in Chapter 3. However, the γ coefficients must be interpreted with caution.

If we look at one equation at a time, each γ represents the degree to which the sales ratio of the associated brand moderates the effect of the promotional variables in that equation on the sales of the brand currently being promoted. That is, γ_{12} measures the degree to which R_{2t} affects the sales ratio for brand 1. These effects are, of course, averaged over weeks when brand 1 was on promotion and those when it was not. If γ_{12} is negative, for instance, the

[3] The terms *structural* and *reduced form* are well established in the literature of econometrics. The latter is something of a misnomer in the present model, as the reduced form equations contain many more coefficients than do the equations of the structural set. However, to change the names to suit the purposes of a single model would invite confusion.

implication is that R_{1t} is smaller when R_{2t} is large than when R_{2t} is small. Hence, we might be tempted to say that the positive effect of $b_{11}X_{1t}$ (which must be greater than zero when brand 1 is on promotion) is reduced because of the effect of brand 2. In addition, we would say that sales of brand 1 in nonpromoted weeks were hurt when brand 2 was on promotion (and hence brand 2's sales were large).

Both of these statements are true, at least so far as the direction of the effect is concerned. But in order to assess the magnitude of the effect, we must have some way of estimating the sales of brand 2 both when brand 1 is on promotion and when it is not. To do this, we turn to (b) of Equation 4.3, which predicts the sales ratio for brand 2 as a function of its promotional variables and the sales of the other brands. But here we find that R_{1t} appears as an *independent variable*, just as was the case for R_{2t} in (a) of Equation 4.3. We have come to an impass: using the set of structural equations we cannot predict the sales of brand 1 without first knowing the sales of brand 2, and we cannot predict the sales of brand 2 without first knowing the sales of brand 1. The situation becomes even more complicated when we include brand 3 in the picture.

In mathematical terms, the equations of the structural set form a simultaneous equations system that jointly determines the values of all the R's conditional on the values of all the X's. The way out of our difficulty thus is to solve the simultaneous equations system for the individual values of the R's, conditional on the X's. The fact that there are three structural equations (in this example) and three unknown R's means that the system is fully determined (i.e., the number of equations equals the number of unknowns), and so a unique solution should be possible.

Let us proceed to solve the structural system given in Equation 4.3 by the method of substitution. First we replace the value of R_3 in (a) and (b) of Equation 4.3 by the prediction for R_3 given by (c). If the t-subscript is left out to simplify the notation this yields

$$\text{(a}'\text{)}\quad R_1 = \gamma_{12}R_2 + \gamma_{13}(\gamma_{31}R_1 + \gamma_{32}R_2 + b_{31}X_3) + b_{11}X_1,$$

$$\text{(b}'\text{)}\quad R_2 = \gamma_{21}R_1 + \gamma_{23}(\gamma_{31}R_1 + \gamma_{32}R_2 + b_{31}X_3) + b_{21}X_2.$$

Then we collect terms and solve (b′) to get R_2 in terms of R_1 and the X's:

$$\text{(b}''\text{)}\quad R_2 = \frac{(\gamma_{21} + \gamma_{23}\gamma_{31})R_1 + b_{21}X_2 + \gamma_{23}b_{31}X_3}{1 - \gamma_{23}\gamma_{32}}$$

Finally, we substitute (b″) into (a′) and solve for R as a function of the X's:

(a″) $R_1 = c_{11}X_1 + c_{12}X_2 + c_{13}X_3$,

where

$$c_{11} = \frac{b_{11}}{D},$$

$$c_{12} = \frac{(\gamma_{12} + \gamma_{13}\gamma_{32})}{(1 - \gamma_{23}\gamma_{32})} \cdot \frac{b_{21}}{D},$$

$$c_{13} = \gamma_{13} + \gamma_{23}\frac{(\gamma_{12} + \gamma_{13}\gamma_{32})}{(1 - \gamma_{23}\gamma_{32})} \cdot \frac{b_{31}}{D},$$

and

$$D = 1 - \gamma_{13}\gamma_{31} - \frac{(\gamma_{12} + \gamma_{13}\gamma_{32})(\gamma_{21} + \gamma_{23}\gamma_{31})}{(1 - \gamma_{23}\gamma_{32})}.$$

Similarly, we can substitute (a″) back into the other equations to obtain solutions for R_2 and R_3 explicitly in terms of the X's.

Summing up, we have the following set of final equations for predicting R_1, R_2, and R_3:

$$\begin{aligned} R_1 &= c_{11}X_1 + c_{12}X_2 + c_{13}X_3, \\ R_2 &= c_{21}X_1 + c_{22}X_2 + c_{23}X_3, \\ R_3 &= c_{31}X_1 + c_{32}X_2 + c_{33}X_3. \end{aligned} \tag{4.4}$$

Each of the c coefficients can be calculated from the values of the γ's and b's estimated with the original structural equation set. Hence, Equation 4.4 is completely determined by the information in Equation 4.3, even though a certain amount of calculation is required in order to make the transition from the structural to the reduced form set of equations.[4]

Comparisons of Equation 4.4 with Equation 4.1 show that the two are equivalent: Equation 4.4 is the reduced form system corresponding to our three-brand, one promotional variable example. Hence, estimations of the coefficients of the structural equation set allows us to obtain estimates of the reduced form coefficients, even though the latter could not be estimated directly.

4.3.3 Extension of the Structural System

The multiple-equation system developed here for the case of three brands and one promotional variable can be extended directly to meet the requirements of the store audit

[4]The calculations are not as tedious as might be implied by the ordinary algebraic solution given here. The matrix algebra solution, which is the one actually used in the computer, is given in Appendix 4A.

data base, with its twenty-four brand-size combinations and seventeen promotional variables. All that is necessary is to include all twenty-three other brand-size sales ratios in each of the structural equations of Equation 4.3 and increase the number of promotional variables and coefficients from one to seventeen. Each equation of the extended structural set would look like this:

$$R_{it} = \sum_{\substack{j=1 \\ (j \neq i)}}^{24} \gamma_{ij} R_{jt} + \sum_{k=1}^{17} b_{ik} X_{ikt}. \tag{4.5}$$

The model specifications developed in Chapter 3 make use of the square root of the sales ratio as the "sales" variable in each regression relation. To be consistent with this result, we will define R_{it} as

$$R_{it} = \sqrt{\frac{Y_{it}}{\overline{Y}_i}}.$$

The structural equations would each contain twenty-three unknown γ coefficients and seventeen b-coefficients. These forty coefficients would have to be estimated from the data for the given brand-size combination.

Although the estimation of forty coefficients from the several hundred observations available for many of the brands and sizes is not impossible, we would expect some difficulties to arise. First, there is likely to be a good deal of collinearity between the various series for R_{it}, especially in regard to the less actively promoted brands and sizes. As twenty-three such series would be included in each structural equation, this could lead to relatively unstable regression estimates.[5] Second, the number of observations available for estimating some of the structural equations is very much less than the general average; this was particularly true for the large container size in some of the store segments. If the number of observations were to drop to one hundred or less, the parameter estimates in a forty-coefficient equation might be unsatisfactory. Finally, the design characteristics of the computer program required to perform the estimation process and make the conversion to the reduced form made it highly desirable to keep the data for all twenty-four structural equations in high-speed core memory at one time. As it turned out, the size of core storage in the IBM 7094 limited the total number of variables in each structural equation (both R's and X's) to twenty-one. Thus, it was deemed

[5]See Farley (1967) for an example of the deleterious effects of collinearity on parameter estimates in multiple-equation systems.

necessary to combine many of the R-variables when estimating the structural equations.

The process of combining variables in a regression equation amounts to specifying that all the variables lumped together have the same coefficient value. Suppose that we have the following regression equation:

$$Y = b_1X_1 + b_2X_2 + b_3X_3,$$

and we wish to combine variables 1 and 2. This yields the equation[6]

$$Y = b^*_{12}(X_1 + X_2) + b_3X_3.$$

The combination process specifies that X_1 and X_2 both have the same coefficient, namely, b^*_{12}. Once we have estimated b^*_{12}, we can always come back to an approximation of the uncombined equation by writing:

$$Y = b^*_{12}X_1 + b^*_{12}X_2 + b_3X_3.$$

By summing X_1 and X_2 we have eliminated one coefficient from the list of quantities to be estimated (i.e., we have gained one degree of freedom) at the expense of the possible misspecification introduced by the assumption that $b_1 = b_2$, but have not otherwise changed the form of the regression relation. Thus, the process of combining R-variables has no effect on our ability to calculate the reduced form coefficients, except to introduce the assumption that the γ-coefficients for some of the brands and sizes are equal.

We chose to combine R-variables in the structural equation system until each equation contained only three "other sales" terms in addition to the dependent variable in the equation. The three new variables have been labeled OSSB, KEYB (ALTB), and OSOB. They are defined as follows:

1. OSSB. The sum of the square roots of the sales ratios for other sizes of the same brand. For example, if we are looking at the equation for the medium size of brand 1, we have

$$\text{OSSB} = R_{\text{Small B1}} + R_{\text{Large B1}}.$$

If we are looking at the brand–2–large–size equation, this variable becomes

$$\text{OSSB} = R_{\text{Small B2}} + R_{\text{Medium B2}}.$$

2. KEYB (ALTB). Read as "key brand" (alternate brand). This variable is the sum of the square roots of the sales ratios for all three container sizes of the key brand in the analysis, if

[6] The coefficient b^*_{12} is an average of the effects b_1 and b_2 as they apply to X_1 and X_2.

the equation in question is *not for one of the key brand sizes*. If the equation does pertain to the key brand, this variable is the sum of the square roots of the sales ratios of the three sizes for the alternate brand used in the analysis.[7] For example, if we are looking at an equation for brands B2 through B8, we have:

$$\text{KEYB (ALTB)} = R_{\text{Small B1}} + R_{\text{Medium B1}} + R_{\text{Large B1}}.$$

If the equation is for brand B1, we have:

$$\text{KEYB (ALTB)} = R_{\text{Small B2}} + R_{\text{Medium B2}} + R_{\text{Large B2}}.$$

3. ASOB. The sum of the square roots of the sales ratios for all sizes of the other brands. It excludes the dependent variable in the given equation (the brand and size for which coefficients are being estimated) and the brands and sizes included in OSSB and KEYB (ALTB).

The sales for all brands and sizes appear in each of the twenty-four structural equations, either as the dependent variable or as an element in the sum making up OSSB, KEYB (ALTB), or ASOB. As the definitions of the three summary (combined) sales ratio variables are mutually exclusive, no sales ratio appears in a given equation in more than one place. Finally, the definitions of the summary variables are such that the sales of a given brand and size will be included in different variables in different equations.

This particular choice of summary variables was chosen for two reasons. First, we believed that the interactions between the promotions of, say, brand 1, size 1 and the sales of brand 1, sizes 2 and 3 were likely to be different than those between brand 1, size 1 and the various sizes for brands 2, 3, and 4. Thus, we did not want to lump sales of other sizes for the same brand with those of other brands and thus assume that the coefficients for the members of the two sets were equal. This led us to the definition of OSSB, which is other sizes, same brand. Second, we wanted to focus on the interactions between the sales of the key brand and the promotions of the various other brands in the study. This led us to separate the key brand coefficients from those for the rest of the brands, as was accomplished by the specification of KEYB (ALTB); hence, we used the alternate brand (B2) to define this variable when dealing with a key brand equation. Finally, our prior decision that the total number of summary sales variables

[7] The key brand is the brand manufactured by the sponsor of our study. It is one of the set B1–B5. The alternate brand, the key brand's main competitor, is another member of this set. Coding requirements preclude identification of the numbers of the key and alternate brands. For purposes of the example that follows, we will assume that B1 is the key brand and B2 is the alternate, although this bears no relation to the brands actually used.

should be limited to three forced us to lump the R's for all the other brands and sizes in ASOB (all sizes, other brands).

In summary, the structural equation for any brand-size combination can be written in terms of the summary sales variables and the promotional variables for that brand and size in the following manner:

$$R_{it} = \gamma_{\text{OSSB}}(\text{OSSB})_{it} + \gamma_{K(\text{A})}(K(\text{A}))_{it} + \gamma_{\text{ASOB}}(\text{ASOB})_{it} + \sum_{k=1}^{17} b_{ik} X_{ikt}. \tag{4.6}$$

In calculating the reduced form coefficients, we set the coefficient of each of the twenty-three R's included in the summary sales variables to γ_{OSSB}, $\gamma_{K(\text{A})}$, or γ_{ASOB}, depending on the variable in which it is included for the given equation.

4.3.4 The Constant Terms in the Multiple-Equation Model

The single-equation regressions reported in Chapter 3 all included an intercept value (also called the constant term in the regression equation). This value is the predicted value of the sales ratio when all the independent variables are zero. When a given brand and size is not being promoted in any way, all the advertising, price, sign, display, and special-offer variables have zero values. In this case the only variables in the equation that are nonzero are CPE and CPM, which represent promotions in competing stores, and YR_{t-1} and YR_{t-2}, which are the lagged values of the sales ratio for this equation. (See Section 3.6 for a discussion of these equations). Thus, the sales ratio, under nonpromotion conditions, is predicted by the sum of the intercept term and the effects of CPE, CPM, and the lagged YR variables. As the latter four variables turned out to have very small coefficients, the predicted sales ratio in weeks with no promotion was usually close to unity (i.e., the sales of the brand and size was close to its average sales in weeks without promotion). Thus, the intercept coefficients in the single-equation regressions should be fairly close to unity, and indeed, that was generally the case.

In the multiple-equation model we followed a somewhat different procedure from that used in the single-equation work. Instead of specifying a constant term in each structural equation and estimating its magnitude from the data, we set up the model so that the predicted sales ratio in each equation was exactly equal to one when there was no promotional activity of any kind in the market. This was accomplished by redefining the sales ratio variable R, as follows:

$$R_{it} = \sqrt{\frac{Y_{it}}{Y_i}} - 1.$$

That is, when sales are equal to $\overline{Y}$, then $R = 0$. This new definition of R was used throughout the model, both for specification of the dependent variable in each structural equation and for computing the sum of R's that yield OSSB, KEYB (ALTB), and ASOB.

Again neglecting the effects of CPE, CPM, and the YRL variables (this loose end will be taken care of later), we can see that when there is no promotion for a given brand *and* the sales ratios for all the other brands and sizes in the market are all equal to unity (which is tantamount to saying that none of them was on promotion either), then all the variables in that given brand's structural equation, including OSSB, KEYB (ALTB), and ASOB, will be zero. Thus, the predicted value of R_{it} in equation (4.6) will be zero. Given the new definition, a zero value for R_{it} is the same as a sales ratio of one, and hence the no-promotion baseline condition is established. While the logic of this translation may be somewhat confusing, we say again that the net effect is to peg the intercept value of each structural coefficient at one rather than allowing it to be estimated from the data.

One reason for making this prespecification of the intercept is derived from the computational procedures used to obtain estimates of the structural equation coefficients. Given the estimation procedures used, the inclusion of an intercept term in the list of quantities to be estimated would have increased sharply the effects of collinearity among the independent variables—particularly OSSB, KEYB (ALTB), and ASOB. Prespecification of the intercept term was the easiest way to circumvent this difficulty. A second reason for the prespecification was to provide a known baseline against which to compare the effects of promotional variables and other brand-size sales on demand. Pegging the intercept at one materially simplified the calculation of the *demand response ratios*, which will be used extensively in our discussion of the multiple-equation model results in Chapter 6. Finally, our experience with the single-equation model indicated that the intercept coefficients were among the most poorly estimated of all the regression coefficients reported in Chapter 3. The existence of a "natural" value of one, which could be specified on the basis of a priori reasoning, eliminated this potential inaccuracy.

The reasoning discussed in the last paragraph was established before we had made our production runs on the multiple-equation model. While our arguments were valid as far as they went, we did fail to consider one important aspect of the model specification. This difficulty has led to a certain degree of difficulty in interpreting the results of the multiple-equation model. (Fortunately, the problem is not crucial to our use of the results.) The difficulty will be discussed in the next subsection, which describes some of the limitations of the multiple-equation model.

4.3.5 Limitations of the Multiple-Equation Model

In Chapter 2 we explained that the figures for mean sales without promotion ($\bar{Y}$) for each brand and size were calculated by averaging the volume of product sold during weeks in which that particular brand did not receive an ad, a price-off promotion, or a display. A difficulty occurs because $\bar{Y}$ does include sales for weeks in which other brands and sizes were being promoted in the same store. Thus, the substitution coefficients estimated by the multiple-equation model are all relative to the average promotional mix used by the store during the sixty-three weeks covered by the audit, rather than to conditions of no promotion.

It is difficult to say what difference this makes in practice, but we can consider an extreme example. Suppose that a store advertised *only* medium-size containers of brands B1 and B2 and that one brand or the other was on sale during every week of the audit. (This was not the case, of course.) Then the $\bar{Y}$ for B1 would be equal to the average sales of B1 when B2 was on promotion, and conversely. In this case the multiple-equation system would tend to indicate that there was *no* promotional interaction between B1 and B2, because except for random noise the sales ratio of each brand would be one (i.e., R would equal 0) for each brand whenever the other one was on sale. Yet a promotional interaction probably exists; the problem is that we cannot measure it from the data in this example. Fortunately, this extreme case would occur only rarely in practice.

Another difficulty is brought about by prespecifying the intercept at one. We argued at the end of the last subsection that the sales ratios of all the brands should be one when *none* of the brands was on promotion. But the $\bar{Y}$'s were obtained by averaging over weeks when no brand-size combinations were being promoted and weeks in which other brand-size combinations were on sale. In fact, the latter conditions are in the majority. If the sales of a given brand and size tended to be greater when there was no competitive promotion than when there was competition (given, of course, that the brand-size was not itself on sale), then the calculated sales ratio should be greater than one when the store was devoid of all promotion. Thus, the prespecification of the intercept at one is somewhat in error. We should have calculated $\bar{Y}$ using only the sales figures for weeks in which there was no competing promotion of any kind, if this had been possible.[8]

The primary effect of this misspecification of $\bar{Y}$ probably is to introduce a positive bias into our estimates of the substitution effects. The nature of this effect is brought out quite clearly by the numerical example used in Section 4.2.2. There we assumed that the three hypothetical brands had identical $\bar{Y}$'s and that the $\bar{Y}$'s were calculated under conditions in which the three brands were promoted equally. We now add the additional assumption that the sales ratios are calculated relative to a $\bar{Y}$ that is obtained by averaging only over weeks when none of the three brands is on promotion, and these new $\bar{Y}$'s are 50 percent greater than the $\bar{Y}$'s used in the original example. To make the conversion we divide all the sales ratios given in the example by an assumed value of 1.5. This results in the time series shown in Table 4.5 (one nonpromoted week is included for comparison purposes). The main difference between this series and the one presented in Section 4.2.2 is that here none of the sales interactions for no-promotion weeks is greater than one, while there the interactions for no-promotion weeks averaged out to one. This is a direct result of the change in definition of $\bar{Y}$.

As the multiple-equation model assigns a positive coefficient to interactions that are greater than one, we would expect to find apparent complementarity if we analyzed the data as originally presented. In the series given in Table 4.5, none of the interactions would have a positive sign; the nearest thing to a positive relation is the effect of brand C's promotion on brand A—where the sales ratio of 1.0 means that brand A gets as much when brand C is on sale as when no other brands are on sale at all.

All this is not to say that promotion of one brand or size cannot produce a positive increment to the sales of another brand-size combination. This may well be the case when

Table 4.5 Promotional Interaction: Third Illustration

Week	Brand Being Promoted	Sales Ratio for Brand: A	B	C	Total
1	A	3.65	0.52	0.46	4.65
2	B	0.33	3.45	0.87	4.65
3	C	1.00	0.80	2.85	4.65
4	—	1.00	1.00	1.00	3.00

[8]The sparseness of weeks without promotion of any kind in certain stores would have made this procedure very difficult.

different container sizes for the same brand are compared, for example. It is just that we must be careful in interpreting positive interaction coefficients. A positive coefficient means only that the two brand-size combinations stand in a relation of *relative* complementarity as compared to other brands and sizes—not that it is necessarily better to have the other brand on promotion than to have no competing promotion at all, as would be implied by the classic economic definition of complementarity. If we keep these factors in mind, we will have no difficulty interpreting the results reported in Chapter 6.

4.4 Estimation Methods for the Multiple-Equation Model

Estimation of the coefficients of a set of multiple equations is, in principle, no different from the estimation of coefficients in single equations. In both cases the objective is to minimize some measure of the discrepancy between the actual values of the y's (dependent variables) and their values as predicted by the x's (independent variables) with respect to the unknown coefficients of the equation system. In single-equation regressions, the chosen measure of discrepancy is the square of the difference between the actual and predicted y's. As all the variables on the right-hand side of the regression are "independent" (i.e., there are no y-values for the current week), the estimation boils down to the simple matter of minimizing the sum of squared errors with respect to the coefficients of the x's.

In multiple-equation work the structural equations include some y-values on the right-hand side—i.e., as "independent variables" along with the x's. But as we noted earlier, the "independent variable" y's in one equation become the "dependent variable" y in some other equation. This leads to complications in the coefficient estimation process.

The nature of the estimation problem can only be sketched here. (See Goldberger [1964] or Johnson [1963] for a complete discussion of this topic.) First, we would like to obtain estimates for all the structural equations simultaneously; that is, by using the data for all brands and sizes to estimate the coefficients for all twenty-four structural equations in one big mathematical calculation. Such procedures exist (they are called "full information" methods), but they are rarely used because of their computational complexity. These methods are ruled out of our study in any case because of the large number of brands, sizes, and promotional variables included in our model. Hence, we are led to estimate the coefficients of each structural equation using only data on the variables actually included in that equation; that is, the twenty-four structural equations are all estimated independently. This procedure falls under the heading of "limited information" methods.

The next problem concerns how each of the structural equations is to be estimated. Two methods are available: standard least squares (regression) and a procedure known as "instrumental variables."[9] Standard least squares is the simpler of the two; in this case we apply single-equation estimation method to each structural equation in turn, ignoring the fact that some of the "independent variables" in each equation are dependent variables in other equations.

Using least squares methods leads to the following problems however: (1) the y-variables that are treated as "independent" in one equation are correlated with the errors in the equation in which they are "dependent"; (2) the errors in one equation are almost surely correlated with the errors in all the other equations; (3) conditions (1) and (2) imply that the independent variable y's in any equation are correlated with the errors in that same equation; which means that (4) the least squares coefficients of the "independent variable" y's are *biased*. Moreover, this bias does not necessarily disappear as sample size increases.

The method of instrumental variables was designed to eliminate this source of bias. The logic of instrumental variables goes like this.

1. We try to obtain reasonably accurate estimates of the y's in each structural equation for each observation in the data base by methods that will ensure that the y's thus predicted are uncorrelated with the errors in that structural equation (i.e., the negation of condition (3) just described).

2. Then we use these predicted y's to help us estimate the y-coefficients in each equation.[10] That is, for every "independent" y-variable in each structural equation there is a predicted "independent" y-value. These predicted y-values are called "instruments"; they are used *only* to obtain estimates of the coefficients associated with the actual "independent" y-variables, and they have no other role in the model. That is, the method of instrumental variables provides a way to obtain unbiased estimates of the y coefficients of the structural equation system given in equation (4.3), but they do not change the interpretation of the model in the slightest degree.

[9]Other limited information methods, such as two- and three-stage least squares and "k-class" procedures have also been developed, but these all require direct estimation of the reduced form as part of the structural estimation process. We have already seen that direct reduced form estimation is impossible in the present study.

[10]The method by which this is done is given in Appendix 4B.

In applying instrumental variables analysis in the present study, we obtained our instruments as follows.

1. Single-equation regressions were run on the data for all thirty stores over a sixteen-week period near the beginning of the audit. (These results were reported in Chapter 3.)

2. The resulting regression coefficients and the current x-values for the associated brand and size were used to predict the value of YR for each brand, size, store, and week included in a given multiple-equation run;

3. The individual predicted YRs for each store-week were added together to produce OSSB, KEYB (ALTB), and ASOB for the given store-week structural equation, according to the summary y-variable definition given in Section 4.2.3. The resulting predicted values of OSSB, KEYB (ALTB), and ASOB are thus based on the full set of x's (promotional variables for all brands and sizes) and the regression coefficients for the all-stores, sixteen-week runs. As the x's are independent of the error terms in all the equations, (this is a fundamental assumption of standard regression analysis as well as in multiple-equation work), and the regression coefficients from the all-stores, sixteen-week runs are almost completely independent of the error in any equation-store-week combination, the predicted values of OSSB, KEYB (ALTB), and ASOB qualify as instruments. Their use leads to unbiased estimates of the y coefficients in the structural equations.

While the instrumental variables method generates unbiased estimates of the y coefficients, it does so at a cost in the *efficiency* of the estimates. Many studies in the econometric literature show that the application of methods such as instrumental variables (for example, two-stage least squares) gives coefficients with larger standard errors than those obtained by applying single-equation least squares to the same data.[11] (These same studies also show up the least squares bias discussed earlier.) Thus, we are faced with choosing between two methods of which one is known to be biased and the other is known to be inefficient (i.e., to have larger standard errors for the coefficients). Where possible, the choice between bias and efficiency should be based on some estimates of the relative sizes of the bias and efficiency loss and in the context of the purpose for which the empirical analysis is conducted.

An empirical analysis was conducted of the size of the bias and efficiency problems inherent in the application of least squares and instrumental variables estimation methods to

[11]See Farley (1967) for a marketing example.

our store audit data base, in order to place the choice between the two procedures on a firm footing. The results of this analysis are reported at the beginning of Chapter 5. That chapter also describes the results of some additional experiments that were designed to sharpen up the model and its variable definitions.

Appendix 4A Matrix Representation of the Multiple-Equation Model

Let $\mathbf{Y}_t$ be the vector of R_{it}'s, defined as follows:

$$\mathbf{Y}_t' = \{R_{1t}, R_{2t}, \ldots, R_{Nt}\}.$$

If $\mathbf{X}_{it}$ is the k-dimensional column vector of promotional variables for brand i, we can define the following composite vector containing the promotional variables for all the brands and sizes:

$$\mathbf{X}_t' = \{\mathbf{X}_{1t}', \mathbf{X}_{2t}', \ldots, \mathbf{X}_{Nt}'\}.$$

Here, $\mathbf{X}_t$ has $N \cdot K$ rows, where K is the number of promotional variables (there are K rows for each of the brands and sizes). Let the structural equation coefficient vectors be defined as follows:

$$\mathbf{\Gamma} = \begin{bmatrix} -1 & \gamma_{12} \cdots & \gamma_{13} & \cdots \gamma_{1N} \\ \gamma_{21} & -1 & \gamma_{23} & \cdots \gamma_{2N} \\ \gamma_{N1} & \gamma_{N2} & \gamma_{N3} & \cdots -1 \end{bmatrix},$$

and

$$\boldsymbol{\beta} = \begin{bmatrix} \mathbf{b}_1 & 0 & 0 \\ 0 & \mathbf{b}_2 & 0 \\ \vdots & \vdots & \vdots \\ 0 & 0 & \mathbf{b}_N \end{bmatrix},$$

where $\mathbf{b}_i$ is the K-dimensional row vector of coefficients for the promotional variables in the ith structural equation. The matrix $\boldsymbol{\beta}$ is block-diagonal, consisting of N rows (one for each structural equation) and $N \cdot K$ columns (K for each brand and size). The matrix $\mathbf{\Gamma}$ is square ($N \times N$), with a row for each structural equation. Each row contains the coefficients of the sales variables as they appear in that structural equation. The diagonals of $\mathbf{\Gamma}$ are the coefficients of the "own" sales variable for each equation; they are set at -1 to indicate that this variable appears on the left side (i.e., as the dependent variable) in that equation.

The structural equation system may now be written compactly as

$$\mathbf{\Gamma Y}_t + \boldsymbol{\beta}\mathbf{X}_t + \mathbf{u}_t = \mathbf{0}, \tag{4A.1}$$

where $\mathbf{u}_t$ is an N-dimensional column vector of random error terms and $\mathbf{0}$ is a vector of zeros. The fact that $\boldsymbol{\beta}$ is block-diagonal implies that only the X's for the ith set of promotional variables appear in the structural equation for that equation. This is the simplification that allows the structural coefficients to be estimated, as pointed out in Section 4.1.2. This fact also insures that the structural equation set meets the *order conditions for identifiability,* without which the transition to a unique set of reduced form equations would be impossible (Goldberger, 1964, p. 316).

Once the coefficients of Γ and $\boldsymbol{\beta}$ have been estimated from empirical data, it is a simple matter to solve Equation 4A.1 to obtain the reduced form. We merely must premultiply by the inverse of Γ:

$$\mathbf{Y}_t = \Gamma^{-1}\boldsymbol{\beta}X_t + \Gamma^{-1}\mathbf{u}_t = \boldsymbol{\pi}\mathbf{X}_t + \mathbf{V}_t,$$

where $\boldsymbol{\pi}$ is the $(N \times N \cdot K)$ matrix of reduced form coefficients. As matrix inversion and multiplication are standard features of scientific computer languages these steps offer little computational difficulty.

Appendix 4B The Instrumental Variables Estimation Procedure

Using the definitions of Appendix 4A, the multiple-equation model is as follows:

$$\Gamma\mathbf{Y}_t + \boldsymbol{\beta}\mathbf{X}_t + \mathbf{u}_t = \mathbf{0}. \tag{4B.1}$$

Let us focus on the ith equation of this system:

$$\boldsymbol{\gamma}_i\mathbf{Y}_t + \boldsymbol{\beta}_i\mathbf{X}_t + u_{it} = 0, \tag{4B.2}$$

where the vectors $\boldsymbol{\gamma}_i$ and $\boldsymbol{\beta}_i$ are the ith rows of $\boldsymbol{\gamma}$ and $\boldsymbol{\beta}$, respectively. We now set γ_{ii} to -1.0 to normalize the equation (i.e., to define the "dependent variable" for the ith equation), and write

$$Y_{it} = \boldsymbol{\gamma}_i^*\mathbf{Y}_t^* + \boldsymbol{\beta}_i\mathbf{X}_t + u_t,$$

where γ_i^* and Y_t^* are the same as $\boldsymbol{\gamma}_i$ and $\mathbf{Y}_t$ except that the ith element in each vector has been deleted. To simplify the notation we let

$$\mathbf{b}_i = \{\gamma_i^*, \boldsymbol{\beta}_i\}, \text{ and}$$
$$\mathbf{Z}_{it} = \{\mathbf{Y}_t^*, \mathbf{X}_{it}\}.$$

That is, we put the "independent" Y-variables and coefficients for the ith equation and their X counterparts into single composite vectors so that we can write the equations as a standard regression relation:

$$Y_{it} = \mathbf{b}_i\mathbf{Z}_{it} + u_{it}, \quad t = 1, \ldots, T.$$

Now let $\mathbf{Y}_i^*$ be the data vector for Y_{it}; that is, let

$$\mathbf{Y}_i'^* = \{Y_{i1}, Y_{i2}, \ldots, Y_{it}\},$$

and similarly for $\mathbf{Z}_i^*$ and u_{it}, let

$$\mathbf{Z}_i^{*\prime} = \{\mathbf{Z}_{i1}, \mathbf{Z}_{i2}, \ldots, \mathbf{Z}_{it}\}, \text{ and}$$
$$\mathbf{u}_i^{*\prime} = \{u_{i1}, u_{i2}, \ldots, u_{it}\}.$$

Thus, the relations among all the observations for the ith equations can be written compactly as:

$$\mathbf{Y}' = \mathbf{bZ}' + \mathbf{u}', \tag{4B.3}$$

where the subscripts i^* are understood.

How can Equation 4B.3 be estimated? The least squares procedure is to postmultiply by $\mathbf{Z}$ and solve the resulting equations for $\mathbf{b}$, as follows:

(a) $\mathbf{Y'Z} = \mathbf{bZ'Z} + \mathbf{u'Z},$

(4B.4)

(b) $b = \mathbf{Y'Z}(\mathbf{Z'Z})^{-1} - \mathbf{u'Z}(\mathbf{Z'Z})^{-1}.$

The equations in (a) of Equation 4B.4 are the "normal equations" of least squares.

If $\mathbf{Z}$ and $\mathbf{u}$ are independent, the expected value of the last term in (b) of (4B.4) is zero, and the least square estimate of $\mathbf{b}$ is unbiased. But in our case, $\mathbf{Z}$ includes $\mathbf{Y}_i^*$, which, as noted in Section 4.2.1, is not independent of $\mathbf{u}$. Hence, we are led to define the matrix of instrumental variables, $\hat{\mathbf{Y}}_i^*$, described in the text.

$$\hat{\mathbf{Y}}_i^* = f(\text{all } x\text{'s, 16-week all-stores regression coefficients}).$$

Thus $\hat{\mathbf{Y}}_i^*$ is almost completely independent of $\mathbf{u}$, and (we hope) its elements are highly correlated with their associated elements of $\mathbf{Y}_i^*$. (The correlations occur because, after all, the $\hat{Y}$'s are predictions of the Y's). We define $\mathbf{W}_i$ as the composite of $\hat{\mathbf{Y}}_i^*$ and $\mathbf{X}_{it}$; just as $\mathbf{Z}_i$ is the composite of $\mathbf{Y}_i^*$ and $\mathbf{X}_{it}$:

$$\mathbf{W}_{it}' = \{\hat{\mathbf{Y}}_i^*, \mathbf{X}_{it}\},$$

$$\mathbf{W}' = \{\mathbf{W}_{i1}, \mathbf{W}_{i2}, \ldots, \mathbf{W}_{it}\}.$$

Then we have another solution to Equation 4B.3:

(a) $\mathbf{Y'W} = \mathbf{bZ'W} + \mathbf{u'W}$

(4B.5)

(b) $\mathbf{b} = \mathbf{Y'W}(\mathbf{Z'W})^{-1} - \mathbf{u'W'}(\mathbf{Z'W})^{-1}.$

As $\mathbf{W}$ is independent of $\mathbf{u}'$, equation (b) of (4B.5) can be shown to be asymptotically unbiased.

Use of instrumental variables leads to new expressions for

the variance of the regression error term and the standard errors of the estimated coefficients (Goldberger, 1964, p. 285).

Aside from computational matters, the main feature of these results is that the efficiency of the instrumental variables procedure depends critically on the correlations between the predicted Y's, used as instruments, and the actual Y's. The higher the correlation, the smaller the error variance for the equations and the standard errors of the coefficients. Conversely, efficiency is reduced as the cross-correlations between instruments and different Y-variables increases. These considerations are important for understanding the empirical results presented in Chapter 5.

5 Experiments with the Multiple-Equation Model

5.1 Introduction

In this chapter we shall report some preliminary empirical work based on the multiple-equation model for predicting consumer demand that was developed in Chapter 4. The first topic to be considered is that of the relative efficacy of two competing methods for parameter estimation: least squares and instrumental variables. These results are presented in Section 5.2. Then we shall turn our attention to the possibilities offered by an alternative set of Y-variable summary definitions. Estimates obtained by estimating the multiple-equation model using the original set of definitions given in Section 4.3.3 are compared with those using another set, which will be defined at the beginning of Section 5.3. Section 5.4 introduces a complication caused by a shift in market conditions that occurred near the middle of the store audit, and explores some methods for extending the model to take account of this change. As these approaches did not perform satisfactorily, another (more drastic) change in the variable specifications of the multiple-equation model is introduced and successfully tested in Section 5.5. The final multiple-equation model, as it emerged from the experiments reported in Chapter 3 and Chapter 5, is summarized in Section 5.6. This model is the one used to obtain the empirical results for the effects of retailer promotions on consumer demand that are reported and interpreted in Chapter 6.

5.2 Empirical Comparison of Least Squares and Instrumental Variables Estimation

In order to check the performance of the two estimation methods discussed at the end of Chapter 4, we ran comparable multiple-equation runs on two of the four store segments. The set of promotional variables used for these runs was the same as that reported at the end of Chapter 3. The two store segments were the "high response segment" (HRS) and the "low response segment" (LRS), also defined in Chapter 3. These two store groups were chosen in order to test least squares and instrumental variables estimation with the best and worst parts of our data base, where "best" and "worst" refer to the predictive efficacy of the model for the medium container size.

The relative efficiency of the two estimation methods will be considered first. Table 5.1 gives R^2 values from least squares and instrumental variables estimation for the twenty-four brand-size combinations and the two store segments included in this analysis. The most striking feature of this table is that the instrumental variables procedure can lead to negative values of R^2. This is readily explainable. If the instrumental variables used in the estimation process are inefficient enough, the variances of the predicted values of Y may well be larger

Table 5.1

R^2 Comparisons for Least Squares and Instrumental Variables Estimation Methods, Weeks 2–62

		High-Response Segment			Low-Response Segment		
Size	Brand	R^2 L.S.	R^2 I.V.	Sample Size	R^2 L.S.	R^2 I.V.	Sample Size
Small	B2	.167	.048	542	.496	−11.000	506
	B5	.079	−.083	500	.464	.415	512
	B1	.068	−.206	535	.380	−12.598	518
	B4	.061	−.016	545	.444	.103	513
	B3	.078	−.253	334	.858	−25.332	229
	B6	.016	−.055	543	.156	−6.742	512
	B7	–	–	–	.180	.660	512
	B8	.199	.058	547	.331	−8.484	487
Medium	B2	.734	.701	530	.387	−3.972	515
	B5	.789	.785	541	.236	−2.062	514
	B1	.782	.761	537	.260	−7.693	515
	B4	.675	.665	524	.421	.295	513
	B3	.666	.645	393	.113	−2.502	298
	B6	.714	.041	383	.116	−6.612	466
	B7	–	–	–	.364	−2.895	502
	B8	.536	.449	485	.188	−132.158	486
Large	B2	.314	.227	298	.288	.095	486
	B5	.481	.368	259	.510	.510	78
	B1	.581	.507	280	.137	−1.620	262
	B4	.407	.287	225	.373	.321	105
	B3	.309	*	51	–	–	–
	B6	–	–	–	–	–	–
	B7	–	–	–	.530	−2.655	123
	B8	–	–	–	–	–	–

*Calculation impossible because of small sample size.

than that of the original Y's, which, in turn, causes the proportion of Y-variance explained to be negative. (Obviously, negative R^2's are undesirable.)

Table 5.1 shows that there is a very serious drop-off in R^2 when using the instrumental variables estimation method. (Recall that the model and data are the same for both runs; only the method of parameter estimation has been changed.) This loss is not necessarily fatal in the HRS store group, where the all-important medium size yields R^2's of .6 or .7 for both methods of estimation in the case of brands 1 through 5. The instrumental variables estimates for the large size also hold up fairly well, and while the instrumental variables R^2's are slightly negative for small containers, their least squares counterparts are also very small.

Unfortunately, however, the instrumental variables method blows up almost completely when applied to the low response segment stores. Sixteen of the R^2's are negative and most of these are less than -1; the R^2 for B8 medium containers is -132.16. Clearly, this loss in estimating efficiency is unacceptable. While R^2 is not the proper criterion to use in evaluating the estimating efficiency for the coefficients, the very large reductions noted in Table 5.1 leave no doubt that the least squares procedure is producing the better results.

Why does the instrumental variables procedure work fairly well for the HRS and not work at all for the LRS stores? The answer lies partly in the degree of correlation between the instruments and their associated Y-values, and partly in the amount of collinearity among the Y-values themselves. In the HRS, the simple correlations between instruments and actual Y's ran between .4 and .5 for the important brands and sizes. In some cases they were as high as .6, especially for the OSSB and KEYB (ALTB) variables. The collinearity among OSSB, KEYB (ALTB), and ASOB was also moderate for the HRS. In contrast, the correlations between instruments and Y's were seldom above .1 or .15 in the LRS, and collinearity among the Y-summary variables was often quite high. These differences are due to the fact that there is little promotional activity in the LRS stores, and when there are promotions, the response is not as great as in the HRS group. (See the definitions of the various store segments in Chapter 3.) This both reduces the ability of the instrumental variables to predict their corresponding Y's and makes the various Y-time series highly correlated with one another. These two conditions combine to reduce sharply the efficiency of the instrumental variables estimates and destroy the predictive efficacy of the model.

Thus, the least squares procedure, which is unaffected by the correlations between the Y's and the instruments and less sensitive to collinearity among the Y's, must be used in the LRS. As many of the same conditions would doubtless occur in the "mixed response, low volume segment" (MRLV), the same conclusion also applies there. Finally, the need for the estimates from the various store segments to be comparable dictates that least squares be used throughout the analysis.[1]

The size of the bias in the estimates of the substitution inter-

[1]It is possible that these difficulties with instrumental variables in the LRS can be solved. However, time did not permit further experimentation prior to making the production runs that form the basis for this monograph.

action coefficients can be assessed roughly by comparing the coefficient values from the instrumental variables and least squares runs. These are given in Table 5.2 for the HRS stores, where the instrumental variables estimates were good enough to warrant interpretation. The table gives the mean coefficients and standard errors for brands 1 through 6 for small, medium, and large containers, as estimated by each of the two methods. The difference between the instrumental variables (I.V.) and least squares (L.S.) estimates, which is an estimate of the size of the L.S. bias, is reported at the bottom of the table. The ratio of the L.S. to I.V. standard error, whose square provides another assessment of relative efficiency, is also given.

Table 5.2 shows that the least squares results are approximately 0.075 too large (i.e., more positive) for the small and medium equations and 0.22 too large for the large-size equations. These results are fairly consistent over brands and apply to all three substitution variables. On balance it appears that (1) the least squares coefficient estimates are (for the *Y*-variables) as much as an order of magnitude too small, but

Table 5.2 Mean Values of Regression Coefficients and Standard Errors for Substitution Variables – Least Squares and Instrumental Variables Estimation (HRS weeks 2–62)*

		Mean Coefficient Values			Mean Standard Errors		
Variable	Method	Small	Medium	Large	Small	Medium	Large
OSSB	L.S.	0.004	+0.045†	−0.091	0.018	0.058†	0.092
	I.V	−0.102	−0.051†	−0.280	0.047	0.060†	0.139
KEYB (ALTB)	L.S.	−0.038	−0.032	−0.030	0.015	0.025	0.066
	I.V	−0.077	−0.087	−0.265	0.028	0.049	0.126
ASOB	L.S.	−0.011	−0.002	+0.034	0.011	0.018	0.045
	I.V	−0.083	−0.060	−0.216	0.025	0.036	0.124

	Mean Bias Value			Ratio of Mean Std. Errors		
Container	Small	Medium	Large	Small	Medium	Large
OSSB	+0.105	+0.096†	+0.190	0.400	0.970†	0.662
KEYB (ALTB)	+0.040	+0.075	+0.234	0.533	0.500	0.522
ASOB	+0.070	+0.058	+0.250	0.462	0.526	0.364
Mean	0.072	0.075	0.224	0.464	0.663	0.524

*Recoded as described in Appendix A.
†Average excludes brand 6.

(2) even the unbiased estimates of the Y-coefficients imply that the substitution interaction effects for the product under study are smaller than we expected.

As the bias seems to be relatively independent of brand and substitution variable, we are justified in interpreting the *relative* values of the reduced form coefficients without reference to the least squares bias. We must remember, however, that the demand response ratios (DRR's) reported for OSSB, KEYB (ALTB), and ASOB in Chapter 6 are probably underestimates of the true DRR's. Examination of the coefficients of the promotional variables (i.e., all the variables included in the structural equations in addition to the three substitution variables) showed that the choice of estimation method had little effect on them. Hence, we may ignore the problem of least squares bias when interpreting the advertising, price, and other DRR's.

The last part of Table 5.2 shows that the instrumental variables procedure is relatively inefficient compared to least squares, even when dealing with the "good" data from the HRS stores. The least squares standard errors of estimate for the coefficients average out to only about half their average value for instrumental variables. This means that there is a factor of four between the variances of estimate; hence, we appear to be justified in saying that ordinary least squares perform as well as or better than our present version of the instrumental variables estimation procedure.

5.3 An Alternative Set of Y-Summary Variable Definitions

Recall from Section 4.3 that while the sales variables for all twenty-four brand-size combinations are included in each of the structural equations, the use of summary variable definitions brings the number of separate substitution terms in each equation down to three (plus the dependent variable). A set of definitions for these summary variables was given in Section 4.3.3: the variables are "sales for other sizes same brand," OSSB; "total sales for the key or alternate brand," KEYB (ALTB); and "total sales for all sizes of other brands," ASOB.

We shall now consider the following alternative definitions:

1. Y_1 OSSB. "Other sizes of the same brand"; same as OSSB in the previous definition.
2. Y_2 OBSS. "Other brands, same size"; the total sales for the other seven brands for the size being analyzed in the current equation.
3. Y_3 OSOB. "Other sizes, other brands"; this differs from the ASOB definition in that it includes the sales of the key brand (or the alternative brand) and excludes the sales of the

size being analyzed in the current equation (the latter is included in OBSS).

Table 5.3 reports the values of R^2 for parallel runs on the data for the two stores with the greatest frequency of promotion included in the audit. (These two stores are of the same chain and are included in the nine-store HRS group). The old set of Y-summary definitions, given in Section 4.3.3, is labeled as "definition A." The new set given above is listed as "definition B."

The table shows that the original definitions do better than the new ones in eleven of the fourteen estimations for small and medium container sizes (these stores did not carry the large size). Although the average magnitude of the differences is small, the direction is consistent from equation to equation. There seems to be little doubt that definition set A fits the data for these two stores better than definition set B. This test did not encourage us to try out the second definition set on a larger group of stores, especially because of the desirability of keeping the key brand's sales as a separate summary variable in each structural equation.[2]

Table 5.3

R^2 for Two Multiple-Equation Variable Definitions (two stores, weeks 2–62, least squares estimation)

Size	Brand	Definition A	Definition B	Difference	Sample Size
Small	B2	.644	.629	+.015	90
	B5	.285	.245	+.040	63
	B1	.128	.096	+.032	90
	B4	.257	.107	+.150	89
	B3	.173	.154	+.018	90
	B6	.089	.064	+.026	90
	B7	—	—	—	—
	B8	.091	.094	−.003	90
Medium	B2	.935	.942	−.007	90
	B5	.910	.905	+.005	90
	B1	.798	.800	−.002	89
	B4	.757	.715	+.042	87
	B3	.773	.761	+.012	90
	B6	.931	.930	+.001	88
	B7	—	—	—	—
	B8	.599	.503	+.096	90

Note: The medium-size container is not carried by these stores.

[2] Although it is not apparent from Table 5.3, definition B suffers more from collinearity than definition A. This is another reason for dropping B.

5.4 Time Trend and AD-NPL Interaction Experiments

A significant change in market conditions occurred about the middle of the period covered by our audit of retail stores. It was initiated by a reduction in the wholesale price of the product under study. This, in turn, dropped the shelf price for the product by a more than proportionate amount in some stores. The amount of the change was greater than any change anticipated at the start of the study.

In terms of our model, the price reduction led to a drop in the "normal shelf price" (NPL) variable, and hence to changes in the types of ads that would be considered as AD1, AD2, AD3, AD4, and AD5. For instance, an ad that would have been considered an AD5 during the early part of the audit would be classified as an AD4 or even an AD3 after the reduction in normal shelf price. This procedure was consistent with our initial hypothesis, as explained in previous chapters, that it is the relative price reduction (from shelf price) in the ad that moves the product and not the absolute price given in the ad per se.

Given that all our single-equation experiments were based on data taken primarily from the period before the reduction in shelf price, it was necessary to check our variable definitions on the data base as a whole, using the multiple-equation model. This decision was triggered in part by the finding of anomalies in the first full sixty-three-week runs. The anomalies, which took the form of an apparent double plateau in the response of rates of AD2 through AD5, seemed to be traceable in part to the change in normal shelf price.[3]

Initially, four runs were designed to check the performance of the model during the period of NPL transition. They were as follows:

1. A run using the standard model (as described at the end of Chapter 3) on weeks 2 through 17 only—a period that was believed to include relatively few important shelf price reductions.
2. A run using the standard model on the data for weeks 40 through 62, the period after the major price reductions.
3. A run on weeks 2 through 62 using a model in which each value of AD0 through AD5 was multiplied by the current value of NPL (these are called "AD-NPL interaction" regressions).
4. A run on weeks 2 through 62 using the standard (dummy variable) AD definitions, but including a simple time trend term as the eighteenth X-variable in the equation. The time trend was taken as $(W_t - W)$, where W_t is the current week

[3] The nature of the anomalies will be explained in more detail in Section 5.5.

number and W is the average week number for all the observations.

All four experiments were performed on data for the HRS group of stores, using the original set of Y-summary variables. Instrumental variables estimates were obtained for all the runs, because that was the estimation method being used when these experiments were conceived.

Table 5.4 summarizes the results of these experiments. The first two columns give the number of cases in which the advertising-price coefficients (AD2 through AD5, using the standard model) were larger in the periods before and after

Table 5.4
Comparison of Ad Coefficients in Runs for Weeks 2–39 and 40–62, and R^2 for NPL-AD Interactions and Time Trend Runs (stores 1–5, instrumental variables estimation)

		No. of AD2–AD5 Coefficients		Value of R^2			
Size	Brand	Wks 2–39 Larger	Wks 40–62 Larger	NPL-AD Interaction	Time Trend	Difference in R^2	Sample Size (Wks 2–62)
Small	B2	1	0	.267	.267	.0	302
	B5	0	0	−.120	−.003	−.117	260
	B1	0	0	−.024	−.004	−.020	301
	B4	0	0	−.055	−.055	.0	304
	B3	0	0	.064	.064	.0	193
	B6	0	0	−.033	−.027	−.006	303
	B7	—	—	—	—		
	B8	0	0	.124	.127	−.003	305
Medium	B2	2	1	.905	.903	+.002	292
	B5	3	1	.809	.860	−.051	302
	B1	1	1	.829	.832	−.003	301
	B4	2	1	.689	.689	.0	287
	B3	1	1	.747	.751	−.004	241
	B6	0	1	.691	.695	−.004	262
	B7	—	—	—	—	—	—
	B8	1	0	.618	.632	−.024	304
Large	B2	0	0	.374	.372	+.002	169
	B5	0	0	.766	.770	−.004	109
	B1	0	0	.669	.665	+.004	166
	B4	2	0	.519	.532	−.023	107
	B3	—	—	—	—	—	—
	B6		—	—	—	—	—
	B7	—	—	—	—	—	—
	B8	—	—	—	—	—	—
Total		13	6				

the major shelf price break. Of a total of nineteen possible comparisons, thirteen of the AD2 to AD5 coefficients in the "before" period were larger than the corresponding coefficients in the "after" period. (Cases for which there was no activity for the given variable in either the before or the after period are excluded from the table.) As there is no relation between the sign of the difference and either the brand or the size, it appeared that a given level of advertised discount in the "before" period had a greater response than the same level of discount in the after period. This result is consistent with the following interpretation.

In the "before" period, most customers bought on promotion; sales of a brand in weeks when it was not on promotion tended to be very low. In the "after" period, lower shelf prices caused more people to purchase the brand of their choice in nonpromoted weeks. When a promotion did occur, it no longer was the bargain it used to be, and hence had a somewhat lower response. The two cases are depicted graphically in Figure 5.1. Suppose we assume that the total sales of the brand over a long period of time are unaffected by the change in pricing strategy on the part of retailers (if the shelf prices of all important brands change more or less together, this assumption amounts to saying that total product volume in the store is unaffected by the change in retailer strategy). Then the shaded areas under the two sales series in the figure must be equal, and this, in turn, requires that the increase in sales during weeks without promotion noted in the "after" period must be compensated for by a reduction in the sales response during promoted weeks.

While this interpretation is attractive on theoretical grounds (we developed this hypothesis before the data for the "after" period had been processed), we have been unable to corroborate it by looking at the trends of the average weekly sales for weeks without promotion. The relative cumulative averages for the medium container size in stores 1 through 5 (included in the HRS group) for four of the five major brands are as shown in Table 5.5. The mean weekly sales without promotion seems to have gone up in the "after" period only in the case of brand B4. It went down very sharply for B1 and stayed the same or declined slightly for B2 and B5.

A second interpretation of the decrease in the response to ads with a given discount is that some of the high response stores stopped promoting medium-sized containers in the "after" period, leaving the low response stores as the only ones active in the weeks 40 to 63 regressions. Again, we can

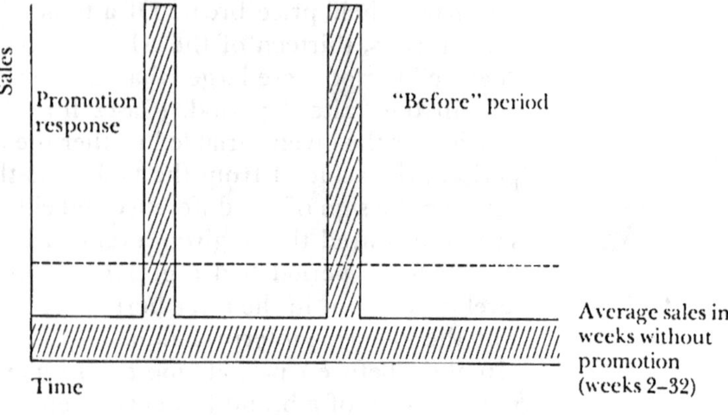

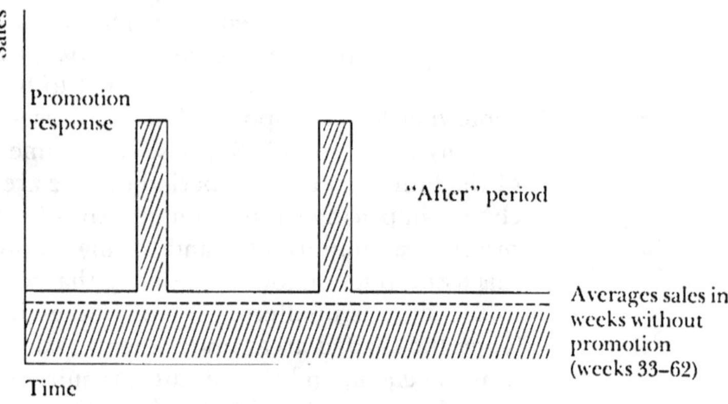

Figure 5.1 Hypothetical sales series in periods before and after shelf price reduction.

get no clear-cut assessment of this possibility from the data (but see the results in Chapter 6 where before-after results for absolute AD-price definitions are interpreted in considerably more detail).

Finally, we should note that the before-after results reported here run counter to the idea that a greater *percentage* price reduction should lead to a greater response. In the "after" period, when NPL is low, a given discount represents a greater percentage reduction from the normal shelf price;

Table 5.5 Relative Mean Weekly Sales Without Promotion: Medium Size

Weeks Included in the Average	Brand B2	B5	B1	B4
1–24	111	99	170	57
1–63 (=100)	100	100	100	100

yet this period yields smaller response coefficients on the average.

Our conclusion from this set of results, and from the aforementioned anomalies in the sixty-three-week runs, was that considerably more effort had to be expended on the advertising-price definitions in order to obtain managerially useful interpretations.

With this conclusion in mind, our next experiment was to try the sixty-three-week NPL-AD interaction and time trend multiple-equation runs described earlier in this section.

Multiplication of the AD variables by NPL amounts to assuming that the response to a given AD variable is greater in the "before" period, when NPL is higher, than in the period after the shelf price reduction. This is consistent with the results of the before-after runs with the standard model reported earlier.

In contrast, inclusion of the time trend term allows sales to be either larger or smaller on the average in the "after" period, depending on the sign of the coefficient. (We did not try a run with both the NPL interaction and time trend terms included, although this would have been desirable.)

The values of R^2 obtained from these runs are reported in the third and fourth columns of Table 5.4, and the differences between them are given in the fifth column. Comparison of the predictive power of the two sets of runs shows that the time trend model does better than the NPL-AD interaction model in eleven of the eighteen brand-size combinations for which data were available, the two are about equal in four cases, and the NPL-AD interaction model performs better in only three cases. In addition, multiplication by NPL in the interaction model failed to eliminate the anomalies in the progression of responses from AD2 to AD5 mentioned earlier. Hence, it appeared that the time trend was a better candidate for inclusion in our final model than was the interaction of the AD variables with NPL.

Table 5.6 reports the time trend coefficients and their standard errors and *t*-ratios. Only one of the eighteen coefficients is statistically significant. Moreover, the signs of the coefficients are mixed: ten of the eighteen are positive, while eight are negative. Thus, the time trend term does not appear to be measuring the effect of the change in shelf prices with any consistency. Given these essentially negative results, we concluded that the time trend approach was not capable of resolving the difficulties inherent in tracking the shelf price reduction, and the hypothesis of a time trend was dropped from further consideration.

Table 5.6

Regression Coefficients, Standard Errors and t-Ratios for Time Trend Variable (stores 1–5 weeks 2–62, instrumental variables estimation)*

Size	Brand	b	σ_b	t_b
Small	B2	−0.000	0.004	−0.127
	B5	+0.010	0.004	+3.342
	B1	+0.002	0.002	+0.361
	B4	−0.002	0.004	−0.382
	B3	−0.002	0.004	−0.337
	B6	+0.001	0.004	+0.657
	B7		—	—
	B8	−0.002	0.002	−1.576
Medium	B2	+0.002	0.004	+0.568
	B5	+0.004	0.006	+0.730
	B1	−0.008	0.006	−1.311
	B4	+0.008	0.008	+0.941
	B3	−0.008	0.006	−1.459
	B6	+0.014	0.008	+1.751
	B7	—	—	—
	B8	−0.010	0.004	−2.107
Large	B2	+0.004	0.010	+0.385
	B5	+0.016	0.018	+0.892
	B1	+0.010	0.014	+0.693
	B4	−0.028	0.009	−1.539
	B3	—	—	—
	B6	—	—	—
	B7	—	—	—
	B8	—	—	—

*Recoded as described in Appendix A.

5.5 Absolute AD-Price Definitions

The failure of the experiments with AD-NPL interactions and the time trend and the persistence of the anomalies in the relative effects of the AD-price variables led us to experiment with an entirely new concept of AD-price definitions. Instead of classifying a given AD on the basis of the difference between the price quoted in the ad and the normal shelf price (NPL), we decided to try a series of runs in which the actual price given in the ad formed the entire basis for classification. For example, under the new definitions an xx¢ ad for a given size is always classified as an AD5, regardless of the value of NPL. We call these new categories "absolute AD-price" definitions, in contrast to the "relative AD-price" definitions defined in Chapters 2 and 3 and used in all the equations for which results have been reported so far.

Six multiple-equation runs were implemented to check the

performance of the absolute AD-price definitions and contrast them with the original relative AD-price model. They were as follows:

1. Relative AD-price; weeks 2 through 62 (overall period).
2. Relative AD-price; weeks 2 through 32 ("before" period).
3. Relative AD-price; weeks 33 through 62 ("after" period).
4. Absolute AD-price; weeks 2 through 62 (overall period).
5. Absolute AD-price; weeks 2 through 32 ("before" period).
6. Absolute AD-price; weeks 33 through 62 ("after" period).

All the runs were performed on the nine HRS stores, using the least squares estimation procedure. The breakpoint between the "before" and "after" periods was reduced from week 39 (as defined in the regressions reported in Section 5.4) to week 32 in order to reflect better the beginning of the period of shelf price reductions by the major stores included in the HRS category.

Our first comparison between the absolute AD-price and relative AD-price models was in terms of predictive efficacy. The values of R^2 were nearly the same for the two models: although the original model performed slightly better in some cases, the new model did better in others. On balance, there was a tendency for the absolute AD-price R^2's to be slightly larger than their relative AD-price counterparts, especially for the "overall" (sixty-three-week) runs, but no consistent pattern of differences could be found. In view of the importance of the differences between the two models in regard to managerial interpretations, the small differences in average predictive efficacy were judged to be unimportant. Thus, the choice between the two models had to be based on the relative interpretability of the two sets of advertising-price coefficients.

The regression coefficients for AD0 through AD5 for the six runs are reported in Table 5.7. This table reports results for the medium-size container of the six major brands in the market area under study. The standard errors of these coefficients are not given, but they run in the range of 0.1 to 0.5. Thus, the AD3, AD4, and AD5 coefficients are almost always statistically significant. The salient features of Table 5.7 are as follows:

1. The overall runs for the relative AD-price variables show the anomaly mentioned earlier in this chapter. The AD2 coefficients for brands B1, B2, B3, and B5 are all considerably higher than the AD3 coefficients for the same brands. In some cases the AD2 coefficients are also larger than the AD4 coefficient, and in the case of B3, AD2 was larger than AD5 as well.

Table 5.7

Regression Coefficients for Relative and Absolute AD-Price Definitions (medium-size container, weeks 2–32, 33–62, and 2–62; HRS; least squares estimation)*

AD-Price Definitions		Brands B1	B2	B3	B4	R5
Relative	AD0	0.20	0.41	—	—	0.60
Weeks 2–62	AD1	—	0.42	—	—	—
	AD2	2.51	2.85	2.54	1.41	3.12
	AD3	1.94	2.09	2.27	2.18	2.55
	AD4	2.51	1.54	—	2.51	2.39
	AD5	3.03	3.78	2.39	2.90	3.25
Weeks 2–32	AD0	—	0.18	—	—	—
	AD1	—	—	—	—	—
	AD2	—	—	3.15	—	—
	AD3	2.23	2.01	2.58	2.02	2.62
	AD4	2.48	1.72	—	2.38	2.47
	AD5	3.41	4.27	2.44	3.13	3.65
Weeks 33–62	AD0	0.30	0.52	—	—	0.71
	AD1	—	0.56	—	—	—
	AD2	2.43	2.61	2.50	1.44	3.27
	AD3	1.46	2.25	2.32	2.23	2.05
	AD4	2.85	2.41	—	2.94	2.29
	AD5	2.33	1.83	3.55	2.67	2.57
Absolute	AD0	—	0.04	—	—	—
Weeks 2–62	AD1	0.42	0.50	—	—	—
	AD2	0.37	0.43	—	—	0.60
	AD3	2.33	2.06	—	2.81	2.46
	AD4	1.62	2.11	2.41	2.06	2.41
	AD5	2.99	2.76	2.31	2.66	3.07
Weeks 2–32	AD0	—	0.13	—	—	—
	AD1	—	—	—	—	—
	AD2	—	—	—	—	—
	AD3	2.34	2.03	—	2.12	2.48
	AD4	2.34	1.73	2.68	2.20	2.53
	AD5	3.34	4.34	2.44	3.12	3.65
Weeks 33–62	AD0	—	0.45	—	—	—
	AD1	0.35	0.57	—	—	—
	AD2	0.16	0.45	—	—	0.67
	AD3	—	—	—	—	—
	AD4	1.69	2.39	2.53	1.55	2.25
	AD5	2.48	2.19	2.34	2.56	2.89

*Recoded as described in Appendix A.

2. There are no large AD2 coefficients in the overall absolute AD-price results. This was a result of the difference in the ad definitions. There were relatively few AD2 ads in the HRS stores, and when offered they did not produce a significant response. This implies that the AD2 ads that sold the product in the relative AD-price runs were classified as such because of the drop in shelf price rather than being ads at the relatively higher price that was applicable in the "before" period.
3. In the overall absolute AD-price results, AD3 and AD4 ads performed about the same, while AD5 ads did much better. The anomaly noted in the overall relative AD-price run was not present in the overall absolute AD-price run.
4. The results for the relative AD-price and absolute AD-price runs on the weeks 2 through 32 data were nearly the same. This is to be expected, since the two definitions do not diverge until NPL begins to drop after week 29. Except for brand B3, there did not appear to be any important anomalies in these results.
5. The relative AD-price run for weeks 33 through 62 showed the AD2 to AD5 anomaly very strongly, whereas the absolute AD-price model applied to the same weeks produced results that are readily interpretable. This implies that the relative AD-price definitions tended to break down during the decline in NPL, due to the change in the meaning of the AD2 ad category.
6. In spite of its apparent good performance when taken by itself, the overall absolute AD-price set of runs yielded rather misleading results when compared to the ad effects as estimated from the data for the "before" and "after" periods separately. The absolute AD-price coefficients for the pooled sixty-three-week data were averages of rather divergent sets of coefficients for the two periods. The differences between the "before" and "after" AD-price coefficients will be analyzed in detail in Chapter 6. It appears that an xx¢ ad produces different effects depending on the level of NPL, and so the average results for the sixty-three-week data period taken as a whole are not as meaningful as we would like.

Our conclusions from this set of empirical results can be stated briefly:

1. Neither the relative AD-price nor the absolute AD-price model does an adequate job of tracking the decline in NPL. (An "adequate" model would have to be capable of producing meaningful AD-price coefficients when applied to the data period as a whole.) Hence, it is necessary to split the

audit into two parts and apply whichever model is chosen to each part separately.

2. The absolute AD-price model did a better job of measuring advertising effects in the "after" period than did the relative AD-price model. As the two models are essentially equivalent during the "before" period, this implies that the absolute AD-price model should be chosen as the basis for the remainder of the analysis.

These conclusions were adopted. The results to be reported in Chapter 6 are all based on the absolute AD-price model. The model is applied to the data for weeks 2 through 32 and 33 through 62 separately for each store segment analyzed.

5.6 The Final Multiple-Equation Model

In this section we will review the multiple-equation model variable definitions as they finally were applied to obtain the results to be reported in Chapter 6. The changes between this model and the one used to obtain the single-equation results reported in Chapter 3 can be summarized briefly as follows:

1. The additions to the single-equation model specification required to accommodate substitution interaction effects, as discussed in Sections 4.2 and 4.3;

2. The change in the AD-price definitions discussed in Section 5.5;

3. Some additional changes in the set of included promotional variables and the store segment groups brought about as the result of experience with the model and data base accumulated during the course of the experiments described in this chapter.

The variables included in the final multiple-equation model runs are as follows:

Substitution Interaction Variables (see Section 4.3.3 for definitions of these variables)

OSSB. Sales of other sizes of the same brand

KEYB (ALTB). Sales of the key brand (or the alternate brand), all sizes

ASOB. Sales of all sizes of other brands

Advertising-Price Variables (see Table 6.2 for definitions of the AD-price categories)

AD0. Ads without a price discount.

AD1. Ads with absolute price in category 1 (dummy variable)

AD2. Ads with absolute price in category 2 (dummy variable)

AD3. Ads with absolute price in category 3 (dummy variable)

AD4. Ads with absolute price in category 4 (dummy variable)

AD5. Ads with absolute price in category 5 (dummy variable)

Unadvertised Price Variables

UAP-ZFM. Amount of unadvertised price discount (from NPL) in weeks when another brand of the same size is on promotion in the store

UAP-NFM. Amount of unadvertised price discount (from NPL) in weeks when no other brand of the same size is on promotion in the store

Other Promotional Variables

SPOPD. Special offer: in- or on-pack premium (dummy variable)

SPORD. Special offer: reusable pack (dummy variable)

SPOCD. Special offer: retailer coupon (dummy variable)

Other Variables

CPE-ZFE. Maximum price discount for this brand and size in competing stores in weeks when this brand and size is on promotion

CPM. Maximum price discount for other brands, same size, in competing stores (taken as a deviation from its mean)

Constant Term

Defined as being equal to 1.0 (see Section 4.3)

The variable CPE is used in conjunction with ZFE for the following reason: when a promotion for a given brand and size meets a big promotion for the same brand and size by some other store, we would expect that the response of the AD or UAP variable would be less than normal. Because ZFE is one when the brand and size is on promotion and zero elsewhere (see Chapter 2), the ZFE-CPE interaction accomplishes this purpose. Its coefficient acts as an offset to the AD and UAP coefficients.

All the variables in the multiple-equation model except CPM are used in their raw form; that is, they are not taken as deviations from their means. Thus, when a variable has a zero value it makes no contribution to the sum that predicts the sales value for the equation. An intercept value of one is built into the multiple-equation model. (See Section 4.3.4 for a discussion of the implications of this specification.) The variable CPM is taken as a deviation from its mean because it is normal for some other brand to be on special in some competing store. Hence the "no-effect" point is taken as the average value of CPM rather than as zero.

Finally, we note the following change in the definition of the store segments. Separate "before" and "after" runs are reported for two segments, each of which is formed by combining two of the segments defined in Chapter 3:

Segment 1: HVS (high volume segment). This is made up of the previous high response (HRS) and mixed response, high volume (MRHV) segments.

Segment 2: LVS (low volume segment). This is made up of the previous mixed response, low volume (MRLV) and low response (LRS) segments.

It was necessary to combine the segments in this manner to provide enough stores in each group to split the data base into two time periods. With fifteen stores in each segment, the sample sizes for weeks 2 through 32 and weeks 33 through 62 were adequate for separate analysis.

The following variables, discussed in Chapters 2 and 3, are not included in the multiple-equation runs:

UODD. Presence of display (dummy variable)

LODC. Location of display code

SISD. Sign in store (dummy variable)

SIWD. Sign in window (dummy variable)

These variables had only very sparse incidence in the data base taken as a whole and almost vanishing incidence in the before-after period store segment data taken separately. The variables were originally included in runs using the relative AD-price definitions for the HRS, MRHV, MRLV, and LRS store groups. The results showed that, given their very infrequent occurrence, (1) the display and sign variables were highly collinear with one another and with the advertising and UAP variables, and (2) even when collinearity was not a problem, the coefficients of these variables were not satisfactory for purposes of interpretation. When collinearity was a problem, the inclusion of UODD, LODC, SISD, and SIWD tended to interfere with the interpretation of some of the AD and UAP variables. Inasmuch as the latter are more important for managerial decision making, we decided to eliminate the display and sign variables from the multiple-equation model.

The effects of displays and signs should be analyzed further. Given their rarity and the fact that they tend to be collinear with other promotional variables included in the model, the best way to analyze them is in terms of the residuals from the fitted multiple-equation model.

The next chapter reports the results of the multiple-equation model. Chapter 7 reports the results of the residual analysis.

6

Results of the Multiple-Equation Analysis

6.1

Introduction

This chapter is divided into three major sections. First is a discussion of the extent to which the multiple-equation model predicts weekly demand by brand and container for each store grouping–time period combination included in the analysis. Next is a discussion of the magnitude of the effects of the various promotional variables on the demand for the brand-size that instigated the promotions. This is followed by a report of the effects of one brand-size promotion on the demand for other brands and sizes.

6.2

Predictive Efficacy

The raw coefficient of determination is a measure of the proportion of the total variation in the dependent variable ($\sqrt{YR}-1$) that is explained by the full set of independent variables. It is computed by the formula $1.0-SSE/SSY$, where SSE is the sum of the squared errors about the regression surface and SSY is the sum of the squares of the dependent variable.

Given the objectives as well as the constraints associated with this project, it is unreasonable to expect that one can explain virtually all the variation of YR in terms of the independent variables that are included in the analysis. For example, some of the variation in our dependent variable could be due to the effects of weather, holidays, and so forth. Still another component of the variation in YR could be associated with inter-store competitive promotion for products other than the one under investigation. Ideally, one would like a measure of the proportion of variation that one could explain out of the total amount of variation attributable to the promotional variations being studied. This is particularly important for some of the small-package-size and low-volume store analyses, in which virtually no promotion for the product occurred. In such a context there is apt to be relatively little total variation in YR, and what is more important, a large percentage of the variation that did occur is attributable to factors other than the product's promotion. The R^2s (coefficients of determination) for a number of these regressions are artificially low if one's purpose is to see how well the regressions do in predicting demand relative only to that component of total variation that is potentially explainable in terms of a brand's promotional activities.

The variance attributable to factors other than those that our analysis attempts to measure will be called "noise variance." We have adjusted the raw coefficients of determination for this source of noise by using the following procedure:

1. For each brand–size–store group–time period combination, the variance of YR was computed based on only those weekly

observations for which there was no promotional activity for that brand-size combination. This variance is therefore an estimate of the magnitude of the noise variance.

2. The amount of variation (based on the preceding estimate) that is due to noise is present in both SSE and SSY. We subtracted our estimate of the noise variance from both terms and recomputed the value of the coefficient of determination.

Both the raw and noise-adjusted coefficients of determination are reported in Table 6.1.

Medium-size containers are the most heavily promoted in the market area under study and therefore constituted the most important component of the market for the product. The average coefficient of determination (based on all eight brands) is higher for medium-size containers than for either of the other two sizes, regardless of time period, in both the all-stores and high-volume stores analyses. The average coefficients of determination in the all-stores analysis for the medium-size containers before adjusting for noise are .54 and .53 in the "before" and "after" time periods, respectively. The "adjusted for noise" coefficients are .71 and .72. In other words, our model accounts for 71 percent of the potentially explainable variation in YR in the "before" period and 72 percent in the "after" period. The model's performance in the high-volume segment is somewhat better. After adjusting for noise, it accounts for 77 and 75 percent of the variation in the "before" and "after" periods. The highest coefficients of determination are for B3 (.84) and B5 (.81) in the medium container size, high-volume store analyses in the before period; and .84 and .78 for the same two brands in the after period. Even for the low-volume store analyses, in which less emphasis is placed on medium-size promotion, the model still explains 73 and 63 percent of the variation in YR after adjusting for noise in the "before" and "after" time periods.

Table 6.1 Coefficients of Determination, Raw and Adjusted for Noise (by container size)

	Raw			Adjusted for Noise		
Brand	Small	Medium	Large	Small	Medium	Large
All Stores						
Weeks 2–32						
B1	.17	.67	.21	.42	.72	.86
B2	.29	.66	.37	.47	.73	.66
B3	.06	.44	.08	*	.68	*
B4	.23	.54	.31	.64	.64	.39

Table 6.1 (*contd.*)

	Raw			Adjusted for Noise		
Brand	Small	Medium	Large	Small	Medium	Large
B5	.32	.65	.05	.55	.73	.58
B6	.12	.50	—	.38	.64	—
B7	.12	.49	.25	.61	.86	.62
B8	.16	.35	—	.38	.66	—
Average	.18	.54	.21	.49	.71	.62
Weeks 33–62						
B1	.07	.55	.44	.15	.65	.48
B2	.09	.51	.27	.21	.59	.33
B3	.55	.59	.25	.93	.79	
B4	.12	.59	.48	.37	.69	.55
B5	.06	.67	.24	.15	.71	.29
B6	.00	.69	—	*	.83	
B7	.26	.17	.58	.25	*	.63
B8	.06	.47	—	.12	.78	—
Average	.15	.53	.38	.31	.72	.46
High-Volume Stores						
Weeks 2–32						
B1	.01	.76	.28	.14	.80	.91
B2	.47	.71	.43	.89	.75	.75
B3	.08	.49	—	*	.84	
B4	.00	.60	.31	.22	.69	.42
B5	.46	.72	.05	.83	.81	.53
B6	.12	.60	—	.33	.91	
B7	—	—	—	—	—	—
B8	.17	.45	—	.61	*	
Average	.19	.62	.27	.50	.77	.65
Weeks 33–62						
B1	.04	.64	.55	.13	.70	.59
B2	.02	.62	.32	.13	.69	.39
B3	.06	.66	—	.37	.76	—
B4	.09	.60	.53	.43	.71	.60
B5	.08	.74	.60	.18	.78	.64
B6	.00	.77	—	.18	.84	—
B7	—	—	—	—	—	—
B8	.02	.54	—	.07	.77	—
Average	.04	.65	.50	.21	.75	.56

Table 6.1 (*contd.*)

Brand	Raw Small	Raw Medium	Raw Large	Adjusted for Noise Small	Adjusted for Noise Medium	Adjusted for Noise Large
Low-Volume Stores						
Weeks 2–32						
B1	.29	.48	.08	.54	.62	*
B2	.39	.54	.30	.57	.77	.67
B3	.16	.46	.06	*	.90	.65
B4	.38	.44	.08	.71	.72	*
B5	.37	.52		.59	.68	—
B6	.16	.06		*	.61	—
B7	.13	.48	.24	.65	.86	.61
B8	.25	.14		.44	.65	—
Average	.27	.39	.15	.58	.73	.64
Weeks 33–62						
B1	.30	.38	.06	.68	.59	.13
B2	.28	.38	.50	.48	.58	.54
B3	.89	.10	—	*	*	—
B4	.28	.62	.64	.65	.76	.69
B5	.28	.53	.0047	*	.63	—
B6	.04	.10	—	*	.56	—
B7	.22	.15	.64	.25	*	.69
B8	.17	.16	—	.30	*	—
Average	.31	.30	.46	.47	.62	.51

*The estimate of noise variance was found to be greater than the raw SSE.

Large container sizes are next in terms of our ability to predict weekly variation in demand. The average coefficients of determination after adjusting for noise are as follows:

	Weeks 2–32	Weeks 33–62
All stores	.62	.46
High-volume stores	.65	.56
Low-volume stores	.64	.51

The model's poorest performance was for small containers; the coefficients are as follows:

	Weeks 2–32	Weeks 33–62
All stores	.49	.31
High-volume stores	.50	.21
Low-volume stores	.58	.47

6.3 Structure: Main Effects

In the four sections that follow we shall discuss the effects of demand for each of four sets of policy variables: (1) retail advertising-price promotions; (2) unadvertised price discounts; (3) special offers, including premiums, reusable packs, and retailer coupons; and (4) competing promotions, that is, those by chains other than the one being analyzed.

6.3.1 Retail Advertising-Price Promotions

Two critical issues underlie the determination of retail advertising-price policy:

1. What determines the response of customer (household) demand to an advertisement? Is it the price that is quoted in the ad or the discount below the normal price (the typical price when the size is not being promoted) that is implied by the quoted price?
2. What is the relationship between the price at which the product is offered in an advertisement and short-run shifts in household demand?

A drop in the normal retail price level for the product under study was initiated in the market area in approximately week 32 of the panel. It was both an asset and a liability from the standpoint of developing a basis for evaluating the effects of advertising and pricing activity on demand. It was a liability in that it necessitated a comparison of the effects of these policy variables both before and after the change as opposed to a simple estimation of their effects over the entire time period. It was an asset in that it created an "artificial experiment" that provided an almost ideal context in which to answer question 1.

6.3.1.1 Advertising-Price Variable Definitions

In each equation included in the analysis there are six advertising-price variables, AD0 through AD5. These variables are coded as dummy variables. That is, during weeks in which there is an advertised price for a given brand-size combination that fell into a particular category, the appropriate AD variable for that category is assigned a value of one, while in weeks in which there is no activity, it is assigned a value of zero. The variables are defined in terms of the absolute value of the retail AD-price quotations they contained.

Because of the competitively sensitive nature of this information, the actual prices have been coded by multiplying the prices for each size by an arbitrarily chosen constant, thereby concealing their (1) absolute level; (2) their relative magnitude over container sizes; and (3) the magnitude of discount off NPL (as reported in Table 6.3). The coded price definitions for each AD category by package size are reported in Table 6.2. It is important that the reader understand these price definitions, which at first may seem painfully obvious, as a basis for understanding our distinction between quoted price and implied discount in the section that follows.

The same definitions are used in the runs for both the weeks 2 through 32 and 33 through 62 time periods. As one goes from an AD0 to an AD5, the price for a given size declines. For example, a medium-size ad (AD3) is defined as a retail ad that quotes a price for a medium-size container between $4.50 and $4.99, whereas an AD5 for the same size container is defined as an ad in which the quoted price is less than $3.99.

6.3.1.2 Quoted Price versus Implied Discount as Demand Determinants

If the price quoted in an ad is the primary determinant of consumer demand, one expects the regression coefficients and their corresponding demand response ratios (hereafter referred to as DRR's) for a given AD category before the drop in normal price to be the same as those observed after it; whereas, if the magnitude of the "implied discount" is the important ingredient, one expects the coefficients and their corresponding DRR's to be lower after the decline in normal price than before it. The DRR for a given average AD coefficient is computed by the following formula:

$$\mathrm{DRR} = (1.0 + b)^2,$$

where b is the average regression coefficient across the top five brands. The 1.0 is added to the coefficient in order to adjust for the fact that 1.0 is subtracted from the value of the

Table 6.2

AD0–AD5 Coded Absolute Price Definitions by Container Size (Dollars)

	Container Size		
Price Variable	Small	Medium	Large
AD0	5.00 or more	6.00 or more	8.00 or more
AD1	4.85–4.99	5.50–5.59	7.50–7.99
AD2	4.70–4.84	5.00–5.49	6.50–7.49
AD3	4.50–4.69	4.50–4.99	5.70–6.49
AD4	4.25–4.49	4.00–4.49	4.50–5.69
AD5	4.24 or less	3.99 or less	4.49 or less

dependent variable prior to running the regression analyses (Section 4.3.4).

Each regression coefficient measures the change in the dependent variable that one expects on average to result from a one-unit change in an independent variable. The dependent variable in our model is the square root of YR − 1 ($\sqrt{YR} - 1$). Our interest is not in the relationship between an independent variable and the square root of YR, but, instead, between it and the magnitude of YR itself. To recover the original metric, we simply square the sum of the regression coefficient and 1.0.

The magnitude of DRR is a measure of the increase over and above normal demand (average demand in weeks without promotion) in the store segment being analyzed associated with the presence of the advertising-price activity.

In addition to comparing the AD coefficients for a given quoted price across time periods, one can also compare the coefficients for AD variables that represented the same (or similar) implied price discounts from one period to the next. Table 6.3 reports estimates of the implied discounts for AD0

Table 6.3 AD0–AD5 Coded Implied Discounts by Container Size (in dollars)

	Container Size		
Price Variable	Small	Medium	Large
Weeks 2–32			
AD0	0.00	0.00	0.00
AD1	0.20	0.50	0.50
AD2	0.35	1.00	1.25
AD3	0.54	1.50	2.16
AD4	0.76	2.00	3.16
AD5	0.97	2.55	4.00
Weeks 33–62			
AD0	–	–	–
AD1	–	0.00	–
AD2	0.15	0.50	0.50
AD3	0.34	1.00	1.41
AD4	0.56	1.50	2.41
AD5	0.77	2.05	3.25
Assumed Normal Prices			
Weeks 2–32	5.13	6.25	8.25
Weeks 33–62	4.93	5.75	7.50

through AD5 by container size for weeks 2 through 32 and 33 through 62. The base prices that are used to compute the discounts are also reported. For example, the discount for AD3's for medium-size containers in weeks 2 through 32 is estimated at $1.50. This figure is arrived at by subtracting $4.75 (the midpoint of the AD3 absolute price range) from $6.25 (our estimate of the normal price—i.e., the price typically quoted in AD0 ads during weeks 2 through 32). The figures are admittedly rough approximations but, nonetheless, are adequate as a basis for the needed comparison.

If the implied discount associated with an advertisement is critical relative to the absolute price quoted in the advertisement, one would expect that the variation in the magnitude of DRR would be less when variables that represented similar price discounts in the period before and after the drop in normal price level are compared than when comparing the DRR's within a given time period.

Table 6.4 reports a comparison of the regression coefficients and DRR's for medium-size containers for the AD variables. These statistics are reported for the all-stores as well as for the high- and low-volume store segments. Each coefficient is an average across as many of the top five brands in the market area as were active with respect to AD promotions in the store segments during the period of the analysis.

The first evidence to be presented is a comparison of the coefficients for the analyses based on weeks 2 through 32 with those from weeks 33 through 62. There are eighteen possible comparisons (six variables times three store groupings). Four of these are automatically eliminated due to the fact that there is no advertising activity in one of the two time periods. An additional three comparisons for AD1 and AD2 are also excluded, as the absolute magnitude of the coefficients is quite small in relation to their standard errors.

Of the remaining eleven comparisons, eight of the average coefficients for the "after" time period (weeks 33 through 62) are less than those for the "before" period. The sharpest drop occurs in the all-stores analysis for AD5's in which the DRR drops from 11.6 to 8.1.

The three before-after comparisons that are not consistent with this finding are for AD4's in the high-volume segment, AD5's in the low-volume segment, and AD3's in the low-volume segment. However, two of these three anomalies can be questioned. For the AD4 result, the coefficients for B3 are unusually high during the "after" period and unusually low during the "before" period. B3 results for advertising consistently show peculiar anomalies (see section 3.4.2).

Table 6.4 Advertising-Price Regression Coefficients and Demand Response Ratios Averaged over Top Five Brands by Store Segment and Time Period for Medium-Size Packages*

	Price Variable					
Time Period	AD0	AD1	AD2	AD3	AD4	AD5
All Stores						
Weeks 2–32						
Reg. Coeff.	0.041(4)	–	0.921(4)	1.166(5)	1.587(5)	2.398(5)
DRR	1.1		3.7	4.7	6.7	11.6
Weeks 33–62						
Reg. Coeff.	−0.003(2)	0.092(4)	0.067(3)	0.968(4)	1.486(5)	1.849(5)
DRR	1.0	1.2	1.1	3.9	6.2	8.1
High-Volume Segment						
Weeks 2–32						
Reg. Coeff.	−0.185(2)	–	1.103(2)	1.723(5)	1.582(5)	2.380(5)
DRR	0.6		4.4	7.4	6.7	11.4
Weeks 33–62						
Reg. Coeff.	−0.023(1)	0.135(4)	0.058(3)	0.800(4)	1.616(5)	1.941(5)
DRR	1.0	1.3	1.1	3.2	6.8	8.6
Low-Volume Segment						
Weeks 2–32						
Reg. Coeff.	0.108	–	0.750(3)	0.731(5)	1.354(5)	0.161(1)
DRR	1.2		3.1	3.0	5.5	1.3
Reg. Coeff.	0.011(2)	0.107(4)	–	1.166(4)	1.008(4)	0.946(3)
DRR	1.0	1.2		4.7	4.0	3.8

*Regression coefficients are recoded as described in Appendix A. Numbers in parentheses indicate the number of brands upon which the average coefficient is based.

If the B3 coefficients are excluded from the calculation of the average, the before-after comparison changes from 1.582 and 1.616 to 1.700 and 1.479—which is consistent with our hypothesis. The AD5 comparison in the low-volume segment is based on the presence of only one advertisement for one brand in the "before" time period, and hence should be discounted because of insufficient data.

Tables 6.5 and 6.6 present the average coefficients and DRR's for small and large container sizes. Using the same logic for excluding comparisons as is used in the case of the medium-size results, all the coefficients for the small-size

Table 6.5 Advertising-Price Regression Coefficients and Demand Response Ratios Averaged over Top Five Brands by Store Segment and Time Period for Small-Size Packages*

Time Period	AD0	AD1	AD2	AD3	AD4	AD5
	Price Variable					
All Stores						
Weeks 2–32						
Reg. Coeff.	0.009(5)	0.014(2)	0.457(1)	—	—	1.156(4)
DRR	1.0	1.0	2.1			4.6
Weeks 33–62						
Reg. Coeff.	0.135(3)	0.072(4)	0.082(4)	0.046(4)	0.033(1)	0.274(5)
DRR	1.3	1.2	1.2	1.1	1.1	1.6
High-Volume Segment						
Weeks 2–32						
Reg. Coeff.	−0.006(4)	—	—	—		2.621(2)
DRR	1.0					13.1
Weeks 33–62						
Reg. Coeff.	0.131(3)	—	0.240(4)	0.056(4)	—	—
DRR	1.3		1.5	1.1		
Low-Volume Segment						
Weeks 2–32						
Reg. Coeff.	0.023(5)	0.047(2)	0.471(1)	—	—	1.089(4)
DRR	1.0	1.1	2.2			4.4
Weeks 33–62						
Reg. Coeff.	—	0.030(4)	0.003(4)	0.024(4)	0.081(1)	0.322(5)
DRR		1.1	1.0	1.0	1.2	1.7

*Regression coefficients are recoded as described in Appendix A. Numbers in parentheses indicate the number of brands upon which the average coefficient is based.

results are lower in the "after" period than in the "before" period. The data for large container sizes are much fewer than for the other two sizes. The averages are often based on only one brand. If one includes only those before-after comparisons in which at least two brands are active in both time periods, the after coefficients are consistently lower than those for the "before" time period.

In addition to a comparison of before-after coefficients for the same AD variable, we have also compared before-after coefficients for AD variables for which the implied discounts are the same. Table 6.3 reports the discounts that are implied by AD0 through AD5 advertisements in both weeks 2 through 32 and weeks 33 through 62. If it is the discount that is impor-

Table 6.6 Advertising-Price Regression Coefficients and Demand Response Ratios Averaged over Brands by Store Segment and Time Period for Large-Size Packages*

	Price Variable					
Time Period	AD0	AD1	AD2	AD3	AD4	AD5
All Stores						
Weeks 2–32						
Reg. Coeff.	−0.148(2)	0.275(3)	0.286(1)	1.564(2)	2.394(2)	3.393(1)
DRR	0.7	1.6	1.7	6.6	11.6	19.3
Weeks 33–62						
Reg. Coeff.		0.072(1)	0.193(4)	−0.008(3)	0.661(3)	2.832(5)
DRR		1.1	1.4	1.0	2.8	14.6
High-Volume Segment						
Weeks 2–32						
Reg. Coeff.	—	0.573(3)	0.282(1)	1.320(2)	2.450(1)	3.325(1)
DRR		2.5	1.6	5.4	11.9	18.7
Weeks 33–62						
Reg. Coeff.	—	0.123(1)	0.369(2)	0.110(3)	1.206(1)	3.351(4)
DRR		1.3	1.9	1.2	4.9	18.9
Low-Volume Segment						
Weeks 2–32						
Reg. Coeff.	0.039(1)	0.132(1)	—	—	2.034(1)	—
DRR	1.1	1.3			9.2	
Weeks 33–62						
Reg. Coeff.	—	—	0.112(4)	—	0.504(2)	1.557(2)
DRR			1.2		2.3	6.5

*Regression coefficients are recoded as described in Appendix A. Numbers in parentheses indicate the number of brands upon which the average coefficient is based.

tant, then one would expect to find less variation *between time periods* for AD variables with different implied discounts. For example, the implied discount for an AD4 in the "after" period for medium-size packages is equal to the implied discount for an AD3 in the "before" time period. Therefore, if it is the discount that determined response, the difference in the DRR values for these two variables should be less than the average difference between AD4 and AD5 taken within each of the two time periods.

Table 6.7 reports the results of a comparison of these two sources of variation. The stub of the table lists those combinations of AD promotional variables in the "before" and "after" time periods (1) which have the same implied discounts;

and (2) for each of which there is sufficient data to make a comparison. The first two columns list the DRR's that correspond to the "before" and "after" time periods. For example, for the all-stores run for medium-size packages an AD5 in the "after" period has an implied discount equal to an AD4 in the "before" period.

The DRR for the AD5 is 8.1, while that for the AD4 is 6.7 (Table 6.4 is used as the source for the medium-size data). The difference between these two DRR's was 1.4, as reported in the next column, which contains the absolute value of the *between*-time-period differences in the appropriate AD DRR's. The next column reports the variation in DRR *within* time periods between the same pair of variables. For example, based on Table 6.4, an AD5 in the "before" time period has a DRR of 11.6, while an AD4 has a value of 6.7, leaving a difference in absolute value of 4.9.

In the "after" time period, the corresponding numbers are 8.1 and 6.2, with a difference of 1.9. Therefore, the average difference is 4.0, which is the number reported at the top of the second-to-last column in Table 6.7. If the hypothesized discount and not the absolute price is correct, then our measure of *between-time-period variation* should be greater than that for *within-time-period variation* in the magnitude of the DRR's. The last column of the table reports the difference for the between-period and within-period variation figures. The hypothesis suggested that they should be negative, and they are in eighteen of nineteen cases. In one case the difference is zero.

In spite of the consistency of these two sets of results, there is, nonetheless, one major source of ambiguity. During the first part of the "after" time period, several of the high-volume stores engaged in extremely intensive AD3, AD4, and AD5 type promotions. They were put on at such a rate that we suspected they might have saturated the market. If this were the case, the after-time-period regression coefficients should be down on the average for one of two reasons: (1) the implied discounts were in fact lower; or (2) the clustering of AD3, AD4, and AD5 promotions temporarily saturated the market. We devised a test of the hypothesis that saturation was a major cause of the lower average coefficients during the "after" time period. A pair of regression runs was made for the high-volume store category. One run included weeks 30 through 49, during which time most of the clustering of AD3, AD4, and AD5 promotions occurred, and the other weeks (50 through 62), during which time stores tended to promote at a normal rate per unit of time.

Table 6.7 Comparison of Demand Response Ratios for AD Promotions with the Same Implied Discounts in Weeks 2–32 and Weeks 33–62

	DRR		Absolute Value of Variation		
Comparisons	After	Before	Between Time Periods	Within Time Periods	Difference
Medium-size containers					
All Stores					
AD5 after vs. AD4 before	8.1	6.7	1.4	4.0	−2.6
AD4 after vs. AD3 before	6.2	4.7	1.5	2.2	−0.7
AD3 after vs. AD2 before	3.9	3.7	0.2	1.9	−1.7
AD2 after vs. AD1 before	1.1	1.1*	0.0	1.4	−1.4
High-Volume Stores					
AD5 after vs. AD4 before	8.6	6.7	1.9	3.3	−1.4
AD4 after vs. AD3 before	6.8	7.4	0.6	2.2	−1.6
AD3 after vs. AD2 before	3.2	4.4	1.2	2.6	−1.4
AD2 after vs. AD1 before	1.1	0.6*	0.5	2.0	−1.5
Low-Volume Stores					
AD5 after vs. AD4 before	3.8	5.5	1.7	2.2	−0.5
AD4 after vs. AD3 before	4.0	3.0	1.0	1.6	−0.6
AD3 after vs. AD2 before	4.7	3.1	1.6	1.8	−0.2
Large-size containers					
All Stores					
AD5 after vs. AD4 before	14.6	11.6	3.0	9.8	−6.8
AD4 after vs. AD3 before	2.8	6.6	3.8	3.9	−0.1
AD3 after vs. AD2 before	1.0	1.7†	0.7	2.7	−2.0
AD2 after vs. AD1 before	1.4	1.6	0.2	0.2	0.0
High-Volume Stores					
AD5 after vs. AD4 before	18.9	11.9†	7.0	10.4	−3.4
AD4 after vs. AD3 before	4.9†	5.4	0.5	5.1	−4.6
AD3 after vs. AD2 before	1.2	1.6	0.4	2.3	−1.9
AD2 after vs. AD1 before	1.9	2.5	0.6	0.8	−0.2

*Regression coefficients are recoded as described in Appendix A. Numbers in parentheses indicate the number of brands upon which the average coefficient is based.

If the market was being saturated, and absolute price, not implied discount, is critical, one would expect the average regression coefficients for AD3, AD4, and AD5 promotions to decrease as one goes from weeks 2 through 32 to 30 through

49 and then to recover in weeks 50 through 62 to the level they were at in the "before" time period.

The data for small- and large-size containers are too few to permit analysis (cutting the time period in half cuts sample size in half). However, the average regression coefficients for the three types of AD promotions for medium-size containers for each of the three time periods are as follows:

	AD3	AD4	AD5
Weeks 2–32	1.743	1.600	2.410
Weeks 30–49	1.082	1.509	2.014
Weeks 50–62	0.589	1.857	1.780

There is a clear-cut drop in the magnitude of the regression coefficients between the "before" period and weeks 30 through 49. Apparently, the rate of AD type promotions oversaturated the market and hence acted to pull down their average response. In weeks 50 through 62 the average coefficients for AD3 and AD5 are down quite sharply, while that for AD4 is up but by a more modest degree than either of the two declines. Although the direction of these results is somewhat mixed, their magnitudes indicate that the decline in the average regression coefficients between the "before" and "after" time periods depends primarily on the implied discount, which is consistent with our previous results.

6.3.1.3 Advertising-Price Variables: Effect on Demand

The discussion that follows concentrates on the relationship between AD0 through AD5 promotional activity and demand by package size for the weeks 33 through 62 time period. We have chosen to focus our discussion on this time period as it is the one that is most relevant for the evaluation of current promotional policies. However, our comments about the relative effects of different types of AD activity or about the response differences between package sizes or store groupings are also true of weeks 2 through 32 with one exception: as noted in our discussion of Tables 6.4, 6.5, and 6.6, the DRR's during the "after" time period are systematically lower than those reported for the "before" period.

Furthermore, our evaluation of advertising-price promotional activity is based on the average performance for brands B1 to B5. The variation in the magnitude of the regression coefficients from one store group to another, one size to another, and/or one time period to another, is considerably greater than that attributed to differences between brands.

We shall evaluate the effect of advertising-price activity in terms of its effect *relative to normal demand* (i.e., in terms of the magnitude of the demand response ratios one would expect if particular levels of advertising-price activity were achieved in a store).

Figures 6.1, 6.2, and 6.3 report the DRR's for each store grouping for weeks 33 through 62 by container size. Where the plot for a given size container is incomplete, there was insufficient data to permit the missing information to be included.

The relationship between advertising-price activity and demand varied considerably from one container size to another as well as from one store group to another. Figure 6.1 reports the relationship between DRR and AD0 through AD5 for the all-stores results. Cuts in normal price for small-size containers, even as represented by AD5 ads, do virtually nothing to increase their sales above their normal value in unpromoted weeks.

In contrast, both medium- and large-size containers are quite sensitive to high levels of advertising-price activity (AD4's and AD5's for large-size containers and AD3's, AD4's, and AD5's for the medium size). An AD5 for medium-size containers, on the average, results in sales that are 8.1

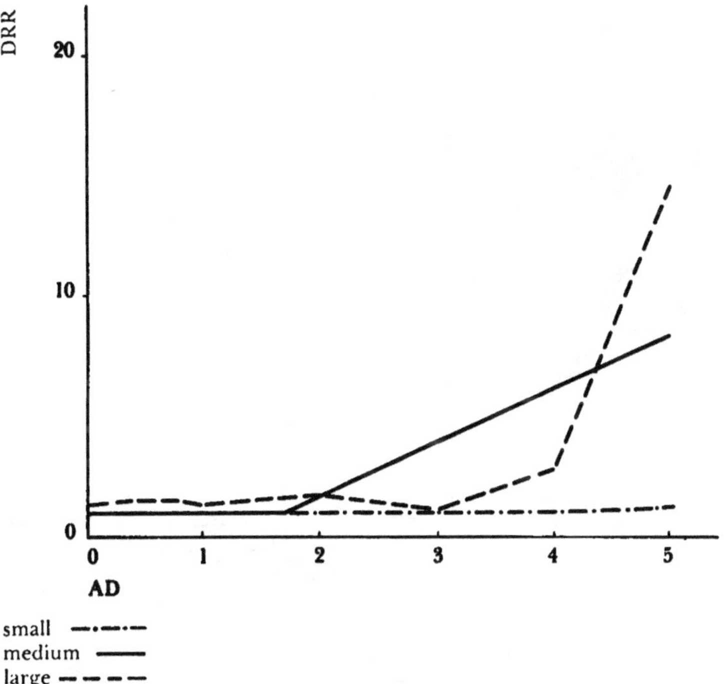

Figure 6.1 Demand response ratios by package size from AD 0–AD 5 for weeks 33–62–all stores.

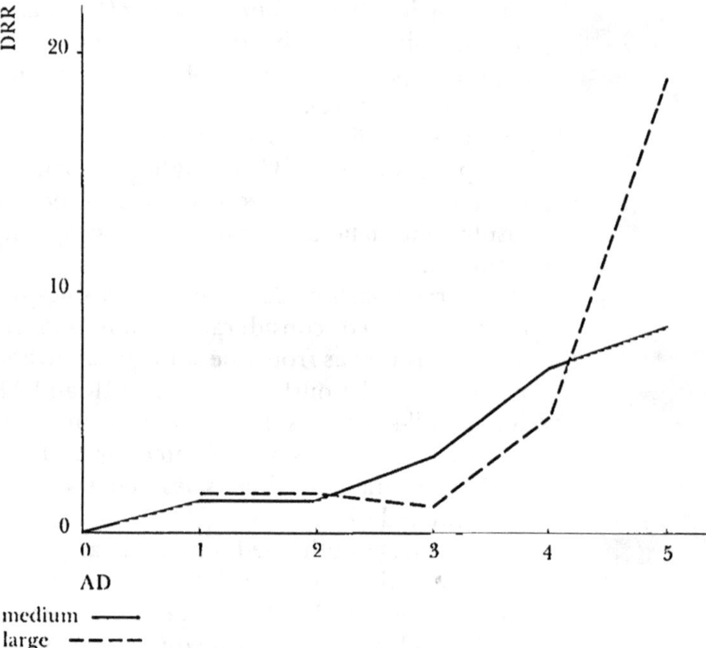

Figure 6.2 Demand response ratios by package size from AD 0–AD 5 for weeks 33–62—high-volume stores.

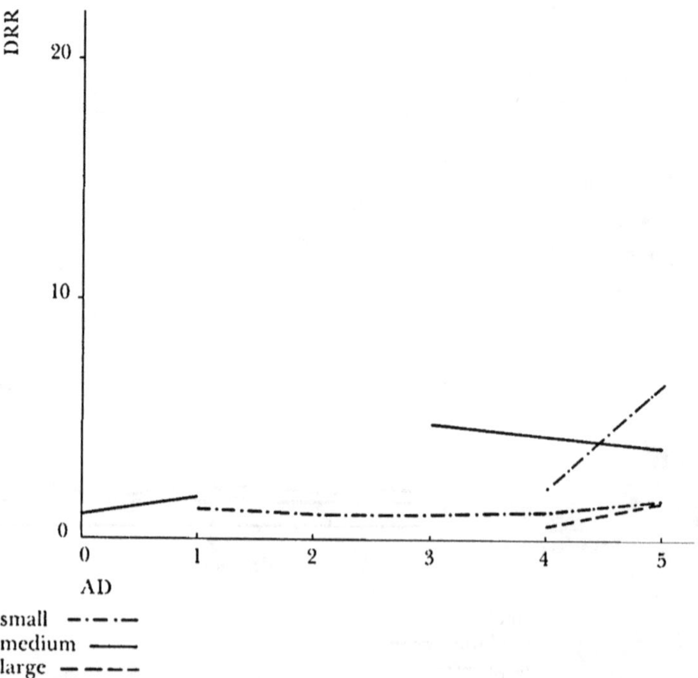

Figure 6.3 Demand response ratios by package size from AD 0–AD 5 for weeks 33–62—low-volume stores.

times the normal value in unpromoted weeks for the stores involved. The corresponding figure for large-container AD5 promotion is 14.6. There appears to be a fairly substantial response threshold such that advertised price promotions as low as approximately 5.25 and 7.00 for medium- and large-size containers, respectively, have virtually no effect on demand. Stated another way, implied discounts up to $1.00 and $1.25 per unit for medium- and large-size containers do relatively little by way of increasing sales.

These effects are not true for all stores, however, as shown by the plots in Figures 6.2 and 6.3. The relationship between DRR and advertising-price activity discussed in the preceding paragraph held up for the high-volume store category but almost completely disappeared in the low-volume store segment. There is still some evidence of a plateau up to AD2 in this group; however, medium and large containers do not do much better than small containers, given high levels of promotional activity, whereas there are sizable differences in response from one container size to another in the high-volume store segment.

6.3.2 Unadvertised Price Discounts

Unadvertised price discounts are split into two categories and measured separately:

1. UAPZFM is defined as the magnitude of a UAP for the brand being analyzed that occurs when another major brand is promoted in the same size in the same store.

6.3.2.1 Variable Definitions

2. UAPNFM. This variable measures the magnitude of UAP's that occur when no competing brand is being promoted.

Our working hypothesis is that the effect of a UAPZFM is less than that for UAPNFM. That is, we believe that the effect of a UAP is reduced if competing brands are present in the same size container in the same store.

6.3.2.2 Findings

Table 6.8 reports the unadvertised price discount DRR's by package size. The DRR's are computed based on a $0.25 discount per unit. This procedure tends to overstate the typical magnitude of their effects due to the fact that a $0.25 per unit discount constituted an extremely high level of UAP activity relative to the norm of the market area. The best UAP performance (the highest DRR values) are recorded for large-size containers during the "after" time period in high-volume stores. Their DRR's were 3.0 and 2.9, respectively.

Contrary to our expectation, the two types of UAP promotions appear to have the same effect. The average DRR for

Table 6.8

Demand Response Ratios for Unadvertised Price Discounts, Assuming a UAP Level of $0.25 Per Unit, by Container Size, Store Grouping, and Time Period*

	Small-Size		Medium-Size		Large-Size	
Time Period	UAPZFM	UAPNFM	UAPZFM	UAPNFM	UAPZFM	UAPNFM
All Stores						
Weeks 2–32	1.4	1.5	2.0	2.9	1.6	1.7
Weeks 33–62	1.3	1.4	1.9	1.8	1.8	2.2
High-Volume Stores						
Weeks 2–32	1.7	1.6	2.0	2.3	2.1	1.7
Weeks 33–62	1.6	1.3	1.9	2.1	3.0	2.9
Low-Volume Stores						
Weeks 2–32	1.3	1.6	1.8	1.4	1.6	1.6
Weeks 33–62	1.2	1.5	1.9	1.4	1.4	1.4

*Regression coefficients are recoded as described in Appendix A.

both UAPZFM and UAPNFM over sizes and store groupings and time periods is 1.7. Both variables tend to be more effective when they are used in high-volume as opposed to low-volume stores. The average UAPZFM is 2.0 for high-volume stores and 1.5 for the low-volume category. The corresponding figures for UAPNFM are also 2.0 and 1.5, respectively. There is little variation of importance in their magnitudes from brand to brand.

6.3.3 Special Offers

Variables designed to measure the effects of three types of special offers were included in the analysis. Each of the variables is a dummy variable that takes on a value of zero if there is no offer of that particular type for a particular store-week-brand-size combination and a value of one if an offer is present. The three variables are as follows:

6.3.3.1 Variable Definitions

1. SPOPD. A measure of whether or not a premium is offered in connection with the sale of the product.
2. SPORD. A measure of whether or not the product is offered in a reusable package.
3. SPOCD. A measure of whether or not a retailer coupon is offered in connection with the sale.

6.3.3.2 Findings

Tables 6.9, 6.10, and 6.11 report the regression coefficients and DRR's averaged over the five major brands by container size.

Table 6.9 Special Offer Regression Coefficients and Demand Response Ratios Averaged over Top Five Brands by Store Segment and Time Period for Small-Size Packages*

Time Period	SPOPD	SPORD	SPOCD
All Stores			
Weeks 2–32			
Reg. Coeff.	−0.114(5)	−0.049(5)	
DRR	0.8	0.9	
Weeks 33–62			
Reg. Coeff.	0.069(4)	0.344(5)	0.443(1)
DRR	1.1	1.8	2.1
High-Volume Stores			
Weeks 2–32			
Reg. Coeff.	−0.086(5)	−0.074(5)	
DRR	0.8	0.9	
Weeks 33–62			
Reg. Coeff.	−0.090(3)	0.335(4)	—
DRR	0.8	1.8	
Low-Volume Stores			
Weeks 2–32			
Reg. Coeff.	−0.028(3)	0.024(4)	
DRR	0.9	1.1	
Weeks 33–62			
Reg. Coeff.	0.115(3)	0.338(5)	0.397(1)
DRR	1.2	1.8	2.0

*Regression coefficients are recoded as described in Appendix A. Numbers in parentheses indicate the number of brands upon which the average coefficient is based.

For premium offers (SPOPD's), the DRR magnitudes are equal to or less than one for fifteen of the eighteen analyses (three sizes times two time periods times three store groupings). The same statement is also true for twelve of the DRR's for reusable pack offers (SPORD's). If the effect of one of these promotions is zero, one would expect the value of DRR to be one. That is, one would expect demand in the week on the average to be equal to the store's average volume during unpromoted weeks. The existence of DRR's less than one means that on the average they tend slightly to *decrease* expected demand for the product.

The pattern of coefficients and their corresponding DRR values is quite different for the retailer coupon variable. During the period of our investigation, this promotional

Table 6.10. Special Offer Regression Coefficients and Demand Response Ratios Averaged over Top Five Brands by Store Segment and Time Period for Medium-Size Packages*

Time Period	SPOPD	SPORD	SPOCD
All Stores			
Weeks 2–32			
Reg. Coeff.	−0.130(5)	−0.364(5)	0.861(5)
DRR	0.7	0.4	3.5
Weeks 33–62			
Reg. Coeff.	−0.014(4)	0.030(5)	2.615(4)
DRR	1.0	1.1	13.0
High-Volume Stores			
Weeks 2–32			
Reg. Coeff.	−0.166(5)	−0.105(5)	1.024(5)
DRR	0.7	0.8	4.1
Weeks 33–62			
Reg. Coeff.	−0.189(3)	−0.243(4)	2.456(4)
DRR	0.7	0.6	12.0
Low-Volume Stores			
Weeks 2–32			
Reg. Coeff.	0.029(5)	−0.219(5)	−0.235(4)
DRR	1.0	0.6	0.6
Weeks 33–62			
Reg. Coeff.	−0.048(4)	0.124(5)	—
DRR	0.9	1.3	

*Regression coefficients are recoded as described in Appendix A. Numbers in parentheses indicate the number of brands upon which the average coefficient is based.

variable was only used for small- and medium-size container promotions. Its value as reported in Tables 6.9 and 6.10 is positive except for the low-volume store segment in the "before" time period. The highest DRR is 13.0 for the "after" time period in the all stores for medium-size containers.

The evidence is quite clear that on the average, premiums and reusable packs tend slightly to retard demand (or, at best, leave it unchanged) as opposed to increasing it. In contrast, retailer coupons serve to increase demand.

6.3.4 Competing Promotions

There are two variables that represent an attempt to measure the effects of a product category's promotions in *competing stores* on the demand for a particular brand-size combination in the store under investigation:

Table 6.11. Special Offer Regression Coefficients and Demand Response Ratios Averaged over Top Five Brands by Store Segment and Time Period for Large-Size Packages*

Time Period	SPOPD	SPORD	SPOCD
All Stores			
Weeks 2–32			
Reg. Coeff.	−0.276(5)	−0.143(4)	—
DRR	0.5	0.7	
Weeks 33–62			
Reg. Coeff.	−0.186(3)	−0.147(4)	
DRR	0.7	0.7	
High-Volume Stores			
Weeks 2–32			
Reg. Coeff.	−0.203(4)	−0.132(3)	
DRR	0.6	0.8	
Weeks 33–62			
Reg. Coeff.	−0.388(3)	−0.475(4)	
DRR	0.4	0.3	
Low-Volume Stores			
Weeks 2–32			
Reg. Coeff.	0.165(3)	−0.031(2)	
DRR	1.4	0.9	
Weeks 33–62			
Reg. Coeff.	−0.080(2)	−0.344(2)	
DRR	0.8	0.4	

*Regression coefficients are recoded as described in Appendix A. "Numbers in parentheses indicate the number of brands upon which the average coefficient is based.

6.3.4.1 Variable definitions

1. CPE. This variable is defined as the lowest advertised price for the same brand-size (as the one under investigation) in competing stores.
2. CPM. This variable is a measure of the magnitude of the lowest advertised price among the major brand competitors of the same size container as the brand being analyzed but in competing stores.

6.3.4.2 Findings

The results for all container sizes were summarized in the same fashion as those for the policy variables evaluated in the preceding sections. Demand response ratios were calculated for each combination of container size, store grouping, and time period. Therefore, for each of the two variables, eighteen DRR's were calculated.

All eighteen of the DRR statistics for the CPM variable are equal to 1.0. Fifteen of those for CPE are also equal to 1.0, while two others had a value of 0.9. Only one DRR calculated out of the full set of thirty-six values for both variables has a value greater than 1.0. It is the DRR for CPE for small container sizes in the high-volume segment during the "before" time period; it is equal to 2.5.

A DRR of 1.0 is expected if a particular policy variable has no impact on demand. Should we therefore conclude that interstore competition does not on the average have an effect on the demand for the product regardless of the container size or the brand involved? (There is relatively little variation present in the DRR statistics from brand to brand.)

Our specification of the competing store variables is the poorest of any of the promotional variables included in the study. Within the constraints of our data base, we attempted to develop an effective set of variable definitions. However, having data available only for the stores in the panel limited our ability to measure the competitive environment that each of the stores faces in a particular week. Even if one had data for the product category being analyzed by brand, size, and week for virtually all the stores that surround each store in our panel, there still would be a serious gap in our data base. The effect of interstore competition on the volume of demand for the product in a particular week in a panel store depends not only on the product's own promotions in competing stores but also on the stores' promotional offerings of other products in a particular week.

Obtaining a measure of the full bundle of promotional activities across a wide range of products for the full set of stores surrounding each panel store was far beyond the economic constraints on this investigation.

However, one can legitimately ask, regardless of the economic justification for not measuring this vast range of competing store behavior: What effect is its exclusion apt to have on the results that are reported for the promotional variables included in the study?

A more general way of stating this question is to ask: What effect does the exclusion of one or more independent variables that are, in fact, correlated with the dependent variable under study (in our case the demand for a particular brand-size combination in a given store-week) have on the magnitude of the regression coefficients and the corresponding DRR values of the promotional variables that are included (such as AD0 through AD5 advertising-price variables)?

The answer to this question depends on the extent to which

the excluded variable is correlated with one or more of the explanatory variables included in the analysis. If the degree of correlation is zero, then our estimates of the effects of the included variables are unbiased. If it is other than zero, then an element of bias is present. The closer the value of the correlation to zero, the lesser the degree of bias.

To what extent are the weekly promotional activities of one particular store correlated with those of another? It is our contention that the degree of correlation is relatively low. In our previous work (Massy and Frank, 1966), we conducted an investigation of this issue and found virtually no intercorrelation in the *weekly* promotional activities of one chain versus those of another in a market similar to the one under investigation. Hence, promotions in competing stores should not lead to bias in the results we have reported.

6.4 Reduced Form Analysis

The regression equation results that have thus far been discussed provide a measure of the effect of a given brand-size's promotional activity on its demand. In addition to these "main effects," the promotional activities for a given brand-size combination also affect the demands for competing brands and sizes. In order to arrive at an estimate of the effect of each brand-size combination's promotional activities on itself, as well as on all other brand-size combinations, we included the following three variables in each of the individual store group–brand–size specific regressions.

OSSB
KEYB (ALTB)
OSOB

These variables are defined in Section 4.3.3. In and of themselves these variables are unimportant. However, when the estimates of their coefficients are combined with those for the other promotional variables for each brand-size combination, they can be used to solve a set of twenty-four simultaneous equations (eight brand categories and three sizes). The solutions of these equations provide estimates not only of the effect of each brand-size combination's promotional activities on its own demand, but also estimates of the effect of its promotional activities on all the demands for other brand-size combinations. This is done simultaneously for every promotional variable included in the model. If every promotional variable is active for each brand-size, this amounts to estimating 312 coefficients (eight brands, three sizes, thirteen variables) for each brand-size combination (of which there were twenty-four) for a total of 7,488 reduced form coefficients.

We shall use the coefficients determined by the reduced form solution to discuss two questions:

1. If B5 initiated a particular type of promotion such as an AD5, what brand-size combinations did it harm the most? To which did it do the least harm?

2. What brand-size promotions have the greatest impact on B5's demand when they are initiated by its competitors? Which have the least impact?

Separate reduced form analyses are performed for each store grouping–time period combination. The results discussed in the following paragraph are based on the high- and low-volume store categories in weeks 33 through 62. The aforementioned questions are centered on B5 purely for illustrative purposes. It is one of the brands in which the sponsors of the study are especially interested.

6.4.1 Impact of B5's Promotions on the Demand for Other Brand-Size Combinations

In order to shed light on the effect of B5's promotional activity for each of its container sizes on the demand for other brand-size combinations, we will focus our attention on the impact of whatever B5 promotional variable has the greatest effect on its own brand-size demand. For example, for B5 small-size containers in high-volume stores, AD2s had the largest DRR of any promotional variable on B5's small-size container demand. Therefore, we will examine the average effect of a B5 AD2 promotion for its small-size container on the weekly demand for other brand-size combinations than those represented by B5's offerings. In contrast, for B5's medium-size containers in high-volume stores, the variable with the highest DRR is AD5. Therefore, for the medium-size analysis we report the impact of a B5's AD5 on competing brand-size combinations.

Table 6.12 reports these results. The stub of the table lists, by container size, the B5 promotional variable that has the largest effect on its own demand. The first set of three columns records (1) the three brand-size combinations on which the B5 promotional variable listed in the stub has the "most injurious" effect; (2) the reduced form coefficient that measures the average magnitude of that effect; and (3) the DRR that corresponds to the coefficient. The last three columns report the same information for the three brand-size combinations on which B5 has the "least injurious" effect. Within the most injurious and least injurious summaries, the three brand-size combinations are ranked by the relative magnitude of their impact (1) from low to high for the reduced form coefficient with the "most injurious" category; and (2) from high to low for the "least injurious" category.

Table 6.12 Impact of B5's Promotional Activities on Other Brands (weeks 33–62)

Container Size Promotional Variable	Most Injurious Brand-Size	Reduced Form Coeff.	DRR	Least Injurious Brand-Size	Reduced Form Coeff.	DRR
High-Volume Stores						
Small, AD2	B4-L	−0.001	1.0	B2-L	0.045	1.1
	B1-L	0.017	1.0	B1-L	0.032	1.1
	B4-S	0.020	1.0	B3-S	0.029	1.1
Medium, AD5	B4-L	−0.072	0.9	B2-L	0.076	1.2
	B1-L	−0.015	1.0	B1-M	0.032	1.1
	B4-S	−0.006	1.0	B3-S	0.024	1.1
Large, AD5	B4-L	−0.174	0.7	B2-L	0.119	1.3
	B1-L	−0.061	0.9	B1-L	0.033	1.1
	B4-S	−0.044	0.9	B3-S	0.017	1.0
Low-Volume Stores						
Small, AD5	B2-M	0.052	1.1	B8-S	0.184	1.4
	B3-M	0.057	1.1	B4-S	0.175	1.4
	B4-M	0.057	1.1	B1-S	0.164	1.4
Medium, AD5	B2-M	0.061	1.1	B8-S	0.240	1.5
	B3-M	0.067	1.1	B4-S	0.237	1.5
	B4-M	0.068	1.1	B1-S	0.221	1.5
Large, AD5	B2-M	0.047	1.1	B8-S	0.151	1.3
	B3-M	0.051	1.1	B4-S	0.144	1.3
	B4-M	0.051	1.1	B1-S	0.135	1.3

On the average, B5's small-size container promotions have their most injurious effect on the demand for B4's large containers. The reduced form coefficient for B4's large size is −0.001 and its corresponding DRR is 1.0. But what does it mean to say that a B5 AD2 promotion on the average generates a 1.0 DRR for B4 large-size containers and that this constitutes the most injurious effect that B5's AD2s have on any competing brand-size combination?

The results cited imply that when B5's small size receives an AD2 promotion, the demand for B4's large size is unchanged relative to the average of B4's large size demand in weeks in which the latter is not being promoted. B4, in effect, paid no penalty in magnitude of its average demand in unpromoted weeks when it was opposed by B5's small-size AD2 promotion. If B4 also offers some type of promotion during the same week, then the fact that a B5's AD2 is also present leaves B4's expected DRR for that promotion unchanged. In the case of B5 small-size AD2 promotions, this impact on competitors represented the greatest degree of relative competitive injury that occurred for any competing brand-size combination.

In contrast, the least injurious effect of a B5 small-size AD2 is the demand for B2 large-size containers, where the DRR was 1.1. An AD2 promotion by B5 on the average added 0.1 more to the DRR for B2's large size than would be expected, given whatever promotional activity B2 engaged in that week.

Based on Table 6.12, B5's major promotional activities have the following effects on competing brands and sizes in high-volume stores:

1. A small-size AD2 type promotion (a) has its most injurious effects on B4's large-size container demand and its least injurious effect on B2's large-size container demand; (b) tends to affect all competing brand-size combinations to about the same degree, as illustrated by the fact that the lowest DRR for any brand-size combination is 1.0, whereas the highest DRR is only 0.1 greater (i.e., 1.1).
2. A medium-size AD5 type promotion has its most injurious effect on B4's large size, which has a DRR of 0.9, and its least injurious effect on B2's large size, with a DRR of 1.2.
3. A large-size AD5 type promotion has its most injurious effect on B4's large size, with a DRR of 0.7, and its least injurious effect on B2's large size, with a DRR of 1.3.
4. As one goes from small- to large-size promotions, the impact of B5's promotional activity tends to be less evenly spread across competing brand-size combinations, as evidenced by the increase in the range between the extreme values for DRR associated with each container size (e.g., the range for small-size container DRR's is 0.1, for the medium-size container 0.3, and for the large-size container 0.6).
5. Regardless of which B5 container size one analyzes, the primary impact of its major promotional activity was on competing large-size containers. For example, medium-size container B5 AD5 promotions have a greater impact on competing large-size containers than on those of the same size as the one being promoted. This finding was checked by comparing it with similar analyses of the effects of B1, B2, and B4 promotions on competing brand-size combinations. With virtually no exceptions, regardless of the size being promoted, the primary impact of the promotion on the demand for competing sizes is on large-size containers.
6. Regardless of the container size it promotes, B5 affects B2 large container demand the least and B4 large containers the most.

The findings for the low-volume stores deviate sharply from those for the high-volume category:

1. Regardless of container size, the most injurious effect of a B5 promotion is on B2 medium-size containers and the least injurious effect is on the store's private brand.
2. Even the most injurious effects had DRR's greater than or equal to 1.1. In the context of the low-volume stores, B5 has a "most injurious effect" on these brand-size combinations in the sense that one of its AD5 promotions does less by way of increasing competing brand-size expected DRR than it does for other competitors. For example, it increases B2's DRR in the case of a small container size AD5 promotion by 0.1, whereas in the case of the store's private brand, a B5 AD5 on the average results in an increase of 0.4 in its DRR.
3. As one goes from small to large container sizes, there is virtually no difference in the variation in impact it has between competing brand-size combinations (i.e., the range of DRR's is 0.3 for small containers, 0.4 for medium-size containers, and 0.2 for the large size).

This tendency for highly effective B5 promotions to be associated with increments in the DRR's for competing brand-size combinations in low-volume stores is also present in the effects of promotions by other major brands on their competitors. Two possible explanations for this behavior in low-volume stores are (1) that low-volume stores consistently underestimate the demand that is generated by major promotions to a greater extent than high-volume stores (and, furthermore, once they run out of stock they try to switch customers to competing brand-size combinations, possibly with a UAP type promotion); and (2) that low-volume stores deliberately tend to order less than they expect by way of demand to minimize their total markdowns due to the product's promotion. It seems reasonable to believe that in the face of a temporary stock-out of the promoted brand, customers will switch to a competitor.

6.4.2 Impact of Promotions by Other Brand-Size Combinations on B5's Demand for Each Container Size

Our analysis is based on the three brand-size combinations that have the most injurious effect on the demand for each of B5's container sizes and the three that have the least injurious effect on each.

The findings for the high-volume stores are as follows:

1. For B5's small- and medium-container-size demand, the impact of competing brand-size promotions is about the same from one brand-size combination to another.
2. For B5 large-size containers, however, there are marked differences. The most injurious promotions are those put on

by B2 for its medium- and large-size containers, which tend to reduce B5's large-size DRR in unpromoted weeks from 1.0 to 0.5. The least harmful promotion on the average is an AD5 type for B4 large-size containers, which increased B5's DRR from 1.0 to 2.6.

In low-volume stores we found the following:

1. There is more variation in the effect of competing brand-size combinations from one brand to another on B5 DRR's for both small- and medium-size containers than is true in high-volume stores. Although the DRR's are of about the same magnitude in the low-volume stores, those that are least injurious had high values.
2. In contrast to the high-volume stores, there is no clear-cut pattern as to which brands have the greatest impact on large container size demand.
3. In the low-volume (as well as the high-volume) stores, the variation in DRR from one competing brand-size combination to another is greater for large-size containers than for the other two sizes.

6.4.3 Summary of Brand-Size Interaction Effects

Two main points emerge from the results given in Sections 6.4.1 and 6.4.2. The first concerns the degree to which the demands for different brands are linked and the second concerns linkage among sizes. We will discuss each in general terms.

Major interbrand effects can be inferred by examining the following sets of extreme coefficients in the reduced form table:

1. *Maximum* injury *by* a brand: what brand is hurt most by a given brand when that brand is on promotion? (The most *negative* set of coefficients in a given *row* of the reduced form table.)
2. *Maximum* injury *to* a brand: what brand hurts a given brand most, when the other brand is on promotion? (The most *negative* set of coefficients in a given *column* of the reduced form table.)
3. *Minimum* injury *by* a brand: what brand is hurt least by a given brand when that brand is on promotion? (The most *positive* set of coefficients in a given *row* of the reduced form table.)
4. *Minimum* injury *to* a brand: what brand hurts a given brand least, when the other brand is on promotion? (The most *positive* set of coefficients in a given *column* of the reduced form table.)

The following diagrams report our results for "maximum

injury *by* a brand" and "maximum injury *to* a brand" (points 1 and 2) for the high-volume store group, weeks 33 through 62. (Arrows indicate the directions of the demand shift; e.g., in diagram A, the arrow from B4 to B5 indicates that when B5 is on promotion it hurts B4 the most; in diagram B, the same arrow means that B4 is hurt more by B5 when B5 is on promotion than by any other brand's promotions.) These diagrams are based on a summarization of both medium and large container sizes. This is practical because the effects for the two sizes are usually consistent.

A. Maximum injury by a brand:

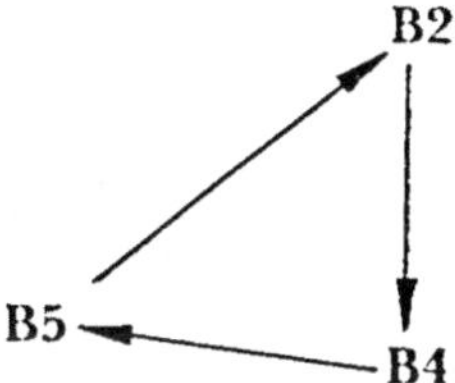

B. Maximum injury to a brand:

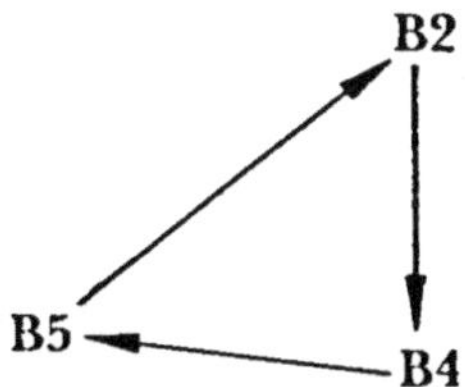

These results indicated (1) that B5's promotions draw relatively more from B4 than other brands, B2 draws most from B5, and B4 draws most from B2 (diagram A); and (2) B5 is hurt more by B2 than by other brands' promotions, B2 is hurt most by B4, and B4 is hurt most by B5 (diagram B). Equivalent diagrams for "least injury" (points 3 and 4) show essentially the same results, but with a few anomalies.

Thus, we found a somewhat peculiar (though potentially very interesting) set of relative interactions in this market area:

1. Extreme shifts in demand tend to flow in a circle: from B2 to B4 to B5 to B2, and so forth, rather than being traded among a single pair of brands.
2. Other brands, including B1 and B3, did not figure in the extreme vulnerability statistics, even though some of them have a high incidence of promotions.

6.5 Concluding Statement

The multiple-equation model results reported in this chapter were for the following variables: (1) advertised-price promotion; (2) unadvertised price discounts; (3) special offers; and (4) competing store promotions. Two categories of in-store promotional variables were deliberately excluded from the model: signs and displays. These are discussed in Chapter 7.

7 Results of the Residuals Analysis

7.1 Introduction

Estimates of the effects of signs and displays were deliberately omitted from the multiple-equation analysis reported in the preceding chapter. The residuals analysis was planned initially in order to provide estimates of their effects. In addition, experience gained in interpreting the results of the multiple-equation model, together with feedback from the sponsor's top management, led us to extend the residuals analysis in order to answer the following questions:

1. What is the effect on sales of special offers such as bonus packs and mail-ins (i.e., consumer contests and premiums that have to be sent for)? Originally, our analysis included the effects of three other types of special offers—on-pack premiums, reusable packs, and retailer coupons.
2. What is the relationship between major ads (i.e., those in the AD3, AD4, and AD5 categories) and in-store promotional support? That is, what is the probability that a grocer will engage in in-store activity if he runs a major ad? Also, what are the types of in-store activity that he is most likely to engage in under these circumstances?
3. What is the effect on its sales of changes in a brand's normal price? One price variable was originally included in our analysis to measure unadvertised price discounts (UAP's). Our intention was to measure discounts off a given brand-size's normal price that were being offered at retail in a given week. Although this class of price activity is the principal category of unadvertised price promotions, there is still another way in which price affects demand—namely, via changes in a brand's normal price (long-run changes in the retail store's pricing policy with respect to a given brand-size).
4. What is the effect of timing of major advertised-price promotions (those in the AD4 and AD5 categories that offer the product to households at substantial implied discounts)? Stated another way, if a retailer engages in an AD4 or AD5 promotion in the current week, is the effect of that promotion on sales in any way influenced by whether or not he engaged in a similar type of promotion for the *same brand and size* in the previous week, the week before that, and so forth? Is the impact on current promotions for a given brand-size combination contingent upon the number of weeks since similar types of promotions were offered by the *same brand for any size*?

Because we found no systematic differences in the effects of any of the promotional variables from one brand to another, we adopted earlier the convention of averaging our estimates of these effects over the major brands. A similar convention has been adopted in this section. It is based on data for the four brands with the highest market shares in the metropolitan area. The estimated effects, which shall be discussed in succeeding sections of this chapter, are estimates of the average effects over these four brands. Wherever our data permit, separate analyses will be reported by container size. However, this is not always possible, as some types of promotional activity occur rarely if ever for certain of the package sizes.

7.2
Needed: A "Cleaner" Measure of Sales

The dependent variable in the multiple-equation model was computed on a weekly basis for each store and within each store for each brand-size combination, as follows:

1. *Actual sales were divided by normal sales.* Normal sales were defined as the average weekly sales in that store for the brand-size under investigation, based on those weeks during which the brand-size was not being promoted. The ratio of actual sales to normal sales was computed for the purpose of adjusting for differences in sales levels associated with differences in stores, brands, and sizes that were not a function of short-run promotional activity. This ratio was given the mnemonic YR.
2. *One was subtracted from YR.* This accounting convention scales the YR series so that a zero YR is what one would expect in a week when the brand was not being promoted.
3. *The square root was taken of YR minus one.* This was done for technical reasons involving the assumptions made in multiple regression analysis (see Section 3.4.3).

The dependent variable was therefore the square root of the quantity YR minus one (hereafter this measure is referred to as sales). We could have used this sales measure once more as the dependent variable. We did not.

In order to understand the rationale underlying the measure that was chosen, suppose that we had used it as our dependent variable to study, say, the effect of the presence of a sign-in-window. Suppose, further, that the presence of a sign-in-window *always* occurred in weeks with AD4 or AD5 advertised price promotions (promotions offering unusually steep price discounts to the consumer). What would happen if we conducted two separate analyses? Suppose that in one we correlated AD4 and AD5 activity with sales and found that on the average such promotions would increase demand by a factor of twenty. Now further suppose that in the other analysis we correlated the presence or absence of signs-in-window with demand. Because we have assumed that signs-in-window always occur with AD4 or AD5 activity, we would again find that on the average demand would be increased by a factor of twenty. However, we would now ascribe this increase in demand to signs-in-window instead of to AD4 or AD5 activity. If the two sets of policy variables were completely correlated, that is, if they always occurred together, we would overestimate by a factor of two what would happen to sales if we were to engage in both types of promotions. That is, we would be saying sales on the average would increase by a factor of forty if we were to engage in both signs-in-window and AD4 or AD5 activity. What we really want to do is to hold one set of promotional variables constant and let the other vary.

In fact, in the "real world," in-store sign activity is only partly correlated with AD4 and AD5 activity. There is still an element of double counting present, but it is nowhere near as extreme as in our hypothetical case.

Our problem is to find some way of eliminating the possibility of double counting. To do this we need to find some way of controlling (adjusting) for the effects on sales of variables we have previously analyzed.

Here is how we handled the problem:

1. As a result of our previous analysis for each brand-size combination for both high- and low-volume stores, we had a regression equation containing estimates of the effects of each of the policy variables included in that analysis.

2. The raw data, together with the regression coefficients (our estimates of the effects of each of the policy variables), were used to compute an *expected sales* figure for each store-brand-size-week combination. This series of *expected sales* figures varies from observation to observation because of differences in the promotional variables included in our analysis, and for no other reason. The actual sales figure varies for three reasons: (1) the effects of those variables included in our original analysis; (2) the effects of variables excluded from the original analysis (many of which we now choose to study); and (3) variations due to random fluctuations or errors in the data.

3. For each observation we subtracted the *expected sales* from *actual sales* (i.e., we computed a residual sales figure). If the model developed in our original analysis constitutes an adequate description of the relationships under investigation, the *residual sales* figures will vary from observation to observation only due to the effects of this second category of variables; that is, the *residual sales* figure is a new measure of sales that is *adjusted* for the effects of the variables included in the original analysis.

In effect, we have used statistical procedures to control for (figuratively, hold constant) effects of one set of policy variables on sales in order to obtain a "cleaner" measure of the effects of another set of policy variables.

The dependent variable used in this analysis is the *residual sales* series, which was computed in the fashion we have just described.

7.3 Method of Analysis

Cross-classification procedures were used to generate the results reported in this chapter. The logic required to transform the results reported in a given table into a form consistent with the regression coefficients and the demand response ratios (DRR's) reported in our previous analysis is, with one exception, virtually the same regardless of which policy variable is being analyzed. In order to avoid repetition, we shall discuss the procedure involved in this section.

Two types of policy variables are included in this analysis. One type takes the form of a dummy variable (e.g., sign-in-store is either on or off), while the other is continuous (e.g., normal price). The transformation required is a bit more complex for the second type than for the first.

7.3.1 Dummy Variable Transformation

Suppose that we were interested in estimating the effect of a sign-in-window on sales for medium-size containers in high-volume stores. The first step in the transformation process would be to sort our observations into two categories: (1) those store-brand-weeks in which there was a sign-in-store; and (2) those in which there was not. Next we would compute the average residual sales for each of these two categories. Suppose that the results of that calculation were as follows:

Average residual sales, sign-in-store: 0.60

Average residual sales, no sign-in-store: −0.02

The difference between these two numbers (0.60 − (−0.02) = 0.62) is logically equivalent to the average regression coefficients that were used in the previous analysis as estimates of the average effect of a given policy variable. The demand response ratio (DRR, which is equal to the number of times that actual sales is greater than normal sales, given that the policy variable is turned "on") is calculated as it was before by adding one and squaring. In our example this would give us a demand response ratio of 2.65. In other words, window signs increase normal sales by a factor of roughly two and two-thirds.

7.3.2 Continuous Variable Transformations

For the purpose of this illustration, suppose that we want to estimate the effect on residual sales of normal price for medium-size containers in high-volume stores. As in the previous example, we would first classify our observations into a number of categories representing different normal price levels. For each category we would then compute the average value of residual sales. So far the procedure is the same as for the dummy variable illustration. Next, however, we plot the results of our hypothetical calculations as illustrated by Figure 7.1. We can describe that relationship by drawing an approximate regression line through the scatter. The slope of that line is our estimate of the effect on sales of a change in normal price. In our illustration, for a thirty-cent change in normal price, on the average there is a 0.50 change in residual sales. Our estimated regression coefficient would be −0.50.

Now, suppose that one cuts the normal price by thirty cents. Thirty cents is equal to one unit of change in our analysis. In addition, the change amounts to a decrease or a negative one-unit change. Therefore, the calculation of the resulting demand response ratio would be as follows:

$$DRR = (-0.50(-1) + 1)^2 = 2.25.$$

We would expect that the effect of a thirty-cent decrease in normal price would be to increase sales by two and one-quarter times their normal volume.

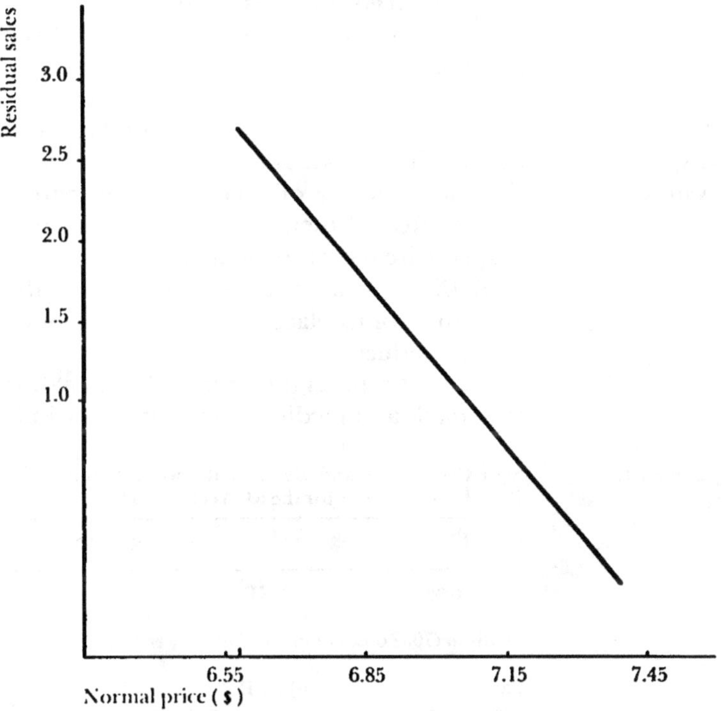

Figure 7.1 Hypothetical plot of residual sales and normal price.

7.4
Results

The discussion that follows concentrates on the relationship between the presence or absence of signs (in-store or in-window) and sales, by package size. The two sign variables that were used are as follows:

7.4.1
Sign Variables

1. SIWD. A measure of whether or not a sign-in-window was present in connection with the sale of the product.
2. SISD. A measure of whether or not a sign-in-store was present in connection with the sale of the product.

Table 7.1 reports these results. If the effect of sign promotions were zero, one would expect the value of DRR to be one. That is, one would expect demand in the week on the average to be equal to the store's average volume during weeks in which the brand-size in question was not on promotion. However, since the DRR's are greater than one in all cases, we conclude that signs do tend to *increase* demand for the product. *That is, the effects of SIWD's and SISD's are positive,* and effects of SIWD's are greater than those of SISD's.

A look at the coefficients for each of the three container sizes reveals that size differences do occur. The highest DRR's occur for the large-size containers, for which the values are 8.6 and 5.6, respectively, for SIWD and SISD. The smallest effects for signs occur in the medium-size containers, for which the respective DRR's for SIWD and SISD are 1.1 and 1.0.

7.4.2
Display Variable

It was intended originally to conduct separate analyses of displays in and out of the product's display section. However, their infrequency of occurrence permitted an analysis only of the effect of their presence or absence, not their location. Displays are therefore defined as follows:

UODD. A measure of whether or not a display was present, regardless of its place in the store, in connection with the sale of the product.

Table 7.2 reports the results of the analysis. The DRR's for the small- and medium-size container displays of 1.8 and 1.6,

Table 7.1. Sign Coefficients and Demand Response Ratios Averaged over Top Four Brands in All Stores for the 63-Week Period

Size	SIWD*	SISD*
Small (6826 observations) DRR	2.1	1.4
Medium (7002 observations) DRR	1.1	1.0
Large (2790 observations) DRR	8.6	5.6

*All significant at the 95 percent level.

Table 7.2. Display Coefficients and Demand Response Ratios Averaged over Top Four Brands in All Stores for the 63-Week Time Period

Size	UODD
Medium (7,002 observations) DRR	1.8*
Large (2,790 observations) DRR	1.6†

*Significant at the 95 percent level
†Significant at the 90 percent level

respectively, indicate that the effect of displays is to increase base sales by about 70 percent.

7.4.3 Special Offer Variables

Variables designed to measure the effects of the three most prevalent types of special offers had been previously analyzed by the multiple-equation method (see Section 6.3.3). By way of review, these special offers were:

1. SPOPD. A measure of whether or not a premium was offered in connection with the sale of the product.
2. SPORD. A measure of whether or not the product was offered in a reusable package.
3. SPOCD. A measure of whether or not a *retailer* coupon was offered in connection with the sale.

Analyses of the effects of three additional types of special offer activity are included in this report, as follows:

1. SPOBD. A measure of whether or not bonus product was offered in connection with the sale of the product.
2. SPOMD. A measure of whether or not mail-ins were offered in connection with the sale of the product. This would cover any type of offer in which the consumer would have to mail in something to partake of the offer (i.e., contests, mail-in premiums).
3. SPOLD. A measure of whether or not an in-pack coupon for later purchase was offered in connection with the sale of the product.

The frequencies for two other special offers (manufacturer's coupon and a tie-in with other products) were so small as to render analysis of them meaningless. Table 7.3 reports the results of the DRR's for SPOBD, SPOMD, and SPOLD. Because occurrences of these are so infrequent, their results are averaged over the whole sixty-three-week period as well as over high- and low-volume stores. By way of comparison, the DRR values for SPOPD, SPORD, and SPOCD from the multiple-equation analysis are also given in the same table.

Recapping earlier conclusions on SPOPD, SPORD, and SPOCD, we find the evidence quite clear that on the average premiums and reusable packs tended to retard sales slightly

Table 7.3 Special Offer Coefficients and Demand Response Ratios Averaged over Top Four Brands in All Stores

		Regression Results			Cross-Classification Results		
Time Period		SPOPD	SPORD	SPOCD	SPOBD	SPOMD	SPOLD
Small-Size Container (6826 observations)							
Weeks 2–32	DRR	0.8	0.8	—			
Weeks 33–62	DRR	1.0	1.8	1.9			
Weeks 1–63	DRR					0.8	
Medium-Size Container (7002 observations)							
Weeks 2–32	DRR	0.7	0.4	2.3			
Weeks 33–62	DRR	1.0	1.1	7.0			
Weeks 1–63	DRR				1.2	0.5	0.3
Large-Size Container (2790 observations)							
Weeks 2–32	DRR	0.5	0.7	—			
Weeks 33–62	DRR	0.7	0.7	—			
Weeks 1–63	DRR				—	—	2.3*

*Significant at 95 percent level

rather than increase them. In contrast, retailer coupons tended to increase demand.

To this we can now add that mail-ins appear to retard demand. Although the DRR's for mail-ins are not statistically significant by themselves, the fact that both the figures for small and medium container sizes are less than one would indicate that the effect of mail-ins is probably negative.

The effect of bonus packs on medium-size containers appears to be slightly positive. However, again the results are not statistically significant. Turning next to coupons for later purchase we see that for the large size this type of activity tends to increase normal demand by slightly over three times. The comparable figure for medium-size containers is disappointingly low. However, this DRR of 0.3 is not statistically significant. Looking at these figures relatively, though, the coupon for later purchase activity for the large-size containers appears to elicit a much stronger response than for the medium size. This particular finding is consistent with earlier findings about the greater responsiveness of large-size than of medium-size containers to promotional variables.

7.4.4 The Incidence of In-Store Promotion with Major Ads

In this section we deal with the question of the extent to which getting a "good" ad (AD3–AD5) leads to getting other in-store supporting activity. Since the major part of the merchandising and advertised-price activity occurred for the medium container size, we shall confine ourselves to it. Table 7.4 shows the probability of in-store promotional support occurring with major ads.

It is evident from Table 7.4 that the majority of in-store promotional support occurs when there is a large (AD3–AD5) ad.[1] The probability with these major ads ranges from about 75 percent to 85 percent, whereas it is generally less than 25 percent with anything below an AD3. The most prevalent kind of in-store help is in the form of sign activity. This occurs to a greater degree in low-volume than in high-volume stores. However, in high-volume stores, displays are used much more than in low-volume stores. *Since three-fourths or more of the in-store activity occurs with large ad activity, it appears as if the chance of obtaining this type of activity is greatly enhanced when a large ad can be obtained. Conversely, if a large ad cannot be obtained, the chances are very slim for getting in-store merchandising support.* This leads us to conclude that a grocer's decision to give in-store support is contingent upon two primary questions: (1) what price he wants to charge for the product; and (2) whether he wants to advertise it.

7.4.5 Effect of Change in Normal Price on Sales

One variable that was computed each week for each brand-size in each store was the normal price level (NPL). This represented the normal or average price for a particular brand-size-store-week. *The inclusion of NPL was an attempt to track the long-run effects of price level.* This should be differentiated from the AD0 to AD5 and UAP variables, which measured the short-run effect of promotional price discounts off the normal price. The level of NPL, once established,

Table 7.4

Probabilities of In-Store Promotional Support Occurring with Major Ads for Medium-Size Containers, Averaged over Four Top Brands

Type of Support	<AD3	AD3	AD4	AD5	Total	≥AD3	Base
High-Volume Stores							
Display	0.240	0.135	0.260	0.365	1.000	0.760	104
Sign	0.230	0.159	0.294	0.317	1.000	0.770	126
Display and Sign	0.164	0.149	0.299	0.388	1.000	0.836	67
Any Support	0.264	0.147	0.270	0.319	1.000	0.736	163
Low-Volume Stores							
Display	1.000	0.000	0.000	0.000	1.000	0.000	2
Sign	0.156	0.511	0.333	0.000	1.000	0.844	141
Display and Sign	—	—	—	—	—	—	0
Any Support	0.168	0.503	0.329	0.000	1.000	0.832	143

[1] Large refers to size of discount, not size of ad.

tended to change very slowly in comparison to the change in the advertising-price variables.

A demand curve can be constructed by looking at the variations in base demand for the product, as measured by the residuals, in relation to the normal price of the product. Figure 7.2 shows this relationship for the high-volume stores and Figure 7.3 shows it for the low-volume stores. Since there are only two data points within which to fit a demand curve for the small-size container, it will not be included in the analysis.

Table 7.5 shows what the average demand is at varying price levels in the high-volume stores. The large container size appears to be the most responsive to price changes, with the medium size the next most responsive.

Demand in low-volume stores is not very responsive to price. The only indication of responsiveness to a lowering of the NPL is when the normal price for the large container size is reduced below $7.50. At an average price of $7.10 for large containers, demand is increased three and one-half times.

Additional caution with respect to interpreting the NPL effects should be advised. These effects may be confounded by three factors: (1) effects from other brands lagging behind the price reduction started during the middle of the sixty-third-week period; (2) store substitution effects as some stores drop their price and others do not; and (3) some increase in primary demand for the product as a result of a drop in shelf price. However, overall, it appears that price is a fairly powerful determinant of demand; for example,

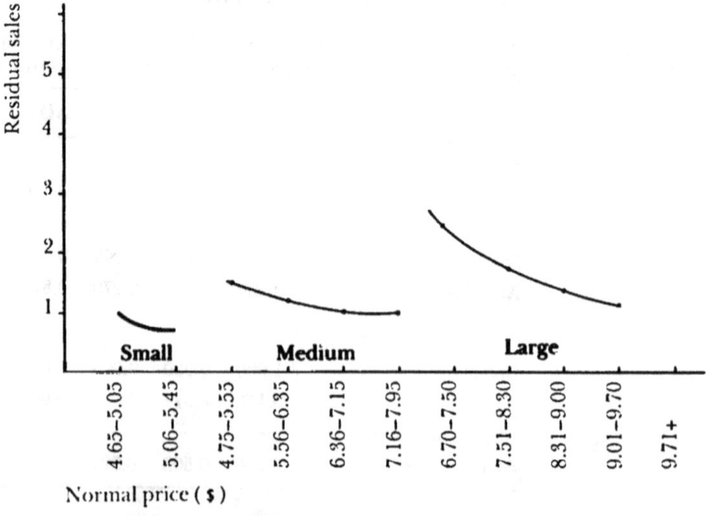

Figure 7.2 Demand curve for high-volume stores.

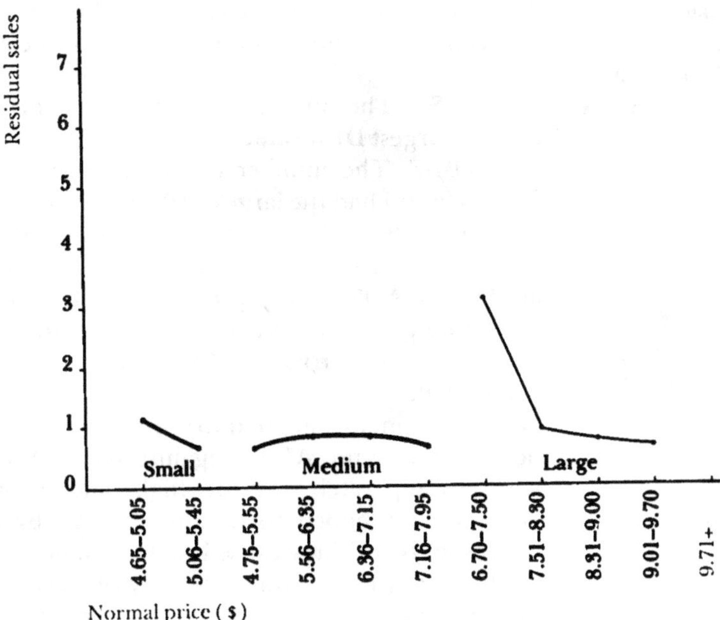

Figure 7.3 Demand curve for low-volume stores.

a large-size container price of approximately \$7.00 in high-volume stores sustained over six weeks (in the absence of competition) implies a total DRR equal to approximately $2.4 \times 6 = 14.4$.

Table 7.5 **Demand as a Function of NPL, Averaged over the 63-Week Time Period and the Top Four Brands**

		DRR	
Container Size	NPL* \$	High-Volume Stores	Low-Volume Stores
Small	4.85	1.0	1.0
	5.25	0.8	0.9
Medium	5.15	1.8	0.7
	5.95	1.3	0.8
	6.75	0.9	0.9
	7.55	0.8	0.8
Large	7.00	2.4	3.5
	7.90	1.7	1.1
	8.65	1.3	1.0
	9.35	1.0	1.0

*Price levels coded as reported in Section 6.3.1.1, Table 6.2.

7.4.6. The Effect of Promotional Timing on Demand

To answer the question of what effect the time interval between promotions has on demand, two new variables were created.

1. NWBS. The number of weeks since this brand and size had the largest DRR value in this store.
2. NWBA. The number of weeks since any container size for this brand had the largest DRR value in this store.

The rationale behind defining these variables in this manner was that when a brand had a good promotion in a store, say an AD4 or AD5, then it probably would have the maximum DRR among all brands and sizes in that store. Hence, NWBS and NWBA are surrogates for the presence of a major retail promotion.

It was originally intended to cross-classify the major promotions, AD4's and AD5's, against the NWBS and NWBA variables separately for the high- and low-volume stores. We had also hoped to do this analysis by container size. However, two things caused us to change these plans. First of all, we found that the frequency of AD4 and AD5 promotions for the small and large containers was too low to permit analysis. This is also true of medium-size containers in the low-volume stores. Second, the relationships using NWBA are identical to those observed for NSBA. This is probably due to the fact that the two measures overlap. Hence, we restricted our analysis to the medium container size in the high-volume stores, using only NWBA as a measure of the number of weeks since last promotion. We measured the carry-over effects of past promotions not only on the effects of current AD4 or AD5 activity but also on the effects of current UAP activity.

As the number of weeks increases since any container size for a brand has enjoyed outstanding performance relative to its normal volume, the expected sales resulting from engaging in an advertised price promotion at first increases and then appears to decline. This is true for both AD4 and AD5 promotions. The peak in expected sales for an AD4 promotion in terms of the interval since the brand's last period of outstanding performance is about seven to eight weeks, while the peak in the sales one would expect from an AD5 promotion occurs after approximately eleven to twelve weeks. The same general relationship holds for UAP's, for which the peak occurs in about the eighth or ninth week.

The DRR's for AD4 and AD5 type promotions that are reported in Chapter 6 are measures of the average effect of each type of promotion without taking into account the effects of timing which have just been discussed. These average effects can now be adjusted for the influence of timing. Instead of having only one DRR as a measure of AD4 activity, as a result of the adjustment process, we will now have a schedule of DRR's that measures the relationship of the DRR one would expect, from, say, an AD4 as a function of NWBA. Table 7.6 reports the results for AD4, AD5, and UAP promotions. For example, the DRR one would expect from an AD4 type promotion for medium-size container that occurred two weeks after the last major promotion is 4.9. By waiting two weeks to initiate the promotion, the expected DRR would increase from 4.9 to 6.7.

Looking first at AD4's and AD5's, it is apparent that in the first two weeks immediately following a major promotion, the effect of a large AD is not fully realized. However, as the weeks go by without a major promotion, the effect of having a large AD becomes greater and greater. As was graphically illustrated earlier, the effect for an AD4 peaks out at seven or eight weeks after a major promotion. At this time an AD4 will have an average DRR of 8.6, as compared with a normal DRR of 6.2. From this high point, the effect falls slightly. The effect for an AD5 seems to take longer to reach its peak. Its maximum effect occurs at eleven to twelve weeks, when the DRR reaches 13.7, compared to a normal DRR of 8.1 for an AD5. After this period the effect falters, as was the case for

Table 7.6 Demand Response Ratios Adjusted for Carry-over Effects Averaged over Top Four Brands for High-Volume Stores, Medium-Size Containers

	Type of Promotion					
No. of Weeks since Major Promotion	AD4		AD5		UAP*	
	Coeff.	DRR	Coeff.	DRR	Coeff.	DRR
Base Effect	1.49	6.2	1.85	8.1	0.39	1.9
	Adj. Factor		Adj. Factor		Adj. Factor	
1–2	−0.27	4.9	−0.09	7.6	−0.25	1.3
3–4	0.08	6.7	−0.06	7.8	0.11	2.3
5–6	0.33	8.0	0.01	8.2	0.25	2.7
7–8	0.45	8.6	0.15	9.0	0.30	2.9
9–10	0.41	8.4	0.60	11.9	0.30	2.9
11–12	0.36	8.1	0.85	13.7	0.24	2.7
13–14	0.30	7.8	0.83	13.5	0.12	2.3
15–16	0.24	7.5	0.78	13.1		
17–18	0.18	7.1	0.71	12.7		
19–20	0.11	6.8	0.62	12.0		
21 or more	0.02	6.3	0.53	11.4		

*UAP based on average discount of $0.25.

the AD4. This faltering may indicate that those consumers who were waiting to buy their favorite brand on sale could wait no longer and bought it at shelf price or switched to another brand on sale.

Turning now to the UAP variable, which was taken as an average of $0.25 for the medium-size container, we can see much the same type of curve that existed for the ads. That is, demand response is below normal for a UAP the first two weeks after a major promotion, but after that demand increases over normal demand, reaching a peak at eight or nine weeks. Past the peak, demand falls off slightly, just as in the case of the AD variables. The UAP curve thus corroborates our findings about carry-over effects.

7.5 Concluding Statement

The estimates of the response of demand to promotion, which we have reported in Chapters 6 and 7, are of *central importance* to the development of a model capable of evaluating the profitability of alternative promotional programs. However, they provide only one of several pieces of information required for a comprehensive economic analysis. In order to translate the regression coefficients and their corresponding DRR's into meaningful terms, one needs a system capable at the very least of the following:

1. Relating manufacturer allowances to retailers (on a manufacturer-by-manufacturer basis) to the types of retail promotional activity that occur in a given promotional period (i.e., one must assign probabilities to the various types of retail promotional activities given to a particular allowance package). We have implicitly assumed probabilities of 1.0—all stores will do the same thing. Obviously the probability of an AD5 is not 1.0 and, in addition, will differ from that of other promotional variables, such as a UAPNFM. The probabilities will also vary over time.
2. Using these probabilities together with the results of the multiple-equation model plus data on the volume of the product sold by the two store segments, to generate a series of unit volume estimates.
3. Transforming the volume estimates into revenue estimates and combining this with cost data to obtain profit estimates for a particular manufacturer.

In addition, one would like a system that would be sufficiently flexible in the sense that it would permit the evaluation of a wide range of alternative promotional programs in a short span of time.

The need for such a system is clear-cut; however, it imposes a substantial calculation burden. Hand calculations would be of little use and fortunately are completely unnecessary.

The need for such a system has led us to the development of what we can call an "economic analysis simulation," which is capable of meeting these requirements. It will be discussed in the following chapter.

8 Simulation of Promotional Effects

The results reported in Chapters 6 and 7 provide estimates of the effects of retailer promotions on consumer demand for the product under study. However, estimates of regression coefficients and demand response ratios do not by themselves lead to forecasts of sales volume. These forecasts depend on the base figures used to calculate the normalized sales ratios used as dependent variables in the regressions and cross-classifications, the frequency of the incidence of different kinds of retailer promotions, and so forth. In addition, some method for relating retailer promotional activity to the types of allowance packages offered by manufacturers in the market must be found if we are to close the loop between manufacturers' actions and consumer demand.

A simulation model designed to permit exploration of the effect of different degrees of retailer activity on sales and profits was constructed as part of the research project being reported. The model also can be used to make rough predictions of retailer promotional activity, conditional on whatever allowance package is specified by the user. The model has been used effectively to predict sales (and profits) as a function of different mixes of retailer promotion activity, and to a lesser extent to predict retailer activity on the basis of test promotional packages.[1]

First we will present an overview of the model. This will be followed by a more detailed description of the model's inputs and outputs. Part of this discussion will be couched in terms of a set of operating instructions for the simulation, as this is the best way to represent its functions. Technical considerations relevant to the operation of the model will be presented in the third and last section of this chapter.

8.1 Overview of the Model

A macro flow chart of the allowance effect simulator is presented in Figure 8.1. Major inputs (provided by the user) are listed along the left margin of the figure and major outputs are described on the right. The main functions performed by the program are indicated in the boxes down the center of the figure.

The program is divided into five major segments, each of which will be discussed in the following paragraphs.

[1]The success of the prediction of retailer activity using the procedure built into the model depends critically on the stability of the marketplace during the historical data period. (The reason for this will be apparent presently.) As was discussed in Chapters 6 and 7, this requirement is not met well in our data. Hence this part of the model has been used sparingly. A new model for the prediction of retailer activity is being constructed for the sponsors of the study. We hope to report on this at a future date

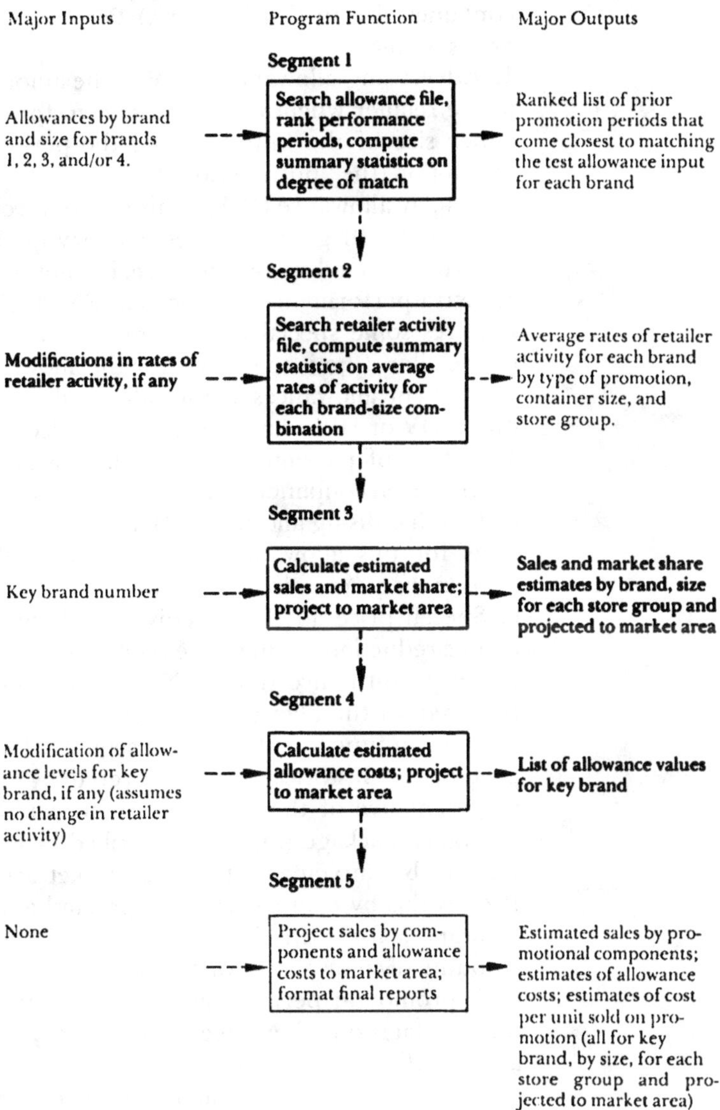

Figure 8.1 Macroflow chart of promotion simulation.

8.1.1 Segment 1: Allowance Inputs

The program starts by requesting input describing the *allowance package* to be offered by each brand for the promotion period to be simulated. Allowances are typed in at the teletype terminal, in terms of dollars per unit[2] to be offered for each container size for each of the four major brands active in the market. (Allowances are specified separately for each

[2]The exact units of quality and price used in the simulation are disguised.

container size in this industry.) Permissible allowance types are as follows:

1. Advertising allowance (ADV). The amount offered is paid to the retailer whenever he runs an ad for the indicated container size of the brand during the period covered by the promotion (the "push period").
2. Display allowance (DIS). This covers special displays in the retail store. In general, a retailer may qualify for either an advertising or a display allowance, but not for both.
3. Extra performance as specified (EXT). The manufacturer requires some special kind of promotional performance by the retailer if he is to qualify for the allowance. This and the subsequent allowances are usually paid in addition to whatever ADV or DIS allowances are to be received by the retailer.
4. Picture of package in ad (PIC). This is paid when an ad for the given container size includes a picture of the package.
5. Merchandising allowance (MER). The performance conditions for this allowance vary, but generally they relate to signs in the store or in the window.
6. Special price ad (PRI). This is paid when an ad offering a price reduction is run by the retailer.
7. No performance (NOP). No performance of any kind is required for this allowance; all retailers automatically qualify.

The main function of program segment 1 is to find out what part of the historical period covered by the audit is most representative of the conditions that would exist if the test allowance package (input as described by types 1 through 7) were to be implemented in the market area being studied. It does this by comparing the types and amounts of the test allowances for each size of each brand with the types and amounts of allowances for the same size that existed during each promotion period covered by the audit data. The historical data on allowances, stored in computer memory as an *allowance file*, were obtained from the sponsoring company's records. The allowance packages for the small, medium, and large container sizes for the four major brands for each week of the retail store audit are included in the file.

The program searches the historical allowance file to find the allowances that are most like the test allowance package. The rules by which this search is conducted are described in Section 8.2.1. The search is conducted for each brand separately, using whatever portion of the allowance file is specified by the operator. (For instance, allowances offered by certain brands at given times may be excluded from consideration if desired.)

The output of program segment 1 is a set of tables showing

which historical allowance packages are most like the test package input for each brand. Statistics giving the degree of "likeness" for each comparison are also provided. The operator can scan these results and cause the program to repeat the search for any brand using different portions of the historical allowance file if he desires. When the assignment of representative historical periods to each test allowance package is complete, the program transmits its results to program segment 2 for further processing.

8.1.2
Segment 2:
Retailer Activity

The main function of program segment 2 is to determine the rates of retailer activity associated with the historical promotion periods assigned to each test allowance package by segment 1. The information needed to accomplish this has been extracted from the store audit data records and stored in a *retailer activity file* that is accessible to the simulation program. This file contains the proportions of stores engaging in AD0, AD1, and other kinds of promotional activity for each brand and size for the weeks included in the performance period of each historical promotion package. Average values of UAP and other continuous promotion variables are provided, as well as the values of certain other variables to be defined in Section 8.2.2. (Most of the variables for which demand response ratios were reported in Chapters 6 and 7 are included in the file.) The retailer activity information is stored separately for the high- and low-volume store segments.

The program identifies the brand and period of weeks associated with each historical promotion period assigned to a test allowance package by segment 1. The data corresponding to them are loaded from the retailer activity file. The major output from this segment is a set of tables showing the retailer activity to be associated with the test allowance package for each brand. (These results form an important input for the calculations in subsequent program segments.) Provision has been made for the operator to modify the forecasted activity for any variable, for any brand or size, by typing in new values from the console. When everyone has agreed that the set of retailer promotional activities is reasonable, the program is instructed to transmit its results to segment 3 for further processing.

8.1.3
Segment 3:
Sales Outputs

This program inserts the retailer activity variables into a modified version of the multiple-equation demand response model described in Chapters 5 and 6 (the modifications are described in Sections 8.2.3 and 8.3.1). Next it uses the model to estimate the sales volume for each brand, size, and store segment. In addition to the retailer activity estimates provided by program segment 2, the model makes use of information on the base sales levels (for each brand and size) for each store in the sample. (The details of this and other modifications to the model will be described in Section 8.2.3.) This procedure translates the demand response ratios (as reported in Chapters 6 and 7) to quantitative estimates of sales volume.

The model provides sales estimates (in units) for each size of the four major brands in the market area under study. A single aggregate estimate for all sizes of the other brands is also provided. Separate estimates are given for the high- and low-volume store segments. Market-share statistics are calculated from the total sales volume figures.

In addition to making estimates of sales for the particular stores included in the audit, the model attempts to project these estimates to the market area as a whole. The projection factors were obtained by comparing the total sales volumes for the high- and low-volume store groups with Nielsen data for the area covering equivalent time periods. This analysis produced a pair of constants that can be used to inflate the sales estimates for the two store groups to the area as a whole. Market-share statistics for the area are calculated from the projected sales figures.

The estimates of sales and market share for each brand and size, by store group and for the total market area, form the major outputs of program segment 3. In addition, this program performs certain calculations required for segments 4 and 5.

8.1.4 Segment 4: Intermediate Outputs

Program segment 4 calculates estimates of the cost of the allowance package for one of the four brands included in the simulation. This brand is called the "key brand"; its identity is input in program segment 3. As the reports pertaining to allowance costs are output from program segment 5, a description of the calculations will be postponed until our discussion of that segment.

The major output of program segment 4 is a table showing the test allowance package for the key brand. This information is a repeat of the data input in program segment 1 for this brand. The program allows the operator to change the allowance package for the key brand at this point in the simulation if he so desires. However, such a change affects only the cost calculations, not the estimates of sales and market share. The purpose of this feature is to allow an examination of the sensitivity of allowance costs to small changes in the promotional package, assuming that there is no significant change in sales during the performance period.

8.1.5
Segment 5:
Cost and
Profit Outputs

Program segment 5 provides reports on sales, costs, and contributions to profit for the key brand. No inputs are required for this segment of the simulation. The following tables are reported automatically upon execution of the program:

Table 1: *Estimated sales by components by size.* The "components" of sales are background sales, sales due to ads, sales due to reduced priced ads, sales due to unadvertised price discounts, sales due to displays, and sales due to signs. The "background" component includes sales due to causes not related to the specific promotional activities listed in these categories.

Table 2: *Estimated gross profit by components of sales, by size.* Gross profit is obtained by multiplying the sales volumes reported by a gross margin figure supplied to the program. The gross profit figure is before deduction of the costs of the allowance. The components of sales are the same as defined in Table 1.

Table 3: *Estimated sales due to retailer promotions, by size.* This is the sum of all the sales components involving retailer promotions.

Table 4: *Estimated demand response ratios, by size.* The values in this table are obtained by dividing the sales due to retailer promotions by the volume in the "background" sales component. It is a measure of the effectiveness of the allowance package in multiplying what would have been the sales rate in the absence of retailer promotional activity.

Table 5: *Estimated allowance costs by type of allowance and container size.* Each of the allowance types input in program segment 1 (for the key brand) is costed out by multiplying the allowance rate by the volume of sales generated by the components to which it applies. Care is taken to use the same costing rules as would actually be applied by the offering company's accounting department, and double counting of sales and overlapping allowance types is avoided.

Table 6: *Estimated allowance cost per unit sold on promotion, by size.* These figures are obtained by dividing the total allowance cost for each size (output in Table 5) by the total number of units sold under conditions of retailer promotion (output in Table 3).

They are measures of the cost effectiveness of the allowance package.

Table 7: *Estimated gross profit after deducting allowance costs, by size.* Here the estimated allowance cost for each container size is deducted from the total gross profit for that size (see description of Table 2) to obtain an estimate of the contribution to profit generated by the allowance package.

Each of these tables is output for each store group separately and then projected to the total market area.

8.2 Detailed Description of the Simulation

The teletype printout obtained from a sample run of the economic analysis simulation is presented in Appendix 8A, at the end of this chapter. Information typed in by the console operator is underlined; all other information is output by the computer. Various parts of the printout are identified by circled markings, such as 1A or 4C. (In each case the numeric digit refers to the number of the program segment and the letter to the sequence of items within that segment.) These markings will facilitate cross-referencing between the text and the sample output (Appendix 8A).

We will discuss each part of the printout in detail, considering the inputs necessary to operate the program, the procedures used by the program at each step of the analysis, and the meaning of the various outputs supplied by the program.

8.2.1 Segment 1: Searching for Analogous Allowances

As described in Section 8.1.1, the main function of program segment 1 is to obtain inputs for the test allowance packages to be offered by the various brands, search the allowance file, and rank the performance periods in terms of their degree of match with each test allowance. Before proceeding with our description of the program printout, it will be helpful to consider how this searching and matching procedure operates.

What is meant by how "representative" a historical allowance package is of a test allowance package? First, it is clear that if the two are identical (i.e., exactly the same amounts are offered on each type of allowance, for each container size) the historical allowance package is a perfect match. It is a simple matter for the program to search the relevant parts of the historical allowance file to see whether any past allowance exactly matches the test allowance.

If no perfect match exists (e.g., the test allowance package for a given brand was not tried during the audit), the program finds the allowance that comes closest to being a match.

"Closeness" is defined as the value of the following gross deviation between the test and historical allowance:

$$\begin{aligned}\text{Gross deviation} = \tfrac{1}{2}\,&(\text{sum of the squared differences between the total dollar amounts offered for each size})\\ +\tfrac{1}{2}\,&(\text{sum of the squared differences between the dollar amounts offered on each allowance type for each size}).\end{aligned} \quad (8.1)$$

As an example, consider a hypothetical case in which the system considers only two kinds of allowance (A_1 and A_2) and two container sizes (S_1 and S_2). Suppose that the operator has input the test allowance package shown in Table 8.1 and that the program is calculating the gross deviation between it and the first push period contained in the historical allowance file. Assuming the values given in Table 8.1, we would calculate the gross deviation as follows:

$$\begin{aligned}\text{Gross deviation} &= \tfrac{1}{2}(2.25-2.35)^2+(1.75-2.25)^2\\ &\quad+\tfrac{1}{2}(1.50-1.75)^2+(0.75-0.60)^2\\ &\quad+(1.25-1.60)^2+(0.50-0.65)^2\\ &= \tfrac{1}{2}(0.260)+\tfrac{1}{2}(0.231)\\ &= .245.\end{aligned}$$

The gross deviation depends both on the amounts offered for each type of allowance and on the total amount offered for each container size. (Thus, packages offering identical amounts, but one for an ADV and one for a PRI type allowance, would match on the first term given—that is, the squared deviation would be zero—but would not match on the second term. This would produce a medium-sized gross deviation.)

In addition to finding the historical period whose allowance

Table 8.1 Hypothetical Test Allowance Package

Container Size	Allowance Type	Test allowance input by operator	Allowance in first push period of history
S_1	A_1	1.50	1.75
	A_2	0.75	0.60
	Total	2.25	2.35
S_2	A_1	1.25	1.60
	A_2	0.50	0.65
	Total	1.75	2.25

package provides the best match (i.e., the smallest gross deviation) with the test allowance package, the program may also determine the second, third, and fourth best historical packages. The four are rank-ordered by ascending values of their gross deviation figures. A *weight* is assigned to each historical period according to a rule to be described later. In general terms, the rule requires (1) that each weight be between zero and one, (2) that the sum of the weights for the four periods be equal to one, and (3) that the weights be inversely related to the gross deviations (i.e., the historical period with the largest weight is the one with the smallest gross deviation, etc.). The use of four different historical allowance packages increases the reliability of the calculations in subsequent segments of the simulation program by avoiding possible extreme situations.

The searching and ranking procedure described is performed separately for each brand for which a test allowance package has been provided. The program may also be instructed to use the average of a brand's historical allowance packages (i.e., no test allowance is provided); if this is the case, the average is computed and assigned a gross deviation of zero and a weight of one.

Figure 8.2 presents a macro flow diagram for program segment 1. The diagram is cross-referenced with the line numbers included in the sample output (Appendix 8A) to permit easy examination of the logic of the program.

Line 1A. At line 1A the program reads the results of the last search of the historical allowance file, as currently contained in the SEARCH RESULTS table. (This is the table that is transmitted to program segment 2. As program segment 2 does not alter or destroy the SEARCH RESULTS table, the results contained therein are available for reading and further processing in program segment 1.) After the table has been read by the program, the value of the NUMBER OF ALLOWANCE COMPARISONS (labeled NCT by the program) used in the last run is printed out. As noted earlier, this determines the number of different historical allowance periods that will be brought into the final set of search results for each brand.

Line 1B. The next step is for the operator to tell the program whether the results of the last run should be canceled or used as the starting point for the current run. The query CANCEL LAST RESULTS? IF SO TYPE NEW NCT, ELSE TYPE 0 invites this decision. If the previous search results are to be canceled for all brands, the operator responds with the value of NCT that is to be used for the current run. (The new value

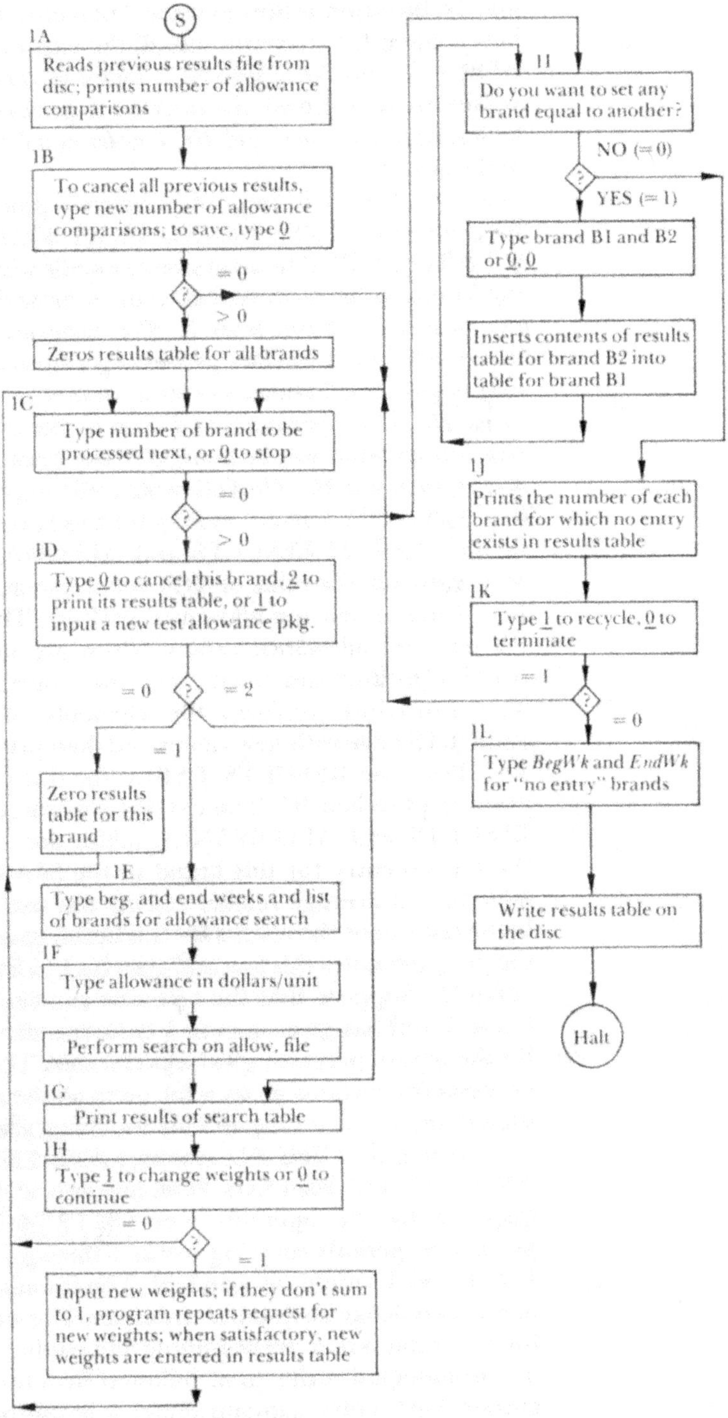

S

1A
Reads previous results file from disc; prints number of allowance comparisons

1B
To cancel all previous results, type new number of allowance comparisons; to save, type 0

= 0

> 0

Zeros results table for all brands

1C
Type number of brand to be processed next, or 0 to stop

= 0

> 0

1D
Type 0 to cancel this brand, 2 to print its results table, or 1 to input a new test allowance pkg.

= 0

= 2

= 1

Zero results table for this brand

1E
Type beg. and end weeks and list of brands for allowance search

1F
Type allowance in dollars/unit

Perform search on allow. file

1G
Print results of search table

1H
Type 1 to change weights or 0 to continue

= 0

= 1

Input new weights; if they don't sum to 1, program repeats request for new weights; when satisfactory, new weights are entered in results table

1I
Do you want to set any brand equal to another?

NO (= 0)

YES (= 1)

Type brand B1 and B2 or 0, 0

Inserts contents of results table for brand B2 into table for brand B1

1J
Prints the number of each brand for which no entry exists in results table

1K
Type 1 to recycle, 0 to terminate

= 1

= 0

1L
Type *BegWk* and *EndWk* for "no entry" brands

Write results table on the disc

Halt

Figure 8.2 Flow chart for program segment 1.

may be the same as the old value, but it must be typed in again here.) Then the program sets all the entries in the SEARCH RESULTS and ALLOWANCE tables to zero. If the last run results are to be saved, the operator types in 0; in this case the tables are not zeroed and NCT is set equal to the value used in the last run.

Line 1C. The main loop of program segment 1 begins with the command, TYPE BRAND TO BE PROCESSED NEXT OR 0 TO STOP. The operator responds with the number of the brand to be processed next or, if he wishes to terminate the processing loop, with 0. The program returns to this line every time it finishes processing a brand. A given brand may be processed as many times as desired.

Line 1D. The operator's response to the query PROCESS? determines what will be done with the brand whose number was input at line 1C. The following codes apply:

0 Cancel the current results for this brand. The elements in the SEARCH RESULTS and ALLOWANCE tables are set to zero, but the value of NCT is not changed.

1 Input a new test allowance package. The program calls for new test allowance values, which are inserted into the search algorithm described earlier (see lines 1E through 1G). This procedure replaces the elements of the SEARCH RESULTS table with new values and then prints the table.

2 Print the RESULTS TABLE for this brand. The program skips to line 1G. The current contents of the SEARCH RESULTS and ALLOWANCE tables are not changed. If there is no entry for this brand in the SEARCH RESULTS table (i.e., if average retailer activity was used for this brand in the last run or the results for this brand have been canceled) the program notes this fact and goes back to line 1C.

Line 1E. Suppose that the operator has decided to process brand 2 and has given a code 1 (new test allowance package) for the type of processing to be performed. Then the program requests instructions as to what parts of the allowance file it should search in trying to find matching allowance periods for this brand: TYPE BEG(inning) AND END(ing) WEEKS AND LIST OF BRANDS FOR (allowance) SEARCH. The response by the operator was 1 63 1 2 3 4 indicating that promotion periods covering weeks 1 through 63, and brands 1, 2, 3, and 4 should be searched. The brands to be included in the search may be listed in any order. The only requirement for this input is that the beginning and ending weeks be typed in chronological order first, followed by a list of four brand entries (each entry contains either a brand number or zero if a brand is not to be included in the search).

Line 1F. The request TYPE ALLOWANCE IN DOLLARS/UNIT FOR S(mall), M(edium), (and) L(arge) container sizes tells the operator that the program is ready to receive the test allowance package for the brand specified at line 1C. The program specifies the allowance type, e.g., ADV, and the operator types in the dollar value of that allowance—first for small containers, then for medium, and then for large. After the large-size entry the program moves to the next allowance type or, after NOP, to the beginning of the search procedure.

Line 1G. After the program completes the search as described, it prints SEARCH RESULTS and then reports its findings for the brand specified in line 1C. The RANK column gives the relative degree to which the given push period matches the test allowance package (rank 1 is the best match and rank 4 is the fourth best match). The column BR/BW/EWeek contains a five digit integer number that defines the brand and the beginning and ending weeks of the performance period to which the given push period applies. For example, the first-ranked push period refers to an allowance period offered by brand 3 which was effective between weeks 60 and 63 of the store audit history. The PUSH INDEX column reports the serial number of this push period. (The push periods contained in the historical allowance file have been assigned serial numbers ascending chronologically for brand 1, then for brand 2, and so on.)

The next four columns of the SEARCH RESULTS table pertain to the degree of match between each push period and the test allowance package. The D-S(mall) column gives the "distance" between the small-size test allowance package and the small-size allowance offered during the historical push period with the serial number indicated for the row. The formula for distance is as follows:

$$\textbf{Distance} = \sqrt{\frac{1}{7}\sum_{i=1}^{7} (\text{test allowance type } i - \text{historical, allowance type } i)^2} \qquad (8.2)$$

where the summation covers the seven types of allowances included in the model (i.e., ADV, DIS, . . . , NOP). All the allowances are expressed in dollars per unit, and all pertain to the container size indicated by the current D-column of the table (in this case the small size). The "distance" measure also has the dimension "dollars per unit"; in the sample, the distance between the test allowance for small containers and the first-ranked historical push period is \$0.114, that between the test package and the second-ranked historical allowance is \$0.371, and so on. This process is repeated for medium and large containers, with the results reported in columns D-M(edium) and D-L(arge) of the table.

The D-TOT**4 column of the SEARCH RESULTS table gives the measure of gross discrepancy used to assign weights to the best four historical allowance push periods. The values are calculated from the gross deviation figure given by Equation 8.1. In the current version of the model, the output of Equation 8.1 is squared to produce D-TOT**4, in order to provide a great deal of discrimination between historical allowance periods. (Equation 8.1 has the dimension "distance squared"; squaring this procedure "distance to the fourth power.")[3]

The figures in the D-S, D-M, and D-L columns differ from those in the D-TOT**4 column in three important respects: (1) The first three are size-specific, whereas the fourth aggregates the distances for the three sizes; (2) the first three pertain only to the discrepancies in the individual allowance types between the test and historical packages, whereas the fourth weights this equally with the discrepancy between the total allowance offered in the two packages (this was shown in Equation 8.1); and (3) the first three have the dimension "dollars per unit of discrepancy," whereas the fourth has the dimension "fourth power of dollars per unit of discrepancy." In general, the size-specific distance measures are easier to interpret, but the total distance measure is necessary for the subsequent calculations.

The last column of the SEARCH RESULTS table is labeled WEIGHT. These values reflect the relative importance that will be assigned to the various historical push periods in later stages of the simulation. As noted earlier, the weights must lie between zero and one, and they must sum to one. They are calculated according to the following formula:

$$\text{Weight}\ (i) = \frac{1/\text{DT}(i)}{\sum_{j=1}^{N} (1/\text{DT}(j))}, \text{ for } i-1, N. \qquad (8.3)$$

Here DT(i) stands for the value of D-TOT**4 for the ith-ranked push period and N is the number of allowance comparisons input to the program at line 1A. As can be seen from the formula, the value of the weight assigned to a given push period becomes larger as its value of D-TOT**4 becomes smaller, that is, as the match between this historical period and the test allowance package gets better.

[3]The symbol X**4 stands for "X to the fourth power of X."

Let us summarize the operation of program segment 1 thus far. The operator tells the program what brand to process next and how the brand is to be processed. If a search is requested, the program is told what portions of the historical allowance file should be searched in connection with this brand (line 1E). Then the operator types in the values of the test allowance package, by type of allowance, for small-, medium-, and large-size containers (line 1F). The program searches the indicated portions of the historical allowance file and reports summary information on the results of the search (line 1G). This information includes the serial number, brand, and beginning and ending weeks of the NCT historical push periods that provide the best match with the test allowance package. A measure of the discrepancy between the test allowance package and the allowances for each of the historical push periods is provided for small-, medium-, and large-size containers separately, and for all sizes aggregated. The aggregate discrepancy measures are then transformed according to Equation 8.3 to yield a set of weights that reflect the comparative relevance of the NCT historical push periods found by the search procedure. These weights, and the serial numbers of the associated historical push periods, are transmitted to program segment 2.

Line 1H. It is possible that the operator may be dissatisfied with the weights assigned to the NCT historical push periods by the simulation program. The program gives him the opportunity to change the set of weights if he so desires. The query CHANGE WEIGHTS? sets up this option. If a 1 is typed, the program responds with TYPE NEW WEIGHTS IN ORDER OF RANK, in which case the operator types exactly NCT new values. These are inserted in the SEARCH RESULTS table in the order in which they are typed, beginning with the first-ranked push period (as indicated in the RANK column of the table). If the new probabilities do not sum to one, the program notes this fact and requests the input again. When an acceptable set of new weights has been provided, the SEARCH RESULTS table may be printed out again by repeating this brand at line 1C. (Note that the distance measures are zeroed out when the weights are modified.)

If the operator's response to the question at line 1H is 0 (no), the program goes back to line 1C to obtain instructions about the next brand to be processed.

Line 1I. When no further brands are to be processed (i.e., a 0 is typed in at line 1C) the program asks SET ONE BRAND EQUAL TO ANOTHER? If the answer is 1 (yes), the program requests the number of the brand that is to be reset and the number of the brand that will provide the information. In the example, we have set brand 1 equal to brand 2; thus all the entries in the SEARCH RESULTS table for brand 1 will be set equal to the corresponding entries for brand 2. The table for brand 2 will not be changed by this process. The program continues to request substitution information until 0 is typed, at which point it goes on to line 1J. (There is no limit to the number of times a given brand may be set equal to another; in every case the last substitution statement input for a given brand will apply.)

Line 1J. Here the program prints out the current status of the SEARCH RESULTS table for each brand as a reminder for the operator. The table, which is labeled CURRENT BRAND ENTRY STATUS contains information on the status of the brand's search results entry and the beginning and ending weeks that apply to that brand. In the STATUS column, a code of "1" indicates that a test allowance package and matching set of historical push periods are available. (These may have been input from the last run and not canceled, provided as the result of a search, or assigned to the brand by setting it equal to another brand.) A code of "0" indicates that no allowance or historical push period indices are currently contained in the SEARCH RESULTS table for that brand. If this is not changed during subsequent operations of the program, average retailer activities will be assigned to this brand.

Line 1K. After seeing the CURRENT BRAND ENTRY STATUS report, the operator is given the option of recycling the program. A 1 response to the query RECYCLE? sends the program back to line 1C without changing the contents of any of the tables. A 0 response sends the program into its termination phase, beginning at line 1L.

Line 1L. The last task before termination is to provide instructions as to the range of weeks that will be used in calculating the average rates of retailer activity to be used for brands that do not have an entry in the SEARCH RESULTS table. The program requests TYPE BEGWK AND ENDWK FOR EACH NO-ENTRY BRAND, followed by the number of the first brand for which a test allowance package has not been provided. The operator responds with the first and last weeks of the period to be used in calculating average retailer activity for that brand. Then the program prints the number of the second no-entry brand, if any, and the process is repeated until all the no-entry brands have been covered. The beginning and ending weeks must be typed in for each no-entry brand, even though this information may have been assigned to the brand in the previous run and not canceled out during the current run.

Following the input of the preceding information the program writes the SEARCH RESULTS and ALLOWANCE tables on a disc for transmission to subsequent program segments and then comes to a halt. If necessary, the whole process may be repeated by reloading program segment 1 and executing, beginning at line 1A.

8.2.2 Segment 2: Retailer Activity Estimates

The main function of program segment 2 is to translate the list of push periods that match the test allowance package (as given in the SEARCH RESULTS table transmitted from program segment 1) to a table of retailer activity variables for each brand. Where no SEARCH RESULTS table entry exists for a given brand, program segment 2 calculates the average retailer activity for the brand for the weeks specified at the end of program segment 1. The flow of this program is rather simple, and can be followed directly from the test output given in Appendix 8A without reference to a separate flow chart.

Before describing the program flow for segment 2 it will be helpful to discuss the historical retailer activity file. The historical allowance information used in program segment 1 is divided into forty-five push periods. Each push period is defined in terms of a given set of weeks for a given brand: for instance, nine push periods might pertain to brand 1, ten to brand 2, eleven to brand 3, and fifteen to brand 4. The historical allowance file contains the values of the allowances in the package offered by the given brand during the weeks included in the push period definition.

The historical retailer activity file also is organized in terms of push periods. For each entry in the historical allowance file there is a corresponding pair of entries in the historical retailer activity file: one for high-volume and one for low-volume stores. Each of the activity file entries contains information on some twenty-five retailer promotion variables for each of the three container sizes of the product under study. Therefore, when program segment 1 identifies a push period whose allowance matches a given test allowance package, it is possible to retrieve the retailer activity that occurred during the historical period represented by the designated push period. As each push period is brand-specific (recall, however, that it is possible for the search procedure to assign a push period pertaining to one brand as a match for a test allowance package input for another brand), the retailer activity associated with that push period is also brand-specific. The entire retailer promotion history for the period covered by the audit is included in the summary entries in the historical retailer activity file.

Definitions of the summary variables whose values are stored in the historical retailer activity file are summarized in Table 8.2. The first seventeen variables are identical to the ones used in Chapters 5 through 7. The "dummy variable" form of AD0–AD5 is used here, and the same is true for the display, sign, and special-offer variables. The UAP, CPE, and CPM variables are continuous. The "%" variables are summaries of the incidence of various combinations of the AD, UAP, and display conditions; these are required in order to cost out a given allowance package (see program segment 4). The variable OSOB (all sizes of other brands) has a slightly different definition than that used in the previous chapters: here it refers to the sum of the sales ratios for brands 5 through 8 (all container sizes), whereas previously this variable included sales for brands 3 through 8. The A SALE variable is the average of the actual sales ratios for the brand in question and T BASE is the average of the $\overline{Y}$ (average sales without promotion) variables for all the stores in the given stores group. More will be said about these variables later.

The entries in the historical retailer activity file are summarized to the level of push period (pertaining to a given brand for a certain period of weeks), container size, and store group. However, the original audit data contain records specific to brand, size, week, and individual store. This required that we develop a method for aggregation. The procedure will be presented here (its justification is given in Section 8.3.1):

Let

L be the week number (1–63)

B be the brand number (1–4)

S be the size number (1–3)

K be the store number (1–31),

PP be the push period number (1–45)

KG be the store group number (1–2),

X be one of the variables defined in Table 8.2 defined at the level of a single brand-size-store-week,

Z be the same variable as X, but now defined at the level of a push period–size–store group.

The rule used for aggregation from the level of a brand-size-store-week to that of a push period–size–store group, as required for input to the historical retailer activity file, can

Table 8.2 Definitions of Variables in the Historical Retailer Activity File*

Variable Number	Name	Description
1	AD0	Dummy ad variable, no price discount
2	AD1	Dummy ad variable, price level 1
3	AD2	Dummy ad variable, price level 2
4	AD3	Dummy ad variable, price level 3
5	AD4	Dummy ad variable, price level 4
6	AD5	Dummy ad variable, price level 5
7	UAPZFM	Unadvertised price discount with competitive activity
8	UAPNFM	Unadvertised price discount without competitive activity
9	UODD1	Dummy display variable, in product section
10	UODD2	Dummy display variable, outside product section
11	SIWD	Dummy sign in window variable
12	SISD	Dummy sign in store variable
13	SPOPD	Dummy special offer variable, premium
14	SPORD	Dummy special offer variable, reusable package
15	SPOCD	Dummy special offer variable, retailer coupon
16	CPEZFE	Maximum price discount for this brand-size offered by competing store when there is a promotion for the same brand and size in this store.
17	CPM	Maximum price discount for another brand offered by a competing store.
18	%UAP	Dummy variable for a store offering a UAP
19	%PIC	Dummy variable for a store offering an ad with picture
20	%PR&PC	Dummy variable for a store offering a reduced price ad with picture
21	%AD&DI	Dummy variable for a store offering an ad & a display
22	%UP&DI	Dummy variable for a store offering a UAP & a display
23	A SALE	Actual sales: the YR for this brand and size
24	T BASE	Base: The $\overline{Y}$ (average sales without promotion) for this brand and size
25	OSOB	Total sales of other brands: the average YR for all sizes of brands 5–8.

*All definitions are in terms of a single brand-size-store-week. For aggregation rule see text. Note that variables 18–24 were not included in the multiple equation model.

now be defined as follows:

$$Z(\mathrm{PP},S,\mathrm{KG}) = \frac{1}{\begin{bmatrix}\text{No. of weeks}\\ \text{in PP}\end{bmatrix}} \cdot \sum_{L \text{ in PP}} \left[\frac{\sum_{k \text{ in kg}} (\bar{Y}(B,X,K) \cdot X(B,S,L,K))}{\sum_{k \text{ in kg}} \bar{Y}(B,S,K)} \right] \quad (8.4)$$

That is, the retailer activity file entry is obtained by (1) taking the weighted average of the values of the given variables across all stores in the store group, using the average sales without promotion for each store as the weight; and (2) averaging the above over the set of weeks in the push period. (Recall that the value of B used in Equation 8.4 is determined by the value of the push period index, L.)

Application of this formula implies that the file entries for the dummy variables in Table 8.2 are weighted proportions of store weeks in which the indicated type of activity occurred during the period and for the brand associated with the given push period. Likewise, the entries for the continuous variables are also weighted averages. In each case the stores with large sales in the absence of promotion receive more weight in calculating the average than do the smaller stores.

Line 2A. Let us now turn back to the flow of program segment 2 (see Appendix 8A). The program begins with an option that allows the operator to bypass the execution of program segment 1 and access the historical retailer activity file directly. The program prints out TYPE 0 TO I/P ALLOWANCE FROM PROGRAM 1, OR 1 TO GIVE A PUSH PERIOD INDEX FOR EACH BRAND NOW. A 0 response causes the program to read the SEARCH RESULTS table, which contains the entries set up in the last run of program 1. Its contents are reported in a SEARCH RESULTS table, which summarizes the results obtained in program segment 1 (this is to insure that the operator has not used the wrong search results file). This table contains between one and four entries for each brand (depending on the value of NCT). Each entry gives the push period index and weight associated with a historical allowance period that is similar to the test allowance. The values of beginning week and ending week used to delimit the historical allowance file during the search procedure (which was performed in program segment 1) are also given for each brand. Brands for which average retailer activity is to be used contain zero entries for push period indices and weights, plus the values of beginning and ending weeks that will be used to compute the averages.

A 1 (no) response to the LOAD SEARCH RESULTS...

question causes the program to print AVERAGE RETAILER ACTIVITY WILL BE USED FOR ALL BRANDS, TYPE BEGWK AND ENDWK FOR EACH BRAND NOW. (This is not shown in the sample output.) This is followed by the line BRAND 1, after which the operator types in the values of BEGWK and ENDWK for that brand. The same process is repeated for brands 2 through 4.

Line 2B. After receiving its input instructions, the program proceeds to process the historical retailer activity file for store group 1 (the high-volume stores). The entry for each push period is read in turn and the SEARCH RESULTS and BEGWK and ENDWK tables are checked to see if this information has been assigned to any of the four brands. For instance, the first record in the file pertains to brand 1, weeks 1 through 4 (push period 1). If push period 1 has been found to match the test allowance package for any brand (in program segment 1), the values of all the retailer activity variables for that push period will be multiplied by the weight associated with that push period (also assigned in program segment 1) and added to the accumulated PREDICTED RETAILER ACTIVITY table for the brand in question. This will be done for each of the three sizes. Moreover, if brand 1 does not have an entry in the SEARCH RESULTS table (i.e., if average promotional activity is to be used for this brand), the program will check to see if weeks 1 through 4 (which delimit push period 1) fall inside the interval defined by BEGWK and ENDWK for brand 1. If they do, then the retailer activity variables from this file record are added to the corresponding entries in the brand 1 CURRENT RETAILER ACTIVITY table. Thus, the net results of the historical retailer activity file processing procedure is to build up a PREDICTED RETAILER ACTIVITY table for each of the four brands.

When this process has been completed (i.e., when all the push period entries in the historical retailer activity file have been read and examined) the program prints SEARCH DONE FOR STORE GROUP 1 and goes on to line 2C.

Line 2C. Here the operator has the option of displaying the predicted average retailer activity in store group 1 for brand 1. A 1 (yes) response causes the program to request instructions as to the list of variables to be output. The operator responds with the number of the first and the last variable to be displayed, after which the program prints out the values of the PREDICTED RETAILER ACTIVITY table for each of the three container sizes, for the variables in this list. (Recall that these entries are weighted averages of the store-week activity for stores in the store group, weeks in each push period, and push periods given by the SEARCH RESULTS table.)

Line 2D. Next the program asks whether the operator wishes to change any of the values in the PREDICTED RETAILER ACTIVITY table with the query MODIFY ACTIVITY? A 1 (yes) response prints TYPE VAR(iable), SIZE, VALUE OR 0, 0, 0 TO PROCEED. The response causes the program to substitute the value typed in (the third field of this input sequence) in place of the table entry defined by the variable number and container size. The program continues to ask for modifications until the termination signal (0, 0, 0) is provided.

The sequence of events defined by lines 2C and 2D is repeated for brands 2 through 4.

Line 2E. When the display and modify PREDICTED RETAILER ACTIVITY loop is completed for store group 1, the program prints RETAILER ACTIVITY LOOP FINISHED... TYPE 0 TO PROCEED OR 1 TO RECYCLE THESE STORES. A 1 response returns the program to line 2C for another round of display and/or modification. A 0 response causes the PREDICTED RETAILER ACTIVITY table to be written on the disc for transmission to program segment 3.

Line 2F. This is the same as line 2B, except that it refers to the historical retailer activity table for store group 2 (low-volume stores). The entire sequence of actions indicated by lines 2B through 2E is repeated for this store group, after which program segment 2 terminates.

8.2.3 Segment 3: Sales Estimates

The purpose of program segment 3 is to use the information in the PREDICTED RETAILER ACTIVITY table to forecast the sales volume for each container size of the four major brands in the market area under study. This is accomplished through the use of the multiple-equation model and cross-classification results for the retailer–consumer demand interface that were described in Chapters 6 and 7. Once again, we will discuss the general nature of the calculations performed by this program segment before turning to a line-by-line description of its operation. The justification for the model to be described here will be presented in Section 8.3.1.

Recall from Chapter 4 that, according to the multiple-equation model, the sales ratio for each brand and size can be predicted from the expression

$$\mathrm{YR}(B,S) = f_{BS}(\mathbf{X}_{B1S1}, \mathbf{X}_{B2S1}, \ldots, \mathbf{X}_{B8S3});\ B = 1,8\ \ S = 1,3. \quad (8.5)$$

That is, the predicted sales ratio for a given brand and size is a function of the promotional variables for all brands and sizes. This form of the model was called the "reduced form" system of equations. In our model, all the f-functions have been assumed to be linear. Their parameters can be calculated from the so-called structural equation system. Estimates of both the structural equation and reduced form system coefficients were obtained from the store audit data for high- and low-volume stores, and weeks 2 through 32 and 33 through 62. The empirical results were discussed extensively in Chapter 6 and extended through cross-classification in Chapter 7.

Program segment 3 makes use of a slightly modified form of Equation 8.5 to make predictions about YR. Since the simulation is concerned primarily with the sales of the three container sizes of brands 1 through 4, it was possible to shorten the predicting equation to include only the promotional variables for these brands. Sales of brands 5 through 8 are taken as given so far as the simulation is concerned; the total YR for all sizes of these brands was calculated from the audit data pertaining to each historical push period and included in the retailer activity file as the variable OSOB (see Table 8.2). In other words, the simulation uses the actual sales for brands 5 through 8 instead of trying to predict their sales from knowledge of their promotional activity. (Sales for all container sizes of brands 1 through 4 are predicted explicitly by the model, however.) This simplification means that we can rewrite Equation 8.5 as

$$\mathrm{YR}(B,S) = f_{\mathrm{BS}}(\mathbf{X}_{B1S1}, \mathbf{X}_{B2S1}, \ldots, \mathbf{X}_{B4S3}, \mathrm{OSOB});\ B = 1,4\ S = 1,3.$$

The advantage of this procedure is that it requires only half the file space for retailer activity variables and regression coefficients (brands 1 through 4 instead of brands 1 through 8) and reduces computation time substantially.

We now turn to the files of response coefficients that have been stored for use by program segment 3. Let the symbol

$$c(i,s,\mathrm{KG})$$

stand for the regression coefficient for the ith independent variable for the size s in store group KG, as estimated by the *structural equation* model.[4] The index i runs from 1 to 18 and includes (1) all the promotional variables (AD0 through

[4]Some of the coefficients were estimated by cross-classifying the residuals of the structural equation model against certain promotional variables, as reported in Chapter 7. These coefficients are treated as part of the structural equation model in this chapter.

SPOCD, variable numbers 1 to 15); (2) the competitive store activity variables (CPEZFE and CPM, variable numbers 16 and 17); and (3) the sales of all sizes for brands 5 through 8 (OSOB, variable number 25 in Table 8.2 and variable number 18 in the list of regression coefficients). Note that the list of regression coefficients is not brand-specific: the coefficients estimated for the four major brands have been averaged to produce a single summary coefficient for use by the economic analysis simulation model. This was done partly to stabilize the regression results before input to the model and partly to conserve file space.

The coefficients used in computing these averages were estimated without the use of the square root transformation for YR (discussed in an earlier chapter). This change was required in order to permit aggregation of retailer activity over weeks and stores, as described in Section 8.2.2. (The reasons behind this requirement will be discussed in Section 8.3.1.) Hence, these coefficients are not directly comparable to those discussed in Chapters 6 and 7, though, of course, they bear a strong relation to the demand response ratios reported there.

The structural equation model predicts the sales ratio YR for a given brand and size as a function of the retailer promotion variables for that brand and size, plus three variables summarizing the sales of other sizes and brands. Translation to the reduced form equations, which predict the sales for a given brand and size as a function of the promotional variables for all the brands and sizes, is accomplished by a mathematical manipulation described in Section 4.3.2.

The promotion simulation model uses these reduced form equations: the program calculates the reduced form coefficients from the structural coefficients before proceeding to estimate sales as a function of retailer activity. The reduced form transformation begins by expanding the coefficients of the sales variables in the structural equations to form a matrix covering all the brands and sizes included in the model. (See Section 4.3.3 for a description of the expansion process.) These will be called the *G*-matrices. They were denoted by Γ in Appendix 4A at the end of Chapter 4. The rows of each *G*-matrix represent the brands and sizes for the structural equations, and the columns represent the effect of sales for each brand and size on the sales of the brand and size for the equation given by the row.

The mathematical procedure for obtaining this solution involves finding the "inverse" of the *G*-matrix for each store group. (The inverse of a matrix is analogous to the reciprocal of a single number: that is, G-inverse $= 1/G$.) The main thing to remember about the G-inverse matrices is that they are calculated from the structural equation regression coefficients according to the well-defined mathematical procedures discussed in Chapter 4.

We are now in a position to present the predicting equation for sales. Using the symbols defined in connection with Equation 8.4, we have

$$\text{SALES}(\text{B,S,KG}) = \text{YR}(\text{B,S,KG}) * \text{TBASE}(\text{B,S,KG}); \qquad (8.6)$$

$$\text{YR}(\text{B,S,KG}) = \overset{\text{Ⓐ}}{\sum_b \sum_s G\text{-inverse}(\text{B,S},b,s,\text{KG})} * \qquad (8.7)$$

$$\left[\sum_{i=1}^{17} \overset{\text{Ⓑ}}{c(i,s,\text{KG}) * Z(b,s,i,\text{KG})} * \right.$$

$$\left. + \quad \overset{\text{Ⓒ}}{c(18,s,\text{KG}) * \text{ASOB}(b,s,\text{KG})} + \overset{\text{Ⓓ}}{\text{const}(b)} \right].$$

Equation 8.6 converts the estimated sales ratio (YR) to sales volume by multiplying through by the average base sales without promotion for the brand, container size and store group. (Recall that TBASE is contained in the historical retailer activity file for each store group.)

Equation 8.7 predicts YR as a function of the promotional activities for all sizes of brands 1 through 4, plus the total sales ratio for brands 5 through 8, as indicated in Equation 8.4. This expression is complicated enough to warrant some additional explanation. The four terms of the equation have been designated by **A**, **B**, **C**, and **D** to facilitate this task.

A. The summation symbols ahead of term **A** indicate that the whole expression is summed over brands (b) and container sizes (s). Each component in the sum is weighted by the appropriate element of G-inverse. (The rows of this matrix refer to the brand and size whose sales ratio is being estimated, i.e., B and S, while the columns designate the brand (b) and size (s) whose effects on B and S are currently being considered.) The largest G-inverse elements occur when $b = B$ and $s = S$—that is, with respect to the effects of the promotional activities for a given brand and size upon itself. The weights assigned to the effects of other brands and sizes are always much smaller than those assigned to the own-brand-size effects.

B. The first term inside the brackets accumulates the effects of the promotional and competitive store effects. This is done by multiplying the element in the PREDICTED RETAILER ACTIVITY for the current brand and size (that is, current with respect to the summation in term **A**) by the regression coefficient for that variable and size.

C. The next term adds the effects due to sales of brands 5 through 8 to the prediction. The rationale for this procedure was discussed earlier in this section.

D. The last term in Equation 8.7 is a constant, specific to each of the four major brands, that represents the expected sales ratio when that brand is not on promotion. For normal operation of the simulation this constant is set to 1.0, as required by our original specification of the multiple-equation model (see Section 4.3.4). However, provision has been made for the operator to adjust its value if special circumstances make this desirable.

Let us summarize the operation of the sales prediction procedure briefly. Equation 8.7 takes the information contained in the PREDICTED RETAILER ACTIVITY table for each brand, as supplied by program segment 2, applies the coefficients obtained by estimating the multiple-equation model for consumer demand from the audit data, and solves the equations for predicting simultaneously the effects of all the brands and sizes on one another to produce an estimate of YR for each container size of the four major brands. Equation 8.6 transforms the estimates of YR to estimates of sales in units. The model predicts sales for brands 1 through 4 from the predicted retail activity for each of these brands, taking the sales obtained by brands 5 through 8 during the push periods used to define predicted retailer activity as given.

Having discussed the procedure used to calculate sales estimates, we may now turn to a line-by-line description of program segment 3. The reader should refer to Appendix 8A for a sample of the output of this program.

Line 3A. The first item of output from program segment 3 is a report of the weights used to project sales from the high- and low-volume stores included in the audit to the total market area. The values used in the example are both 0.431. Their equality indicates that, according to the best estimates of the company, about half the stores in the total market area are like those in the high-volume segment of the audit and half are like those in the low-volume segment. The value 0.431 indicates that each unit of product sold in the average store in either segment represents 431 units sold in the market as a whole. That is, if the average sales per store in the high-volume segment of the audit were 7,000 units per four-week period and the average sales in the low-volume segment were 3,000 units per week, the total market would be estimated at $431 \times 7{,}000 + 431 \times 3{,}000 = 4{,}310{,}000$ units. (Note that while the equality of projection factors indicates that the number of stores of the high- and low-volume type in the market as a whole are judged to be equal, this does not imply that the volume generated by the two types will be the same.)

Line 3B. After printing out the values of the projection factors the program requests that the operator INPUT KEY BRAND AND LENGTH OF PUSH PERIOD IN WEEKS. The key brand is the number of the brand for which cost and profit calculations will be made in program segments 4 and 5. (It must be specified here because program segment 3 makes some preliminary calculations required in the costing process.) The second response to this question determines the length of time for which sales, market share, costs, and profits are to be reported. The program makes all its volume calculations on a "sales per store per week" basis and then multiplies its results by the length of the test push period. In the sample run, the length of the push period was set at six weeks.

Line 3C. The simulation is programmed to adjust the predicted sales figures for each brand and size to come closer to the actual sales recorded in the PREDICTED RETAILER ACTIVITY table. (A SALE, which is variable 23 in the retailer activity tables, is used for this purpose.) The ACT(ual) PROJ(ected) ADJUSTMENT CONSTANT controls this option. The equation used to make the adjustment is as follows:

$$\text{ADJ} \cdot \text{SALES} = (1-K) * (\text{Pred. Sales}) + K * (\text{Actual Sales}),$$

where K is the controlling constant input by the operator. As can be seen, $K=0$ produces no adjustment, whereas $K=1$ substitutes the actual level of sales for the value predicted by the program. A value of K between 0 and 1 produces a weighted average of actual and predicted sales. The value of K is usually set to 0.

Line 3D. The command INPUT NON-PROMO SALES RATIO FOR BRANDS 1–4 provides for entry of the values of "const (b)" for each of the four major brands. This constant, which will usually have a value of 1.0, is used in the last term of Equation 8.7. This option allows the operator to adjust the expected level of YR during weeks when a given brand is not on promotion to take account of special circumstances. The value of this constant applies to all sizes of the indicated brand. Note that "const (b)" is used in the equation that predicts sales levels; it has nothing to do with the adjustment constant input at line 3C.

Line 3E. After receiving the input in lines 3B through 3D, the program passes on to the sales estimation procedure for high-volume stores. Its progress is logged after the data for all the brands of each container size have been processed, and again after the sales information has been written on the disc for use by program segments 4 and 5. (The sales values so written include the adjustment for actual sales, if any.)

Line 3F. The sales estimates (after adjustment, if any) are reported by the program in the ESTIMATED SALES BY BRAND AND SIZE table. This table presents sales figures in units per store for whatever period has been specified as the length of the test push period (entered at line 3B). The results in this and all subsequent tables for high- and low-volume stores are averaged over all the stores in a given group. Hence, the estimated sales for brand 2, medium-sized containers, is read as "795 units per high-volume type store during a six-week period." Average weekly sales per store would be 133 units (795/6).

Row and column totals for brands and sizes are provided in the table of estimated sales. The grand total sales figure (the southeast corner entry in the table) is more than the sum of the row and column total sales figures because it includes the sales of brands 5 through 8 (all sizes). The value of these OSOB sales is given in the line of output following the table.

Line 3G. The next output of the program is the ESTIMATED MARKET SHARE BY BRAND table. These figures are obtained by dividing the total sales for each brand by the grand total sales estimated for all brands and sizes. (They do not sum to one because of the existence of sales for brands 5 through 8.)

Line 3H. After reporting sales and market shares for the high-volume stores, the program goes on to perform the same task for the low-volume segment of the market. Line 3H is identical to line 3E for this group.

Line 3I. When processing of the low-volume segment has been completed, the sales results are projected to the market area as a whole using the procedures described earlier. The output tables are the same as those for the individual store groups except that sales are reported in thousands of units for the total market rather than on a per-store basis, and the market share figures are calculated from the projected sales figures instead of by projection from the individual segment shares.

When all the sales and market share reports are completed the program asks the operator to load program segment 4 and terminates.

8.2.4
Segment 4:
Intermediate
Calculations

Program segment 4 is a transition step between segment 3, which calculates and reports estimates of sales, and program segment 5, which reports cost and contribution to profit for the key brand. Many of the calculations needed for the tables printed in program segment 5 are actually performed in program segment 4, but we will not discuss them here.

Line 4A. The first step in program segment 4 is to print out the values of the key brand, the length of the test push period, and the actual-predicted sales adjustment constant. All three of these parameters were input to program segment 3 and are printed out here for the operator's information only.

Line 4B. Next the program prints out the contents of the TEST ALLOWANCE table for the key brand. These allowance values were input in program segment 1. (If average retailer activity is being used for the key brand, this file will contain all zeros.) Note that the TOTAL column includes the maximum of the ADV and DIS allowances rather than counting both of them. This is in accordance with the standard operating procedures of the company.

Line 4C. The operator is given the option of changing any of the values in the key brand allowance table. A 1 (yes) response to this query causes the program to print GIVE SIZE, ALLOW(ance)TYPE, NEW VALUE, OR 0,0,0 TO CONTINUE. The program substitutes the new value (third field of the response) for the original contents of the indicated cell in the key brand allowance table. This process is repeated until the operator types three fields of zeros, after which the TEST ALLOWANCE table is again printed out (this time without the TOTAL column). It should be noted that changes in the allowance for the key brand at this point in the simulation program flow do not change the predicted retailer activity (this can only be done by rerunning program segment 1). Hence, the predicted level of sales is independent of changes in the allowance values. The purpose of this option is to allow the operator to perform sensitivity analyses on the costs of different allowance packages, holding sales constant.

Line 4D. A 0 response at line 4C or completion of the allowance change process sends the program into the calculation of allowance costs. Its progress is logged at various stages of the processing. The program writes a REPORT file for each store group; this file provides the information necessary for the operation of program segment 5.

8.2.5
Segment 5:
Cost and Profit
Estimates

Program segment 5 is the reporting segment of the simulation program. Its function is to print out tables showing the sales breakdown for the key brand, the gross profit generated by these sales, the estimated sales due to retailer promotions, the demand response ratio for these promotions, the estimated allowance costs, and the contribution to profit generated during the test push period.

Each of these tables refers to the test push period taken as a whole. (In the sample output this has been set at six weeks.) The tables for each of the two store groups are on a per-store basis, just as was the case for the sales and market share reports for the high- and low-volume store segments that were provided in program segment 3. The dimensions of these figures are "units per store" for sales volumes and "dollars per store" for cost and profit tables. The REPORTS FOR ALL STORES AGGREGATED project the sales, cost, and profit estimates to the market area as a whole, using the procedures discussed in Section 8.2.3. Here the tables are dimensioned in "thousands of units" and "thousands of dollars."

The meaning of each of the report tables in program segment 5 was discussed in Section 8.1.5 as part of our overview of the simulation. As most of the labels in the tables are self-explanatory, there is no need to provide a more detailed explanation here. The following comments are all that is necessary to understand the reports.

The sales estimate for each size of the key brand (input in program segment 3) is broken down into COMPONENTS OF SALES to facilitate the process of costing the test allowance package. The nature of these components can be understood by referring back to Equation 8.7, which predicts the value of YR. This equation is broken down as shown in Table 8.3. The ADS component estimates the sales that are due to retailer advertising (whether or not the ad includes a price reduction); PRICE does the same thing, but limits consideration to ads in which a reduced price is offered. Sales due to unadvertised price discounts (UAP), displays (DISPLY), and signs in the store and the window (SIGN) are estimated in a similar fashion. The background (BKGND) sales component consists of sales due to all causes not previously specified, including special offers, competitive store effects, and the effects due to sales of other sizes and brands. With the exception of the overlap between ADS and PRICE, the components of sales are mutually exclusive and exhaustive. The fact that the multiple-equation model can be used to estimate the sales due to each of the number of factors in the retail shopping environment (e.g., ADS and UAP's) means that it is possible to determine what portions of the total sales generated during a test push period will qualify

Table 8.3 Definitions of Components of Sales

Component	Portion of Equation 8.6: Values of b and s in Term **A**	Values of i in Term **B**	Names of Variables in Term **B**
ADS	$b = B, s = S$	$i = 1$–6	AD0–AD5
PRICE	$b = B, s = S$	$i = 2$–6	AD1–AD5
UAP	$b = B, s = S$	$i = 7, 8$	UAPZFM
			UAPNFM
DISPLY	$b = B, s = S$	$i = 9, 10$	UODD1
			UODD2
SIGN	$b = B, s = S$	$i = 11, 12$	SIWD
			SISD
BKGND	$b = B, s = S$	$i = 13$–17	SPORD–CPM
	$b = B, s = S$	Terms C and D	
	$b \neq B, s \neq S$	Terms B, C, and D	
TOTAL	Sum of ADS, UAP, DISPLY, SIGN, & BKGND.		

for each type of performance allowance. This is the reason for breaking retail sales for the key brand down into components.

Let us illustrate how the process of costing a given type of allowance works. (The complete set of equations defining the allowance costing process can be found in Section 8.3.2.) Suppose that the test allowance package consists only of an ADV for medium-sized containers. (This is unrealistic, but it provides a simple example with which to work.) According to the rules used in the program, the following portions of the total medium-sized container volume would qualify for the ADV:

(1) All sales generated by ads; (2) Sales generated by displays in stores running both a display and an ad; (3) Sales generated by signs in store having a sign and running an ad; (4) Background sales in all stores running ads.

The data in the PREDICTED RETAILER ACTIVITY table (e.g., the number of stores that both run an ad and offer a display), plus the estimated levels of the COMPONENTS OF SALES, provide all the information needed to evaluate the allowance package.

A word of explanation is required with respect to the table ESTIMATED COST PER UNIT SOLD ON PROMOTION AND PER TOTAL UNITS SOLD. There will be some cases in which an allowance will be offered but no units will be sold on promotion (e.g., when a small NOP is offered for small containers). Application of the allowance rate to the background sales component will produce an estimated allowance cost, but the denominator of the fraction "cost per unit sold on promotion" will be zero. When this happens, the program arbitrarily assigns the very large number 99999.000 to this ratio.

We will now describe the initialization procedures required for program segment 5. As noted earlier, the tables output by this program were described in Section 8.1.5, so a line-by-line description of them is not needed.

Line 5A. After being loaded the program prints out the values of the weights to be used in projecting per-store sales, costs, and profits for the high- and low-volume store segments to the total market area. The nature and purpose of these weights were described in connection with line 3A of program segment 3.

Line 5B. Then the program requests the operator to input the gross margin to be used in calculating contribution to profit. The gross margin figure is the difference between the wholesale price of the product and the total variable production and distribution costs, all on a per-unit basis. It does not include allocation of any overhead costs, advertising, sales force, or the allowance package. (The gross margin figure used in the sample output is disguised for obvious reasons.)

Line 5C. Next the program prints out the name of the key brand (in this case brand 2), the length of the test push period, and the value of the actual-predicted sales adjustment constant. These variables were input back in program segment 3. The program then proceeds to output the report tables described earlier, first for high- and low-volume stores and then for the total market area. At the conclusion of this output program, segment 5, and the simulation as a whole, comes to a halt.

8.3 Technical Considerations

We will now turn our attention to some of the technical details of the simulation model. First, the procedure used to manipulate the estimated retailer activity figures to obtain forecasts of sales will be considered. This will be followed by a discussion of the problem of assigning costs to the different types of promotional allowances.

8.3.1 Retailer Activity and Sales Forecasts

The procedures used to develop inputs to the PREDICTED RETAILER ACTIVITY table and to forecast sales volume were described in Sections 8.2.2 and 8.2.3. The purpose of this section is to prove that these procedures are consistent with the assumptions of our multiple-equation model, and that the forecasts made by their use have desirable properties.

8.3.1.1 The Restriction to Four Major Brands

The original multiple-equation model consisted of twenty-four simultaneous equations; one for each size of the eight major brands. The version used in the promotional effects simulation considers the four major brands (brands 1 through 4) as endogenous, and the other four brands as exogenous. The original structural equation system of the multiple-equation model was written in matrix terms in Equation 4A.1 of Appendix 4A:

$$\mathbf{\Gamma Y}_t + \boldsymbol{\beta}\mathbf{X}_t + \mathbf{u}_t = \mathbf{0} \quad \text{(24 equations).} \tag{8.8}$$

Let us partition $\mathbf{\Gamma}$ and $\mathbf{Y}_t$ as follows:

$$\mathbf{\Gamma} = \begin{bmatrix} \Gamma_{11} & \Gamma_{12} \\ \Gamma_{21} & \Gamma_{22} \end{bmatrix}; \qquad \mathbf{Y}_t = \begin{bmatrix} Y_{1t} \\ Y_{2t} \end{bmatrix},$$

where the subscript "1" stands for a major brand and "2" stands for a minor brand.

We are taking the historical values of minor brand sales as "given," just like retailer activity (we write the vector of minor brand sales as $\overline{Y}_{2t}$ to emphasize this fact). Hence, we are only interested in the first twelve equations of the system in Equation 8.8:

$$\mathbf{\Gamma}_{11}\mathbf{Y}_{1t} + \mathbf{\Gamma}_{12}\overline{\mathbf{Y}}_{2t} + \boldsymbol{\beta}\mathbf{X}_t + \mathbf{u}_t = \mathbf{0}. \tag{8.9}$$

Now it is clear that all the sales variables in $\overline{\mathbf{Y}}_{2t}$ belong in the OSOB summary variable, so far as all the sizes of brands 1 to 4 are concerned. Hence the coefficients of all the elements of $\overline{\mathbf{Y}}_{2t}$ are the same within a given structural equation. That is, Γ_{12} can be rewritten as follows:

$$\Gamma_{12} = \begin{bmatrix} \gamma_{1.\,\mathrm{ASOB}} & \gamma_{1.\,\mathrm{ASOB}}\ldots \\ \gamma_{2.\,\mathrm{ASOB}} & \gamma_{2.\,\mathrm{ASOB}}\ldots \\ \cdots\cdots & \cdots\cdots\cdots \\ \gamma_{12.\mathrm{ASOB}} & \gamma_{12.\mathrm{ASOB}}\ldots \end{bmatrix},$$

where $\gamma_{i.\mathrm{ASOB}}$ is the estimate of the coefficient of ASOB in the ith structural equation (where $i = 1, 12$ covering the three sizes of the four major brands). Hence, the second term of the ith equation of Equation 4B.2 can be rewritten as follows:

$$[\gamma_{i.\mathrm{ASOB}}, \gamma_{i.\mathrm{ASOB}}, \ldots] \cdot \overline{\mathbf{Y}}_{2t} = \gamma_{i.\mathrm{ASOB}} \sum_{i=13}^{24} \overline{Y}_{i.t} = \gamma_{i.\mathrm{ASOB}}\overline{Y}_T;$$

that is, the "other brand" term in the revised multiple-equation model is equal to the OSOB coefficient for the given (major) brand and size times the sum of the sales for minor brands and sizes.

Thus, the revised multiple-equation model is:

$$\mathbf{\Gamma}_{11}\mathbf{Y}_{1t} + \overline{Y}_T\gamma_{i.\mathrm{ASOB}} + \boldsymbol{\beta}\mathbf{X}_t + u_t = \mathbf{0}, \tag{8.10}$$

where $\overline{Y}_T$ is scalar and $\gamma_{i.ASOB}$ is a twelve-element column vector giving the OSOB coefficients for the twelve major brand equations.

Transformation to the reduced form requires that Equation 8.10 be solved for the endogenous variables, now limited to the elements of $\mathbf{Y}_{1t}$. It is

$$Y_{1t} = -\mathbf{\Gamma}_{11}^{-1}(\overline{Y}_T \gamma_{i.ASOB} + \boldsymbol{\beta}\mathbf{X}_t + \mathbf{u}_t), \tag{8.11}$$

where $\mathbf{\Gamma}_{11}^{-1}$ is the G-inverse matrix discussed in the text. We find that expansion of Equation 8.11, taking note of the fact that β is block-diagonal as shown in Appendix 4A, yields Equation 8.6 in Section 8.2.3.

8.3.1.2 Aggregations over Stores and Weeks

The procedures used in the promotional effects simulation require that retailer activity data be aggregated to the level of store groups and push periods for each brand and size. Yet the estimates of coefficients for the multiple-equation model, which are used as parameters in the simulation, were based on data for individual store-weeks. We wish to show that aggregation does not affect the validity of these coefficients.

We can prove this point by considering a very simple model representing the demand for one brand and size, and only one retailer promotion variable. Let us define the following variables:

- Y_{sl} — The sales volume for the brand and size in question for store S and week L
- $\overline{Y}_s$ — The average sales without promotion variable in store S
- YR_{SL} — The YR value for store S and week L: it is equal to $Y_{SL}/\overline{Y}_S$
- X_{SL} — The value of a retailer activity variable in store S and week L.

Then we may write the following predicting equation for YR in a given store and week:

$$\mathrm{YR}_{SL} = \frac{Y_{SL}}{\overline{Y}_S} = a + bX_{SL}. \tag{8.12}$$

Note that there is no square root transformation on YR in this model; although the results in Chapters 4 through 7 are based on $\sqrt{\mathrm{YR}}$, this transformation was *not* used in the estimation runs that generated the coefficients for the promotional effects simulation.

The objective of the simulation model is to predict sales in units, not the sales ratio. Although Equation 8.12 must be used to estimate a and b, the simulation output is based on the following equation:

$$Y_{SL} = (a + bX_{SL})\bar{Y}_S = a\bar{Y}_S + bX_{SL}\bar{Y}_S. \tag{8.13}$$

Let us now aggregate over S and L to obtain the total sales for the store groups and set of weeks in question.

$$Y_{nL} = \sum_L \sum_S (a\bar{Y}_S + bX_{SL}\bar{Y}_S) = n_L a \sum_S \bar{Y}_S + b \sum_L \sum_S X_{SL}\bar{Y}_S, \tag{8.14}$$

where n_L is the number of weeks in the sum over L, and Y_{nL} is the total sales for the period of n_L weeks.

The simulation provides the option of letting the number of weeks in the test push period differ from the number in the historical push period used as a match to the test allowance package. Hence it is convenient to store all the information in the historical retailer activity file on a per-week basis. This requires that both sides of Equation 8.14 be divided by n_L.

$$Y = \frac{Y_{nL}}{n_L} = a \sum_S \bar{Y}_S + b\left\{\frac{1}{n} \sum_L \sum_S X_{SL}\bar{Y}_S\right\}. \tag{8.15}$$

Format considerations suggested that Equation 8.15 be divided through by the sum of the base sales figures for all the stores in the group

$$\bar{Y} = \sum_S \bar{Y}_S.$$

Hence, our predictions of sales are obtained from

$$Y = \text{YR} * \bar{Y};$$

$$YR = \frac{Y}{\bar{Y}} = a + bZ,$$

where (8.16)

$$Z = \frac{1}{n_L} \frac{X_{SL}\bar{Y}_S}{\bar{Y}_S}. \tag{8.17}$$

The new variable YR is the ratio of aggregate actual sales to average sales without promotions for the store group as a whole; note that YR does *not* equal the average of the YR's for the individual store-weeks. The variable Z is the "average retailer activity" for the store group and set of weeks in question.

We have seen the expressions for "average retailer activity" before, in Equation 8.4 of Section 8.2.2. Examination of Equation 8.17 shows that the retailer activity for a given week is averaged over stores, with the stores' values of $\bar{Y}_S$ (average sales without promotion) used as weights. Then these over-store averages are averaged over weeks. This is exactly the procedure described in connection with Equation 8.4. The development of the last few paragraphs shows that weighted average retailer activity can be used with coefficients obtained from regressions on data for individual store-weeks.

It is easy to generalize Equation 8.16 to include additional promotional variables, both for the brand and size being predicted by the equation and for other brands and sizes. This makes it equivalent to Equations 8.6 and 8.7 in the text. The constant *a* in Equation 8.16 is the same as the variable "const (*b*)" in Equation 8.7; this constant is normally equal to one as required by the multiple-equation model (see Section 4.3.4). The variable ASOB (sales of all sizes of brands 5 through 8) in Equation 8.7 is treated just like any of the retailer promotion variables; that is,

$$\text{Aggregate ASOB} = \frac{1}{n_L} \sum_L \frac{\text{ASOB}_{SL} * \bar{Y}_S}{\bar{Y}_S}$$

where

$$\text{ASOB}_L = \sum_{\text{size}=1}^{3} \sum_{\text{brand}=5}^{8} (\text{YR}_{\text{size, brand}} - 1).$$

Thus, ASOB is the weighted average (over weeks and stores) of the sum of the sales ratios less one for all sizes of the minor brands. (The use of YR − 1 is dictated by the way in which the YR variables enter the structural equations used to estimate the multiple equation model.)[5]

Finally, we should note that use of a square root transformation for YR in estimating the coefficients of the multiple-equation model would cause the linear aggregation performed in Equation 8.14 to fail, thus destroying the entire structure of the simulation system. Hence, the parameter estimates in the simulation must be somewhat less efficient than those used as the basis for the detailed interpretations provided in earlier chapters.

8.3.2 Allowance Cost Calculations

In this section we present a technical description of the procedures used to assign costs to the test allowance package for the key brand. A brief description and an example of the method was presented in Section 8.2.5.

8.3.2.1 Variable Definitions

Let us define the following variables that are available as input to the allowance costing routine. Each refers to a specific size of the key brand for a specific store group.

[5]ASOB is not handled in quite the manner indicated here in the present version of the economic analysis simulation model. The small size of the coefficient of this variable probably makes this error negligible, but it will be changed in a subsequent revision of the model.

Components of Sales (refer to Section 8.2.5 for definitions)

S_1	BKGND	(sales due to background effects)
S_2	ADS	(sales due to any ads)
S_3	PRICE	(sales due to ads at less than shelf price)
S_4	UAP	(sales due to unadvertised price discounts)
S_5	DISPLY	(sales due to displays)
S_6	SIGNS	(sales due to signs)
S_t	TOTAL	(total sales)

Predicted Retailer Activity (refer to Section 8.2.2 and Table 8.2 for definitions)

X_1	AD0	X_7	UAPZFM
X_2	AD1	X_8	UAPNFM
X_3	AD2	X_9	UODD1
X_4	AD3	X_{10}	UODD2
X_5	AD4	X_{11}	SIWD
X_6	AD5	X_{12}	SISD

Q_1 Proportion of stores offering a UAP

Q_2 Proportion of stores offering an ad with a picture of the package

Q_3 Proportion of stores offering an ad with a picture and a reduced price

Q_4 Proportion of stores offering an ad and a display

Q_5 Proportion of stores offering a UAP and a display[6]

Test Allowance Package (see Section 8.1.1 for definitions)

Rates		Total Cost	
A_1	ADV	C_1	ADV
A_2	DIS	C_2	DIS
A_3	EXT	C_3	EXT
A_4	PIC	C_4	PIC
A_5	MER	C_5	MER
A_6	PRI	C_6	PRI
A_7	NOP	C_7	NOP

The X and Q inputs permit the calculation of several additional variables describing the incidence of promotional activities in the retail store group.

Incidence of Retailer Activity

$P_1 = \sum_{i=1}^{6} X_i$; gross proportion of stores with ads.

$P_2 = P_1 - X_1$; gross proportion of stores with reduced price ads.

$P_3 = X_9 + X_{10}$; gross proportion of stores with displays

$P_4 = X_{11} + X_{12}$; gross proportion of stores with signs

[6]Variables Q_1 through Q_5 are recorded as variables 18 through 22 in Table 8.2.

$P_5 = P_1 + P_3 + Q_1 - Q_4 - Q_5$; net proportion of stores offering ads, UAPs, and/or displays.

The first step in the allowance costing procedure is to determine the sales volumes that occur as a result of ads (at shelf price and less than shelf price) in conjunction with displays.

Sales due to ads and displays are determined as follows:

$$T_1 = S_2 + S_5 \frac{Q_4}{P_3}. \tag{8.18}$$

Sales due to price and displays are determined as follows:

$$T_2 = S_3 + S_5 \frac{Q_4}{P_3}. \tag{8.19}$$

In each of these two equations we add the appropriate advertising sales component (ADS or PRICE) to a fraction of the display sales component. In both cases the fraction is Q_4/P_3, the proportion of displays that occur with ads. (This procedure implicitly assumes that to a first approximation all displays offered with ads occur with reduced price ads.)

We also calculate what is called the "background multiplier" as a preliminary step to costing particular allowances:

$$T_3 = S_1 + S_6/P_5. \tag{8.20}$$

This equation will be explained later.

8.3.2.2 Determination of ADV and DIS Costs

Retailers offering both an ad and a display have the option of taking the larger of the ADV and DIS allowances. Hence, the method for determining the cost of these allowances must depend on the relative magnitude of the two. We will take up the two possibilities in turn.

Case 1: ADV ⩾ DIS. The general procedure in this case is to find the sales that qualify for ADV regardless of their qualification for DIS. The remaining DIS sales, if any, are assigned to the display allowance. The equations are

$$\text{ADV:}\quad C_1 = A_1 * (T_1 + P_1 * T_3), \tag{8.21}$$

$$\text{DIS:}\quad C_2 = A_2 * \left[\left(1 - \frac{Q_4}{P_3}\right) * \left(S_5 + S_4 \frac{Q_5}{Q_1}\right) + (P_3 - Q_4) * T_3\right]. \tag{8.22}$$

The first equation calculates the sales due to ads (inside the brackets) and multiples it by the ADV rate to get total ADV cost. Sales due to ads are the sum of the intermediate variable for sales due to ads and displays (T_1) and the product of proportion of stores with ads (P_1) times the background multiplier (T_3). The logic of the background multiplier can now be described: when multiplied by P_1 it estimates the proportion of background sales plus the proportion of sales due to signs that occurred in stores with ads. (Actually, the ratio P_1/P_5 that multiples the SIGN sales component S_6 is the "proportion of stores that have ads, UAPs and/or displays that have ads.")

The logic of Equation 8.22 is much the same as that of Equation 8.21. The first term in the brackets is the proportion of stores with displays that do not have ads (these are the stores that qualify for DIS only). It is multiplied by the DISPLY sales component plus the proportion of the UAP sales component that is associated with stores having displays (the second term in the brackets). The third term is the proportion of stores that have displays but no ads; it is used to scale the fourth term, the background multiplier.

Case 2: ADV < DIS. The logic here is just the opposite of that for Case 1. First, DIS sales are identified without regard to their qualifications for ADV. Any remaining ad sales are assigned to ADV. The equations are

$$\text{ADV:}\quad C_1 = A_1 * \left\{\left(1-\frac{Q_4}{P_1}\right) * (P_1 - Q_4) * T_3\right\}; \tag{8.23}$$

$$\text{DIS:}\quad C_2 = A_2 * \left\{S_5 + S_2\frac{Q_4}{P_1} + S_4\frac{Q_5}{Q_1} + P_3 * T_3\right\}. \tag{8.24}$$

These equations look somewhat different from their counterparts in Case 1 because we have not bothered to define an intermediate variable analogous to T_1 as used in Equation 8.21. However, tracing through their logic in a manner like that discussed for case 1 will show that the two cases are exact opposites.

8.3.2.3 Determination of Other Allowance Costs

Extra allowances (EXT) are given under certain circumstances to retailers who offer ads at less than shelf price.[7] They are offered as an addition to whatever other allowances the retailer may receive. The equation for EXT costs is

$$\text{EXT:}\quad C_3 = A_3 * \{T_2 + P_2 * T_3\} \tag{8.25}$$

The sales qualifying for the EXT allowance are equal to the sales generated by reduced price ads (intermediate variable T_2) plus the proportion of stores running reduced price ads times the background multiplier (T_3).

[7]Other methods of qualification are possible, but this one is by far the most common.

The "picture of package" (PIC) allowance is offered to retailers who run a cut of the package in their ad. While most of these ads also offer a price reduction, this is not a necessary condition for qualification. As was the case with EXT, the PIC allowance is a net addition to any other allowance offerings. The cost equation for PIC is

$$\text{PIC:}\quad C_4 = A_4 * \left\{T_1\frac{Q_2}{P_1} + Q_2T_3\right\} \tag{8.26}$$

The sales volume applied to the allowance rate is equal to the ratio of stores running ads with pictures to all stores with ads (Q_2/P_1) times the estimated ad sales volume (T_1) plus the proportion of stores having PIC's (Q_2) times the background sales multiplier (T_3).

As programmed in the model, merchandising allowances (MER) are given to stores that offer any kind of merchandising activity for the brand. Merchandising activity is defined as ads, displays, or signs. This allowance is also an addition to the ADV or DIS amounts earned by the store. The equation for the cost of this allowance is

$$\begin{aligned}\text{MER:}\quad C_5 = A_5 * \Big\{S_2 + S_5 + S_6 + \left[\frac{Q_5}{Q_1} + (Q_1 - Q_5)\frac{P_4}{P_5}\right] * S_4 \\ + [(P_1 + P_3 - Q_4) + (Q_1 - Q_5)] * S_1\Big\}\end{aligned} \tag{8.27}$$

The three terms inside the braces on the first line of the equation are the sales components for ads, displays, and signs, all of which qualify for MER. The second line takes the ratio of stores with display and UAP to those with UAP (Q_5/Q_1) plus the product of the net proportion of stores with UAP but no display ($Q_1 - Q_5$) and the ratio of stores with signs to stores with signs, ads, UAP's, and/or displays (P_4/P_5), and multiplies this quantity by the UAP sales component. The purpose of this term is to isolate the UAP sales that occur with displays or signs (by definition there are no stores with ads and UAP's), and hence qualify for MER. The last term aggregates the proportion of stores with ads (P_1) and displays (P_3), eliminating the double counting ($P_1 + P_3 - Q_4$), plus the proportions of stores with UAP's but no displays ($Q_1 - Q_5$); this is assumed to be a reasonable approximation of the proportion of stores with signs but no ads or displays, and multiplies this by the background sales component (S_1).

The reduced price ad allowance (PRI) is analogous to PIC. Its equation is

$$\text{PRI:}\quad C_6 = A_6 * (T_2 + P_2 * T_3). \tag{8.28}$$

The PRI intermediate sales variable (T_2) is added to the product of the proportion of stores with ads at less than shelf price and the background sales ratio ($P_2 * T_3$). (Recall that T_2 includes sales due to reduced price ads and displays with reduced price ads.)

The no-performance allowance (NOP) is easy to cost, as it applies to all sales without regard to promotional performance:

$$\text{NOP:} \quad C_7 = A_7 * S_T, \tag{8.29}$$

which is simply the product of the NOP and total sales.

8.3.2.4 Inventory Effects

No attempt has been made to include retailer inventory fluctuations in the promotional effects simulation. The model predicts sales at retail and applies the allowance rates to these figures, not to purchases from the manufacturers. If retailers take advantage of allowances to stock up, and if this stocking-up is not reflected in promotions and retail sales during the performance period of the allowance, the simulation will tend to underpredict allowance costs.

8.4 Conclusions

The promotional effects simulation reported here represents a first step in what we hope will be an ongoing effort to simulate the marketing environment for the product under study.

The advantages of such a simulation are many. The process of constructing the simulation model has led to insights about the structure of the market and the implications of the econometric model used in our empirical work. By running the model we can uncover information about the magnitudes of certain key relationships that are implied by our data. Some of these insights could not have been obtained directly from the empirical results reported in earlier chapters.

The simulation described here is "data-rich." That is, it is closely tied to an extensive empirical data base. The portions of the model that predict retail sales as a function of retail activity (program segment 3) have been subjected to extensive tests and structural interpretation, as reported earlier. The "economic" portions of the simulation (program segments 4 and 5) are made up largely of accounting relationships and identities. Program segment 2 is largely an information retrieval program; it reads historical retailer activity rates from a data bank, processes them according to simple rules, and allows on-line interaction by the analyst with respect to changes in the described inputs. Taken together, these segments provide an easy way to explore the implications of the empirical retailer promotion–consumer demand model that is the major subject of this monograph.

The "model" that makes up program segment 1 is entirely different. Its function is to predict retailer activity as a function of manufacturers' allowance inputs. As the reader will have noticed, the approach is simple and mechanistic. This model has no behavioral underpinnings, and we have no illusions about its predictive efficacy.[8] It was constructed rapidly for the express purpose of providing initial rough estimates of retail promotional activity, based on historical data, to the operator of the information retrieval program (segment 2).

The results of segment 1 invariably are modified by the analyst before the rest of the simulation is run. Hence there is no question of presenting an empirical validation of this part of the model. (In contrast, validation of the retailer-consumer interface model was a major topic of our earlier chapters.) The program and its description are presented with this caveat; it is included in order to make our presentation of the simulation program complete.

We offer the research presented in this monograph in hopes that it may stimulate others to undertake similar efforts. Much of the methodology is new or at least not well known in marketing circles, and hence worth reporting. The specific empirical findings of the study, and the simulation model based upon them, have already been put to good use by the sponsoring company. The same thing can be accomplished by other companies in other markets, as well as by academic researchers.

[8]For a more careful but very incomplete approach to modeling the retailer's advertising behavior decision process, see Massy and Frank (1966).

Appendix 8A
Sample Output from the Simulation

```
-FCRT

FCRTRAN IV A14.03

>LCAD /MPGM1/
SYMBOLIC FILE

>EXEC
(1A) MARKET SIMULATION
     LAST NCT=    4
(1B) CANCEL LAST RESULTS? IF SC TYPE NEW  NCT, ELSE TYPE  0.
     0
(1C) TYPE BRAND TO BE PROCESSED NEXT OR  0  TO STOP
     2
(1D) PROCESS?
     1
(1E) TYPE BEG AND END WEEKS AND LIST OF BRANDS FOR SEARCH
     1 63 1 2 3 4
(1F) TYPE ALLOWANCE IN DOLLARS/UNIT FOR S,M,L
     ADV
     1.00 1.25  1.00
     DIS
     .50 .50 .50
     EXT
     0 C C
     PEC
     0 C C
     MER
     0 0 0
     PRI
     .25 .45 .35
     NCP
     .1C .15 .10

(1G) SEARCH RESULTS
      BEGWK, ENDWK=     1     63

     RANK  BR/BW/EW  PUSH INDEX      D-S     D-M     D-L     D-TOT**4   WEIGHT
        1    36063       30          .114    .421    .085     115.68     .531
        2    45863       45          .371    .226    .278     211.03     .291
        3    26063       19          .571    .121    .475     687.55     .089
        4    35759       29          .571    .121    .475     693.51     .088

(1H) CHANGE WEIGHTS?
     1
     TYPE NEW WEIGHTS IN CRDER OF RANK
     .50 .25 .25 .10
     NEW WEIGHTS DO NOT SUM TO ONE......
     TYPE NEW WEIGHTS IN ORDER OF RANK
     .50 .25 .15 .10
(1C) TYPE BRAND TO BE PROCESSED NEXT OR  0  TC STOP
     2
(1D) PROCESS?
     2
```

```
(1G) SEARCH RESULTS
     BEGWK, ENDWK=    1     63

     RANK   BR/BW/EW   PUSH INDEX        D-S      D-M      D-L       D-TOT**4   WEIGHT
        1    36063         30          0.000    0.000    0.000         0.00     .500
        2    45862         45          0.000    0.000    0.000         0.00     .250
        3    26063         19          0.000    0.000    0.000         0.00     .150
        4    35759         29          0.000    0.000    0.000         0.00     .100

(1H) CHANGE WEIGHTS?
     0
(1C) TYPE BRAND TO BE PROCESSED NEXT OR   0   TO STOP
     4
(1D) PROCESS?
     2

     SEARCH RESULTS
      BEGWK, ENDWK=     1     52
     NO RESULTS TABLE ENTRY FOR THIS BRAND.
(1C) TYPE BRAND TO BE PROCESSED NEXT OR   0   TO STOP
     0

(1I) SET ONE BRAND EQUAL TO ANOTHER?
     1
     TYPE B1 AND B2 FOR THE SUBSTITUTION B1=B2
     1 2

     SET ONE BRAND EQUAL TO ANOTHER?
     1
     TYPE B1 BND B2 FOR THE SUBSTITUTION B1=B2
     4 1

     SET ONE BRAND EQUAL TO ANOTHER?
     0
(1J) CURRENT BRAND ENTRY STATUS,
     BRAND   STATUS    BEGWK   ENDWK
       1        1         1      63
       2        1         1      63
       3        0         1      52
       4        1         1      63

(1K) RECYCLE?
     1
(1C) TYPE BRAND TO BE PROCESSED NEXT OR   0   TO STOP
     1
(1D) PROCESS?
     0
(1C) TYPE BRAND TO BE PROCESSED NEXT OR   0   TO STOP
     0

(1I) SET ONE BRAND EQUAL TO ANOTHER?
     0
(1J) CURRENT BRAND ENTRY STATUS,
     BRAND   STATUS    BEGWK   ENDWK
       1        0         0       0
       2        1         1      63
       3        0         1      52
       4        1         1      63

(1K) RECYCLE?
```

```
  0

(1L) TYPE BEGWK AND ENDWK FOR EACH NC-ENTRY BRAND
       BRAND      1
  1 63
       BRAND      3
  33 62
  NORMAL END OF PGM1.

  LOAD /MPGM2/ AND EXECUTE TO CONTINUE SIMULATION
  STOP



  >LOAD /MPGM2/
  SYMBOLIC FILE

  >EXEC


(2A) TYPE  0  TO I/P ALLOWANCE FROM PROGRAM 1,   OR  1 TO GIVE A PUSH PERIOD
   INDEX FOR EACH BRAND NOW
  0


  PARAMETERS I/P FROM PROGRAM 1.


  PUSH PERIOD INDICES
```

BRAND	NCT	PPI	BR/BW/EW	PROP	LWSPT	LWEND
1	1	0	0	0.000	1	63
1	2	0	0	0.000	1	63
1	3	0	0	0.000	1	63
1	4	0	0	0.000	1	63
2	1	30	36063	.500	1	63
2	2	45	45863	.250	1	63
2	3	19	26063	.150	1	63
2	4	29	35759	.100	1	63
3	1	0	0	0.000	33	62
3	2	0	0	0.000	33	62
3	3	0	0	0.000	33	62
3	4	0	0	0.000	33	62
4	1	30	36063	.500	1	63
4	2	45	45363	.250	1	63
4	3	19	26063	.150	1	63
4	4	29	35759	.100	1	63

```
(2B) SEARCH DONE FOR STORE GROUP     1


(2C) BRAND      1
  O/P ACTIVITY?
  0
(2D) MODIFY ACTIVITY?
  0
```

(2C) BRANC 2
O/P ACTIVITY?
1
FIRST AND LAST VARS ?
1 25

PER CENT RETAIL ACTIVITY FOR BRAND 2

VAR	NAME	S	M	L
1	ADO	0.00000	0.00000	0.00000
2	AD1	0.000CC	.00611	0.00000
3	AD2	.00834	.004C1	0.C0000
4	AD3	.0246C	.00533	C.00000
5	AD4	0.000CC	.0219C	C.000C0
6	AD5	0.00000	.03321	.19575
7	UAPZEM	.01716	.05519	.73620
8	UAPNEM	0.00000	0.0000C	0.CC0C0
9	UCDD1	0.00000	0.00000	0.00000
10	UCDD2	0.000C0	0.C0CCC	C.00000
11	SIWD	0.00000	0.00000	0.C00C0
12	SISD	0.0000C	C.0CC00	0.000C0
13	SPOPD	.0061C	.04753	.00874
14	SPCPD	.0860C	.04392	.28183
15	SPOCD	0.0000C	.C0615	0.00000
16	CPEZFE	.02837	.172C1	2.70025
17	CPM	1.83460	3.93835*	16.665
18	%UAP	.00318	.C09C6	.08053
19	%PIC	0.0000C	.02177	.03467
20	%PR&PC	0.000CC	.02177	.03467
21	%AD&DI	0.0C0C0	0.0C0C0	0.C00C0
22	%UP&DI	C.00000	0.00000	0.00000
23	A SALE	21.3	113.1	260.7
24	T BASE	21.1	59.8	18.4
25	OSCB	514.7	514.7	514.7

(2D) MODIFY ACTIVITY?
1
TYPE VAR,SIZE,VALUE OR C,0,0 TO PROCEED
?
2 3 .CC113
?
3 1 .01119
?
0 0 0
(2C) O/P ACTIVITY?
1
FIRST AND LAST VARS ?
1 4

PER CENT RETAIL ACTIVITY FOR BRAND 2

VAR	NAME	S	M	L
1	ADO	0.00000	0.00000	0.000C0
2	AD1	0.000CC	.00611	.C0113
3	AD2	.01119	.0C4C1	0.0C000
4	AD3	.02460	.00533	0.00000

```
(2D) MODIFY ACTIVITY?
0

(2C) BRAND     3
O/P ACTIVITY?
0
(2D) MODIFY ACTIVITY?
0

(2C) BRAND     4
O/P ACTIVITY?
0
(2D) MODIFY ACTIVITY?
0

(2E) RETAILER ACTIVITY LOOP FINISHED FOR STORE GROUP      1
TYPE 0 TO PROCEED OR 1 TO RECYCLE THESE STORES
0
/PROMO/ FILE WRITTEN FOR STORE GRP      1

(2F) SEARCH DONE FOR STORE GROUP     2

BRAND     1
O/P ACTIVITY?
0
MODIFY ACTIVITY?
0

BRAND     2
O/P ACTIVITY?
0
MODIFY ACTIVITY?
0

BRAND     3
O/P ACTIVITY?
0
MODIFY ACTIVITY?
0

BRAND     4
O/P ACTIVITY?
0
MODIFY ACTIVITY?
0

(2E) RETAILER ACTIVITY LOOP FINISHED FOR STORE GROUP
TYPE 0 TO PROCEED OR 1 TO RECYCLE THESE STORES
0
/PROMO/ FILE WRITTEN FOR STORE GRP      2
```

```
NORMAL END OF PROGRAM 2
LOAD /MPGM3/ AND EXECUTE TO CONTINUE SIMULATION.
STOP


>LOAD /MPGM3/
SYMBOLIC FILE

>EXEC

(3A) PROJECTION FACTORS FOR STORE GROUPS 1 AND 2=
      .431     .431

(3B) INPUT KEY BRAND AND LENGTH OF PUSH PERIOD IN WEEKS
2 6
(3C) INPUT ACT-PROJ ADJUSTMENT CONSTANT, BETWEEN  0 (NO ADJUSTMENT)
      AND   1 (PREDICTED SALES=ACTUAL SALES)
0
(3D) INPUT NON-PROMO SALES RATIO FOR BRANDS 1-4
1 1 1 1

(3E) PROCESSING STORE GROUP      1
END SIZE LOOP      S
END SIZE LOOP      M
END SIZE LOOP      L
/SALES/ WRITTEN FOR STORE GROUP      1


RESULTS FOR STORE GROUP      1
*************************
AVERAGE SALES IN UNITS PER STORE


(3F) ESTIMATED SALES BY BRAND AND SIZE
   FOR STORE GROUP     1


BRAND            1           2           3           4          TOTAL
SIZE
  S          147.7        95.0       115.1       120.7         478.6
  M         1257.9       795.0       687.8       819.6        3560.5
  L           86.6      1940.8      1074.9      1547.3        4649.7

TOTAL       1492.2      2830.9      1877.9      2487.7       11005.2

GRAND TOTAL SALES INCLUDES OTHER BRAND SALES OF       2316.4

(3G) ESTIMATED MARKET SHARE BY BRAND

             BR. 1       BR. 2       BR. 3       BR. 4     TOT. MKT
            .13559      .25723      .17063      .22604     11005.2


(3H) PROCESSING STORE GROUP      2
END SIZE LOOP      S
```

```
END SIZE LOOP      M
END SIZE LOOP      L
/SALES/ WRITTEN FOR STORE GROUP      2
**********************************
AVERAGE SALES IN UNITS PER STORE


ESTIMATED SALES BY BRAND AND SIZE
  FOR STORE GROUP     2

BRAND             1          2          3          4         TOTAL
SIZE
  S             280.5      186.6      181.3      208.6       857.1
  M             515.5      291.5      274.3      254.7      1336.2
  L              75.7      134.6      114.0      214.0       538.5

TOTAL           871.8      612.8      569.8      667.4      3667.7

GRAND TOTAL SALES INCLUDES OTHER BRAND SALES OF     935.7


ESTIMATED MARKET SHARE BY BRAND

                BR. 1      BR. 2      BR. 3      BR. 4     TOT. MKT

               .23772     .16709     .15535     .18469      3667.7
```

(31)

```
RESULTS FOR ALL STORES AGGREGATED
**********************************
PROJECTED SALES IN THOUSANDS OF UNITS


ESTIMATED SALES BY BRAND AND SIZE
  FOR STORE GROUP     0
BRAND             1          2          3          4         TOTAL
SIZE
  S             184.5      121.4      127.7      141.9       575.6
  M             764.3      468.3      414.7      463.0      2110.5
  L              69.9      894.5      512.4      759.1      2236.1

TOTAL          1018.9     1484.2     1054.9     1364.1      6324.0

GRAND TOTAL SALES INCLUDES OTHER BRAND SALES OF     1401.6


ESTIMATED MARKET SHARE BY BRAND
                BR. 1      BR. 2      BR. 3      BR. 4     TOT. MKT
               .16112     .23470     .16681     .21571      6324.0

NORMAL END OF PROGRAM 3
LOAD /MPGM4/ AND EXECUTE TO CONTINUE SIMULATION.
STOP


>LOAD /MPGM4/
SYMBOLIC FILE
```

```
>EXEC


(4A)KEY BRAND IS      2,  PUSH PERIOD LENGTH IS     6.
    ACTUAL-PREDICTED SALES ADJUSTMENT CONSTANT=      0.


(4B)ALLOWANCE IN $/UNIT FOR KEY BRAND


               ADV      DIS      EXT      PIC      MER      PRI      NOP     TOTAL
    SIZE
     S         1.00     .50      0.00     0.00     0.00     .25      .10      1.35
     M         1.25     .50      0.00     0.00     0.00     .45      .15      1.85
     L         1.00     .50      0.00     0.00     0.00     .35      .10      1.45

(4C)CHANGE ALLOWANCE VALUES (WITHOUT CHANGING RETAILER ACTIVITY)?
    1
    GIVE SIZE, ALLOW TYPE, NEW VALUE OR  0,0,0  TO CONTINUE
    ?
    2 6 .35
    ?
    0 0 0


    ALLOWANCE IN $/UNIT FOR KEY BRAND


               ADV      DIS      EXT               MER      PRI      NOP
    SIZE

     S         1.00     .50      0.00     0.00     0.00     .25      .10
     M         1.25     .50      0.00     0.00     0.00     .35      .15
     L         1.00     .50      0.00     0.00     0.00     .35      .10

(4C)CHANGE ALLOWANCE VALUES (WITHOUT CHANGING RETAILER ACTIVITY)?
    0
    PROCESSING STORE GROUP     1
    /SALES/ FILE READ.
(4D)/REPORT/ WRITTEN
    PROCESSING STORE GROUP     2
    /SALES/ FILE READ.
    /REPORT/ WRITTEN
    NORMAL END OF PROGRAM 4.


    LOAD /MPGM5/ AND EXECUTE TO CONTINUE SIMULATION.
    STOP


    >LOAD /MPGM5/
    SYMBOLIC FILE

    >EXEC
```

(5A) PROJECTION FACTOR FOR STORE GROUP 1 AND 2= .431 .431

(5B) INPUT GROSS MARGIN IN DOLLARS PER UNIT OR 0 TO USE STANDARD VALUE
.077

ESTIMATED COST PER UNIT SOLD ON PROMOTION AND PER TOTAL SOLD

	S	M	L	TOTAL
PROMOT	99999.000	.078	.056	.061
TOTAL	.006	.050	.052	.050

ESTIMATED GROSS PROFIT AFTER DEDUCTING ALLOWANCE COSTS

	S	M	L	TOTAL
PROMOT	6.004	21.317	48.518	75.839

REPORTS FOR STORE GROUP 2
****
AVERAGE SALES IN UNITS PER STORE
AVERAGE GROSS PROFIT IN DOLLARS PER STORE
AVERAGE COSTS IN DOLLARS PER STORE
FOR THE 6. WEEK PUSH PERIOD AS A WHOLE.

ESTIMATED SALES BY COMPONENTS FOR BRAND 2, BY SIZE
FOR STORE GROUP 2

	S	M	L	TOTAL
BKGND	149.9	240.2	68.4	458.5
ADS	36.7	51.2	66.2	154.2
PRICE	36.7	51.2	66.2	154.2
UAP	0.0	0.0	0.0	0.0
DISPLY	0.0	0.0	0.0	0.0
SIGN	0.0	0.0	0.0	0.0
TOTAL	186.6	291.5	134.6	612.8

ESTIMATED GROSS PROFIT EXCLUDING ALLOWANCE COSTS
BY SALES COMPONENT

	S	M	L	TOTAL
BKGND	11.542	18.501	5.267	35.311
ADS	2.829	3.948	5.099	11.877
PRICE	2.829	3.948	5.099	11.877
UAP	0.000	0.000	0.000	0.000
DISPLY	0.000	0.000	0.000	0.000
SIGN	0.000	0.000	0.000	0.000
TOTAL	14.372	22.450	10.366	47.188

ESTIMATED SALES DUE TO RETAILER PROMOTIONS

	S	M	L	TOTAL
PROMOT	36.7	51.2	66.2	154.2

ESTIMATED DEMAND RESPONSE RATIO FOR RETAILER ACTIVITY

	S	M	L	TOTAL
DRR	1.245	1.213	1.968	1.336

ESTIMATED ALLOWANCE COSTS BY TYPE AND CONTAINER SIZE

(5C) ESTIMATED SALES AND COST REPORT FOR BRAND 2.
FOR A PUSH PERIOD 6. WEEKS LONG
ACTUAL-PREDICTED SALES ADJUSTMENT CONSTANT= 0.

REPORTS FOR STORE GROUP 1
****
AVERAGE SALES IN UNITS PER STORE
AVERAGE GROSS PROFIT IN DOLLARS PER STORE
AVERAGE COSTS IN DOLLARS PER STORE
FOR THE 6. WEEK PUSH PERIOD AS A WHOLE.

ESTIMATED SALES BY COMPONENTS FOR BRAND 2, BY SIZE
FOR STORE GROUP 1

	S	M	L	TOTAL
BKGND	84.6	284.3	139.3	508.2
ADS	0.0	503.9	1623.0	2127.0
PRICE	0.0	503.9	1623.0	2127.0
UAP	0.0	6.7	178.4	185.2
DISPLY	0.0	0.0	0.0	0.0
SIGN	0.0	0.0	0.0	0.0
TOTAL	84.6	795.0	1940.8	2820.5

ESTIMATED GROSS PROFIT EXCLUDING ALLOWANCE COSTS
BY SALES COMPONENT

	S	M	L	TOTAL
BKGND	6.514	21.897	10.726	39.138
ADS	0.000	38.802	124.977	163.779
PRICE	0.000	38.802	124.977	163.779
UAP	0.000	.519	13.742	14.262
DISPLY	0.000	0.000	0.000	0.000

SIGN	0.000	0.000	0.000	0.000
TOTAL	6.514	61.219	149.446	217.179

ESTIMATED SALES DUE TO RETAILER PROMOTIONS

	S	M	L	TOTAL
PROMOT	0.0	510.6	1801.5	2312.2

ESTIMATED DEMAND RESPONSE RATIO FOR RETAILER ACTIVITY

	S	M	L	TOTAL
DPR	1.000	2.795	13.932	5.549

ESTIMATED ALLOWANCE COSTS BY TYPE AND CONTAINER SIZE

	S	M	L	TOTAL
ADV	.126	27.291	68.771	96.188
DIS	0.000	0.000	0.000	0.000
EXT	0.000	0.000	0.000	0.000
PIC	0.000	0.000	0.000	0.000
MER	0.000	0.000	0.000	0.000
PRI	.031	7.641	24.069	31.743
NOP	.352	4.969	8.086	13.408
TOTAL	.510	39.902	100.927	141.340

	S	M	L	TOTAL
ADV	2.644	3.661	3.079	9.385
DIS	0.000	0.000	0.000	0.000
EXT	0.000	0.000	0.000	0.000
PIC	0.000	0.000	0.000	0.000
MER	0.000	0.000	0.000	0.000
PRI	.661	1.025	1.077	2.764
NOP	.777	1.822	.560	3.160
TOTAL	4.083	6.508	4.718	15.310

ESTIMATED COST PER UNIT SOLD ON PROMOTION AND PER TOTAL SOLD

	S	M	L	TOTAL
PROMOT	.111	.126	.071	.099
TOTAL	.021	.022	.035	.024

ESTIMATED GROSS PROFIT AFTER DEDUCTING ALLOWANCE COSTS

	S	M	L	TOTAL
PROMOT	10.288	15.942	5.647	31.877

REPORTS FOR ALL STORES AGGREGATED
****
PROJECTED TOTAL SALES IN THOUSANDS OF UNITS
PROJECTED TOTAL GROSS PROFIT IN THOUSANDS OF DOLLARS
PROJECTED TOTAL COSTS IN THOUSANDS OF DOLLARS
FOR THE 6. WEEK PUSH PERIOD AS A WHOLE.

ESTIMATED SALES BY COMPONENTS FOR BRAND 2, BY SIZE
FOR STORE GROUP 0

	S	M	L	TOTAL
BKGND	101.0	226.1	89.5	416.7
ADS	15.8	239.2	728.0	983.2
PRICE	15.2	239.2	728.0	983.2
UAP	0.0	2.9	76.9	79.8
DISPLY	0.0	0.0	0.0	0.0
SIGN	0.0	0.0	0.0	0.0
TOTAL	116.9	468.3	894.5	1479.7

ESTIMATED GROSS PROFIT EXCLUDING ALLOWANCE COSTS
BY SALES COMPONENT

	S	M	L	TOTAL
BKGND	7.782	17.411	6.893	32.087
ADS	1.219	18.425	56.062	75.708
PRICE	1.219	18.425	56.062	75.708
UAP	0.000	.224	5.992	6.147
DISPLY	0.000	0.000	0.000	0.000
SIGN	0.000	0.000	0.000	0.000
TOTAL	9.002	36.061	68.879	113.942

ESTIMATED SALES DUE TO RETAILER PROMOTIONS

	S	M	L	TOTAL
PROMOT	15.8	242.2	805.0	1063.0

ESTIMATED DEMAND RESPONSE RATIO FOR RETAILER ACTIVITY

	S	M	L	TOTAL

DRR	1.156	2.071	9.992	3.550

ESTIMATED ALLOWANCE COSTS BY TYPE AND CONTAINER SIZE

	S	M	L	TOTAL
ADV	1.194	13.340	30.967	45.502
DIS	0.000	0.000	0.000	0.000
EXT	0.000	0.000	0.000	0.000
PIC	0.000	0.000	0.000	0.000
MER	0.000	0.000	0.000	0.000
PRI	.298	3.735	10.838	14.872
NCP	.487	2.972	3.727	7.141
TOTAL	1.979	20.002	45.533	67.516

ESTIMATED COST PER UNIT SOLD ON PROMOTION AND PER TOTAL SOLD

	S	M	L	TOTAL
PROMOT	.125	.082	.056	.063
TOTAL	.016	.042	.050	.045

ESTIMATED GROSS PROFIT AFTER DEDUCTING ALLOWANCE COSTS

	S	M	L	TOTAL
PROMOT	7.022	16.058	23.345	46.426

NORMAL END OF PROGRAM 5.
TERMINATION OF SIMULATION RUN.
STOP

Appendix A: Coding Conventions

The competitively sensitive nature of our findings has necessitated the coding of our results. This is a small price to pay for the opportunity to report in sufficient detail to permit replication of both methods and findings.

In addition to suppressing the identification of the product category, the metropolitan area, and the time period, the following coding conventions have been used:

1. *Brands.* Codes B1 to B7 refer to the seven major brands in the product category. B8 is an all-other category. The brands are not necessarily ordered by the magnitude of their market shares.

2. *Sizes.* The codes small, medium, and large are used for the three dominant size categories in which the product is merchandised to the ultimate consumer.

3. *Stores.* Codes S1 to S8 refer to eight specific supermarket chain categories (e.g., an S5 might be A&P) to which the various stores in the panel belong. As in the case of the brand codes, the last code, S9, is an all-other category.

4. *Geographic Areas.* Codes G1 to G6 refer to six specific communities within the metropolitan area under investigation. G7 is an all-other category that includes all communities in the metropolitan area other than the six that have been coded in separate categories.

5. *Regression Coefficients and Standard Errors.* All the regression coefficients and standard errors reported as the result of the multiple-equation model have been coded using the following conventions:

$$b^* = (c + db)/k;$$

$$S_b^* = |(S_b b^*)/b|,$$

where b^* and S_b^* are the coded value of the regression coefficient and its standard error, respectively; b and S_b are their original values; and c, d, and k are arbitrarily chosen constants. Although the absolute values of b and S_b are coded, the recode conventions leave intact the ratio of b to S_b.

For the purpose of coding, the variables included in the multiple-equation model were divided into the following five categories: (1) AD0 to AD5; (2) UAPNFM and UAPZFM; (3) SPOPD, SPORD and SPOCD; (4) CPE and CPM; (5) OSSB, KEY (ALT) and OSOB.

The constant k is the same across all five categories; however, the constants c and d vary from one category to another. This convention preserves the relative magnitude of the coefficients within each of the five categories. However, comparisons between categories are no longer possible.[1]

6. *Demand Response Ratio* (DRR). The DRR is computed in the same fashion as described in the text except that it is based on b^* instead of b:

$$\text{DRR} = (1 + b^*)^2.$$

[1]The constant c is equal to zero for category (5) variables to preserve the efficacy of the matrix inversion calculations needed to produce the reduced form coefficients.

Appendix B: Tables

Regression Coefficients and Standard Errors by Brand for All Stores for Small Packages for Weeks 2–32

Table B.1

	Brand 1		Brand 2		Brand 3	
	Reg. Coeff.	Std. Error	Reg. Coeff.	Std. Error	Reg. Coeff.	Std. Error
OSSB	0.015	0.019	0.102	0.023	0.028	0.042
KEYB(ALTB)*	0.036	0.017	0.070	0.021	0.034	0.034
OSOB	0.021	0.009	0.023	0.011	0.004	0.019
AD0	0.031	1.442	0.063	0.123	−0.135	0.151
AD1	—	—	—	—	—	—
AD2	—	—	—	—	—	—
AD3	—	—	—	—	—	—
AD4	—	—	—	—	—	—
AD5	0.807	0.063	1.161	0.071	—	—
UAPZFM	0.049	0.039	0.025	0.010	0.075	0.202
UAPNFM	0.074	0.040	0.078	0.035	0.114	0.028
SPOPD	0.146	0.209	−0.106	0.051	0.078	0.056
SPORD	0.052	0.035	0.064	0.361	0.067	0.647
SPOCD	—	—	—	—	—	—
CPE	0.008	0.004	0.236	0.114	—	—
CPM	0.122	0.091	—	—	0.113	0.061
R^2	0.18		0.30		0.10	
R_a^2†	0.17		0.29		0.06	
Number of Observations	858		850		260	

— Variable was zero over all observations.
*Variable is YR for all sizes of KEYB except for the KEYB results for which it is the YR for all sizes of ALTB.
†Adjusted for sample size.
‡Variable deleted because of collinearity.

Brand 4		Brand 5		Brand 6		Brand 7		Brand 8	
Reg. Coeff.	Std. Error	Reg. Coeff.	Std. Error	Reg. Coeff.	Std. Error	Reg. Coeff.	Std. Error	Reg. Coeff.	Std. Error
−0.002	0.021	0.059	0.025	—	—	0.165	0.089	0.072	0.025
0.017	0.019	0.038	0.019	0.019	0.017	0.095	0.061	0.034	0.013
0.023	0.009	0.021	0.011	0.034	0.008	0.036	0.025	0.023	0.006
0.090	0.107	0.004	0.005	0.092	0.083	—	—	0.121	0.082
−0.114	0.137	0.143	0.342		—	—	—	—	—
0.457	0.265	—	—	0.677	0.135	−0.035	0.071	0.077	0.272
—	—	—	—	—	—		—	—	—
—	—	—	—	0.631	0.235	—	—	—	—
1.225	0.078	1.430	0.086	—	—	0.450	0.102	0.247	0.048
0.047	0.032	0.155	0.014	0.046	0.046	0.043	0.038	0.075	0.014
0.074	0.035	0.078	0.043	0.105	0.013	0.105	0.032	0.088	0.008
−0.117	0.085	0.417	0.162	0.038	0.084	−0.068	0.174	0.021	0.012
−0.333	0.176	0.093	0.094	0.045	0.152	0.378	0.217	0.294	0.160
—	—	—	—	—	—	—	—	—	—
0.029	0.008	†	‡	—	—	−0.006	0.005	0.150	0.108
0.132	0.099	0.122	0.091	—	—	0.109	0.101	0.128	0.384
0.25		0.33		0.13		0.16		0.18	
0.23		0.32		0.12		0.12		0.16	
859		848		852		246		853	

Table B.2

Regression Coefficients and Standard Errors by Brand for All Stores for Small Packages for Weeks 33–62

	Brand 1		Brand 2		Brand 3	
Variables	Reg. Coeff.	Std. Error	Reg. Coeff.	Std. Error	Reg. Coeff.	Std. Error
OSSB	0.025	0.009	0.053	0.021	0.059	0.036
KEYB(ALTB)*	−0.008	0.008	−0.017	0.008	0.011	0.009
OSOB	0.062	0.009	0.045	0.008	−0.008	0.011
AD0	0.093	0.365	0.090	0.238	—	—
AD1	−0.058	0.108	−0.007	0.035	—	
AD2	0.061	0.125	0.003	0.005	—	
AD3	0.040	0.288	0.031	4.740	—	—
AD4	—	—	0.033	4.981	—	—
AD5	0.227	0.113	0.458	0.068	−0.440	0.038
UAPZFM	0.059	0.039	0.057	0.029	0.035	0.003
UAPNFM	0.097	0.023	0.050	0.061	0.020	0.005
SPOPD	−0.179	0.059	−0.064	0.057	0.057	0.149
SPORD	0.039	0.026	0.130	0.815	−0.002	0.002
SPOCD	—	—	—	—	—	—
CPE	0.138	0.123	0.114	0.068		—
CPM	0.124	0.124	0.122	0.091	—	—
R^2	0.08		0.11		0.57	
R_a^2†	0.07		0.10		0.55	
Number of Observations	857		851		360	

— Variable was zero over all observations.
*Variable is YR for all sizes of KEYB except for the KEYB results for which it is the YR for all sizes of ALTB.
†Adjusted for sample size.

Brand 4		Brand 5		Brand 6		Brand 7		Brand 8	
Reg. Coeff.	Std. Error	Reg. Coeff.	Std. Error	Reg. Coeff.	Std. Error	Reg. Coeff.	Std. Error	Reg. Coeff.	Std. Error
—	—	0.015	0.008	0.051	0.028	−0.214	0.119	0.134	0.026
−0.023	0.006	0.013	0.021	−0.002	0.006	−0.011	0.015	−0.008	0.004
0.032	0.008	0.008	0.009	0.009	0.006	0.125	0.015	−0.002	0.004
	—	0.223	0.313	0.122	0.111	—	—	0.056	0.328
0.245	0.176	0.109	0.266	−0.281	0.180	—	—	—	—
0.036	0.570	0.230	0.086	0.112	0.115	—	—	−0.082	0.059
0.006	0.014	0.108	0.133	—	—	—	—	0.132	0.093
—	—	—	—	—	—	—	—	—	—
0.259	0.083	0.864	0.197	—		0.058	0.148	0.125	0.079
0.049	0.007	0.073	0.022	0.063	0.125	0.052	0.014	0.070	0.016
0.051	0.027	0.099	0.032	0.063	0.250	0.074	0.032	0.094	0.046
0.463	0.358	—	—	0.158	0.508	—	—	−0.005	0.002
0.969	0.383	0.583	0.271	−0.114	0.174	−0.039	0.039	0.088	1.635
—	—	0.443	0.933	0.550	0.543	—	—	—	—
0.140	0.140	0.119	0.198	0.131	0.348	0.097	0.131	0.132	0.560
—	—	0.124	0.186	—	—	0.111	0.056	—	—
0.13		0.08		0.01		0.29		0.07	
0.12		0.06		0.00		0.27		0.06	
827		828		859		267		836	

Table B.3

Regression Coefficients and Standard Errors by Brand for All Stores for Medium Packages for Weeks 2–32

	Brand 1		Brand 2		Brand 3	
Variables	Reg. Coeff.	Std. Error	Reg. Coeff.	Std. Error	Reg. Coeff.	Std. Error
OSSB	0.104	0.078	0.227	0.051	0.354	0.106
KEYB(ALTB)*	−0.019	0.036	0.004	0.034	−0.021	0.038
OSOB	0.013	0.019	0.023	0.017	−0.036	0.021
AD0	0.110	0.649	−0.108	0.106	—	—
AD1	—	—	—	—	—	—
AD2	1.367	0.472	0.311	0.196	—	—
AD3	1.297	0.070	1.133	0.068	1.318	0.203
AD4	1.509	0.077	1.810	0.089	1.289	0.133
AD5	2.578	0.108	2.959	0.104	1.853	0.162
UAPZFM	0.100	0.012	0.071	0.039	0.074	0.016
UAPNFM	0.107	0.016	0.085	0.017	0.085	0.029
SPOPD	0.147	0.353	−0.125	0.048	−0.282	0.122
SPORD	−0.153	0.046	−0.858	0.292	−0.164	0.057
SPOCD	2.051	0.368	−0.397	0.233	1.523	0.440
CPE	—	—	0.129	0.259	0.120	0.144
CPM	0.124	0.062	0.124	0.062	0.122	0.061
R^2	0.68		0.67		0.46	
R_a^2†	0.67		0.66		0.44	
Number of Observations	857		856		526	

— Variable was zero over all observations.
*Variable is YR for all sizes of KEYB except for the KEYB results for which it is the YR for all sizes of ALTB.
†Adjusted for sample size.

Brand 4		Brand 5		Brand 6		Brand 7		Brand 8	
Reg. Coeff.	Std. Error	Reg. Coeff.	Std. Error	Reg. Coeff.	Std. Error	Reg. Coeff.	Std. Error	Reg. Coeff.	Std. Error
−0.004	0.045	0.176	0.061	0.087	0.104	0.329	0.098	−0.165	0.106
−0.021	0.032	−0.011	0.032	0.009	0.030	0.070	0.059	0.006	0.026
0.021	0.017	0.025	0.017	0.017	0.013	0.055	0.023	0.019	0.013
0.134	0.250	0.030	3.432	−0.153	0.138	—	—	—	—
—	—	—	—	2.041	0.339	—	—	—	—
1.361	0.438	0.644	0.238	2.156	0.114	—		0.029	4.066
0.982	0.083	1.100	0.074	2.311	0.176	0.241	0.119	0.417	0.118
1.470	0.080	1.858	0.073	—		0.285	0.126	0.577	0.069
2.158	0.127	2.444	0.104	—		1.441	0.106	1.264	0.073
0.096	0.015	0.085	0.017	—	—	0.080	0.033	0.083	0.025
0.051	0.033	0.069	0.069	0.087	0.014	0.073	0.017	0.085	0.020
−0.295	0.159	−0.095	0.158	−0.413	0.209	−0.016	0.021	0.068	0.465
−0.334	0.218	−0.309	0.311	−0.197	0.227	−2.114	0.575	−0.130	0.074
1.509	0.439	−0.378	0.213	−0.375	0.334	−1.467	0.567	0.189	0.338
0.146	0.058	0.122	0.122	—	—	—	—	0.151	0.143
0.128	0.128	0.123	0.041	—	—	0.132	0.066	0.129	0.194
0.55		0.66		0.51		0.51		0.37	
0.54		0.65		0.50		0.49		0.35	
855		863		644		241		771	

Table B.4 Regression Coefficients and Standard Errors by Brand for All Stores for Medium Packages for Weeks 33–62

	Brand 1		**Brand 2**		**Brand 3**	
Variables	**Reg. Coeff.**	**Std. Error**	**Reg. Coeff.**	**Std. Error**	**Reg. Coeff.**	**Std. Error**
OSSB	−0.009	0.011	0.038	0.034	0.178	0.083
KEYB(ALTB)*	−0.013	0.009	−0.015	0.011	−0.019	0.011
OSOB	0.026	0.013	0.002	0.013	0.013	0.017
AD0	—	—	−0.149	0.161	—	—
AD1	0.097	0.140	0.067	0.164	—	—
AD2	−0.050	0.129	0.122	0.373	—	—
AD3	1.154	0.127	0.972	0.142	—	—
AD4	1.124	0.066	1.600	0.083	2.189	0.161
AD5	1.930	0.078	1.453	0.091	1.913	0.090
UAPZFM	0.080	0.014	0.077	0.026	0.073	0.011
UAPNFM	0.078	0.016	0.074	0.032	0.071	0.039
SPOPD	−0.194	0.057	−0.084	0.049	−0.508	0.195
SPORD	−0.033	0.021	0.359	0.850	0.102	1.491
SPOCD	—	—	4.412	0.908	4.906	0.810
CPE	0.129	0.388	0.145	0.072	0.142	0.154
CPM	0.129	0.065	0.124	0.062	0.131	0.087
R^2	0.56		0.52		0.60	
R_a^2†	0.55		0.51		0.59	
Number of Observations	861		846		475	

— Variable was zero over all observations.
*Variable is YR for all sizes of KEYB except for the KEYB results for which it is the YR for all sizes of ALTB.
†Adjusted for sample size.

Brand 4		Brand 5		Brand 6		Brand 7		Brand 8	
Reg. Coeff.	Std. Error	Reg. Coeff.	Std. Error	Reg. Coeff.	Std. Error	Reg. Coeff.	Std. Error	Reg. Coeff.	Std. Error
−0.025	0.036	−0.011	0.013	0.479	0.112	0.127	0.072	1.001	0.134
−0.015	0.013	0.019	0.032	−0.015	0.011	−0.030	0.009	−0.028	0.009
−0.019	0.013	−0.021	0.013	−0.017	0.009	0.019	0.011	−0.034	0.009
0.142	0.315	—	—	0.059	0.209	—	—	—	—
0.129	0.130	0.076	0.172	0.317	0.306		—	0.106	0.158
	—	0.128	0.275	1.122	0.221	−0.088	0.087	0.021	0.401
0.977	0.225	0.767	0.130	2.691	0.083	0.240	0.096	0.288	0.303
0.992	0.071	1.522	0.064	3.124	0.278	0.014	0.092	0.807	0.091
1.942	0.071	2.005	0.070	—		0.380	0.081	0.916	0.043
0.080	0.017	0.085	0.014	0.076	0.013	0.069	0.059	0.079	0.026
0.082	0.020	0.079	0.023	0.072	0.012	0.059	0.029	0.057	0.144
0.728	0.640	—		0.495	0.590	0.076	0.359	0.015	0.032
−0.459	0.354	0.179	1.143	0.295	0.528	—	—	−0.717	0.097
1.304	0.530	0.164	0.295	—	—	—	—	−0.193	0.091
0.141	0.077	0.123	0.164	0.115	0.102	—	—	0.071	0.020
0.129	0.129	0.128	0.256	0.125	0.125	0.124	0.124	0.133	0.053
0.60		0.68		0.70		0.20		0.48	
0.59		0.68		0.69		0.17		0.47	
853		857		613		265		731	

Table B.5 Regression Coefficients and Standard Errors by Brand for All Stores for Large Packages for Weeks 2–32

	Brand 1		Brand 2	
Variables	Reg. Coeff.	Std. Error	Reg. Coeff.	Std. Error
OSSB	−0.009	0.026	0.042	0.032
KEYB(ALTB)*	0.009	0.025	−0.064	0.032
OSOB	0.044	0.013	0.025	0.015
AD0	–	–	0.067	0.462
AD1	0.287	0.112	0.291	0.161
AD2	0.286	0.203	–	–
AD3	1.640	0.182	1.489	0.195
AD4	–	–	2.053	0.208
AD5	–	–	3.393	0.346
UAPZFM	0.070	0.047	0.065	0.259
UAPNFM	0.054	0.025	0.074	0.015
SPOPD	−0.144	0.039	−0.363	0.068
SPORD	0.002	0.001	−0.218	0.031
SPOCD	–	–	–	–
CPE	0.138	0.568	0.140	0.084
CPM	–	–	–	–
R^2	0.24		0.38	
R_a^2†	0.22		0.37	
Number of Observations	453		88	

– Variable was zero over all observations.

*Variable is YR for all sizes of KEYB except for the KEYB results for which it is the YR for all sizes of ALTB.

†Adjustment for sample size.

‡Variable deleted because of collinearity.

Brand 3		Brand 4		Brand 5		Brand 7	
Reg. Coeff.	Std. Error	Reg. Coeff.	Std. Error	Reg. Coeff.	Std. Error	Reg. Coeff.	Std. Error
0.025	0.161	−0.104	0.182	−0.061	0.045	−0.093	0.091
0.019	0.108	−0.174	0.123	0.053	0.040	0.062	0.110
0.132	0.055	0.021	0.074	0.047	0.026	0.095	0.030
—	—	—	—	−0.363	0.314	—	—
—	—	—	—	0.247	0.292	—	—
—	—	—		—	—	—	—
—	—	—	—	‡	‡	—	—
	—	2.734	0.355	—	—	—	—
—	—	—	—	—	—	0.088	0.183
—	—	0.067	0.201	0.072	0.132	0.049	0.036
—	—	0.080	0.021	0.072	0.060	0.060	0.045
−0.899	0.716	0.302	0.943	−0.277	0.101	−0.002	0.009
−0.335	0.176	—	—	−0.020	0.014	0.129	0.496
—	—	—	—	—	—	—	—
—	—	0.059	0.043	0.140	0.209	—	—
0.125	2.257	0.088	0.035	0.118	0.067	0.136	0.155
0.15		0.36		0.11		0.37	
0.08		0.31		0.05		0.25	
151		151		190		62	

Table B.6 Regression Coefficients and Standard Errors by Brand for All Stores for Large Packages for Weeks 33–62

	Brand 1		Brand 2	
Variables	Reg. Coeff.	Std. Error	Reg. Coeff.	Std. Error
OSSB	0.011	0.129	0.153	0.081
KEYB(ALTB)*	−0.009	0.028	—	—
OSOB	0.089	0.042	−0.025	0.025
AD0	—	—	—	—
AD1	—	—	—	—
AD2	0.302	0.442	0.197	0.187
AD3	0.286	0.883	0.088	0.988
AD4	—	—	0.833	0.472
AD5	3.209	0.210	2.087	0.154
UAPZFM	0.094	0.011	0.075	0.019
UAPNFM	0.091	0.020	0.072	0.030
SPOPD	−0.399	0.224	−0.157	0.124
SPORD	−0.751	0.154	−0.253	0.076
SPOCD	—	—	—	—
CPE	—	—	0.128	0.512
CPM	0.123	0.164	0.140	0.028
R^2	0.46		0.29	
R_a^2†	0.44		0.27	
Number of Observations	417		647	

— Variable was zero over all observations.

*Variable is YR for all sizes of KEYB except for the KEYB results for which it is the YR for all sizes of ALTB.

†Adjusted for sample size.

‡Variable deleted because of collinearity.

Brand 3		Brand 4		Brand 5		Brand 7	
Reg. Coeff.	Std. Error	Reg. Coeff.	Std. Error	Reg. Coeff.	Std. Error	Reg. Coeff.	Std. Error
0.390	0.146	−0.114	0.051	−0.125	0.138	0.212	0.108
−0.102	0.072	−0.028	0.023	−0.136	0.119	‡	‡
0.115	0.064	0.047	0.026	−0.023	0.076	−0.006	0.006
	–	–	–	–	–	–	–
	–	–	–	0.072	1.962	–	–
	–	0.257	0.262	0.016	0.797	–	–
–	–	−0.398	0.213	–	–	−0.130	0.114
	–	1.342	0.238	−0.192	0.917	–	–
–	–	3.695	0.339	2.337	0.270	–	–
0.055	0.032	–	–	0.072	0.036	0.054	0.008
–	–	0.059	0.039	0.097	0.032	0.060	0.036
–	–	–	–	−0.001	0.007	–	–
	–	0.169	1.669	0.249	0.433	–	–
–	–	–	–	–	–	–	–
	–	–	–	0.140	0.126	–	–
0.161	0.263	–	–	0.116	0.087	0.131	0.131
0.34		0.51		0.28		0.63	
0.25		0.48		0.24		0.58	
55		179		272		63	

Table B.7 Regression Coefficients and Standard Errors by Brand for High-Volume Stores for Small Packages for Weeks 2–32

	Brand 1		Brand 2		Brand 3	
Variables	Reg. Coeff.	Std. Error	Reg. Coeff.	Std. Error	Reg. Coeff.	Std. Error
OSSB	−0.002	0.021	0.028	0.023	0.019	0.047
KEYB(ALTB)*	0.019	0.019	0.032	0.019	0.009	0.040
OSOB	–	–	0.002	0.011	−0.028	0.023
AD0	0.021	0.120	0.061	0.130	–	–
AD1	–	–	–	–	–	–
AD2	–	–	–	–	–	
AD3	–	–	–		–	–
AD4	–	–	–	–	–	–
AD5	–		3.265	0.164	–	–
UAPZFM	0.090	0.077	0.017	0.010	0.077	0.191
UAPNFM	0.066	0.240	0.055	0.055	0.122	0.029
SPOPD	0.158	0.202	0.018	0.020	−0.062	0.053
SPORD	0.022	0.013	−0.024	0.040	0.026	0.111
SPOCD	–	–	–	–	–	–
CPE	0.872	0.346	–	–	–	–
CPM	0.123	0.164	0.124	0.248	0.111	0.065
R^2	0.03		0.48		0.12	
R_a^2†	0.01		0.47		0.08	
Number of Observations	455		457		201	

– Variable was zero over all observations.

*Variable is YR for all sizes of KEYB except for the KEYB results for which it is the YR for all sizes of ALTB.

†Adjusted for sample size.

Brand 4		Brand 5		Brand 6		Brand 8	
Reg. Coeff.	Std. Error	Reg. Coeff.	Std. Error	Reg. Coeff.	Std. Error	Reg. Coeff.	Std. Error
−0.017	0.021	0.057	0.026	−0.011	0.032	0.040	0.026
−0.002	0.021	−0.008	0.021	—	—	0.013	0.013
−0.011	0.011	−0.025	0.011	0.006	0.011	0.006	0.008
−0.020	0.037	−0.086	0.050	0.044	0.322	0.171	0.084
—	—	—	—	—	—	—	—
—	—	—	—	0.601	0.264	—	—
—	—	—	—	—	—	—	—
—	—	—	—	0.604	0.265	—	—
—	—	1.977	0.181	—	—	0.207	0.104
0.041	0.047	0.236	0.015	0.047	0.270	0.110	0.024
0.056	0.062	0.052	0.077	0.105	0.015	0.143	0.017
-0.139	0.094	−0.403	0.152	0.144	0.457	0.023	0.016
-0.194	0.350	−0.198	0.172	−0.544	0.277	0.449	0.251
—	—		—	—		—	—
—	—	—	—	—	—	0.133	0.373
0.129	0.259	0.123	0.164	0.124	0.124	0.122	0.122
0.02		0.47		0.14		0.20	
0.00		0.46		0.12		0.17	
458		448		459		455	

Table B.8

Regression Coefficients and Standard Errors by Brand for High-Volume Stores for Small Packages for Weeks 33–62

	Brand 1		Brand 2		Brand 3	
Variables	Reg. Coeff.	Std. Error	Reg. Coeff.	Std. Error	Reg. Coeff.	Std. Error
OSSB	−0.034	0.021	−0.013	0.009	0.011	0.044
KEYB(ALTB)*	−0.013	0.009	−0.015	0.008	−0.006	0.011
OSOB	−0.009	0.009	—	—	0.006	0.013
AD0	0.094	0.391	0.152	0.181	—	—
AD1	—	—	—	—	—	—
AD2	0.101	0.139	0.061	0.162	—	—
AD3	0.148	0.133	0.064	0.347	—	—
AD4	—	—	—	—	—	—
AD5	—	—	—	—	—	—
UAPZFM	0.081	0.020	0.080	0.022	0.066	0.153
UAPNFM	0.064	1.474	0.055	0.118	−0.008	0.003
SPOPD	−0.017	0.017	−0.020	0.025	−0.233	0.086
SPORD	0.075	0.275	0.338	0.365	−0.164	0.088
SPOCD	—	—	—	—	—	
CPE	0.151	0.119	0.110	0.068	—	—
CPM	0.125	0.502	—	—	0.128	0.768
R^2	0.07		0.05		0.10	
R_a^2†	0.04		0.02		0.06	
Number of Observations	440		442		198	

— Variable was zero over all observations.
*Variable is YR for all sizes of KEYB except for the KEYB results for which it is the YR for all sizes of ALTB.
†Adjusted for sample size.

Brand 4		Brand 5		Brand 6		Brand 8	
Reg. Coeff.	Std. Error	Reg. Coeff.	Std. Error	Reg. Coeff.	Std. Error	Reg. Coeff.	Std. Error
−0.011	0.017	—	—	0.042	0.032	0.049	0.028
−0.038	0.008	−0.038	0.013	−0.009	0.008	−0.008	0.004
—	—	−0.023	0.017	−0.006	0.008	−0.002	0.004
—	—	0.147	0.425	0.120	0.278	0.077	0.221
—		—	—	−0.281	0.184	—	—
0.101	0.201	0.697	0.174	0.195	0.175	−0.109	0.071
−0.265	0.172	0.277	0.264	—	—	—	—
	—	—	—	—	—	—	—
	—	—	—	—	—	—	—
	—	0.085	0.020	—	—	0.038	0.024
0.060	0.107	0.103	0.044	0.065	0.162	0.085	0.257
—	—	—	—	—	—	0.021	0.016
—	—	1.093	0.383	—	—	0.284	0.309
—	—	—	—	—	—	—	—
0.107	0.107	0.096	0.060	—	—	—	—
0.131	0.131	—	—	—	—	0.125	0.376
0.12		0.11		0.03		0.05	
0.09		0.08		0.00		0.02	
419		416		444		447	

Table B.9

Regression Coefficients and Standard Errors by Brand for High-Volume Stores for Medium Packages for Weeks 2–32

	Brand 1		Brand 2		Brand 3	
Variables	Reg. Coeff.	Std. Error	Reg. Coeff.	Std. Error	Reg. Coeff.	Std. Error
OSSB	−0.132	0.123	0.129	0.078	0.409	0.136
KEYB(ALTB)*	−0.004	0.045	−0.011	0.044	−0.055	0.047
OSOB	−0.015	0.026	−0.017	0.025	−0.053	0.026
AD0	—		−0.347	0.326	—	—
AD1	—	—	—	—	—	
AD2	—	—	0.854	0.516	—	—
AD3	1.690	0.104	1.345	0.110	2.320	0.325
AD4	1.718	0.100	1.568	0.125	1.111	0.172
AD5	2.541	0.123	2.880	0.123	1.830	0.186
UAPZFM	0.103	0.015	0.081	0.030	0.073	0.022
UAPNFM	0.130	0.017	0.094	0.023	0.090	0.032
SPOPD	0.124	0.724	−0.107	0.067	−0.294	0.223
SPORD	−0.165	0.076	−1.012	0.441	0.967	0.829
SPOCD	1.870	0.445	0.192	0.809	1.745	0.509
CPE	0.151	0.056	0.151	0.056	0.123	0.287
CPM	0.128	0.256	0.125	0.251	0.120	0.072
R^2	0.77		0.72		0.51	
R_a^2†	0.76		0.71		0.49	
Number of Observations	457		458		314	

— Variable was zero over all observations.
*Variable is YR for all sizes of KEYB except for the KEYB results for which it is the YR for all sizes of ALTB.
†Adjusted for sample size.

Brand 4		Brand 5		Brand 6		Brand 8	
Reg. Coeff.	Std. Error	Reg. Coeff.	Std. Error	Reg. Coeff.	Std. Error	Reg. Coeff.	Std. Error
−0.036	0.062	0.219	0.085	0.072	0.142	−0.178	0.189
−0.021	0.044	−0.047	0.045	0.002	0.040	−0.013	0.036
−0.026	0.025	−0.034	0.025	−0.004	0.021	−0.026	0.019
−0.023	0.123	—	—	−0.129	0.157	—	—
—	—	—	—	1.995	0.394	—	—
1.351	0.519	—	—	2.196	0.133	0.079	0.682
1.507	0.169	1.755	0.134	2.365	0.206	0.415	0.161
1.642	0.110	1.872	0.091	—	—	0.582	0.085
2.140	0.152	2.510	0.127	—	—	1.255	0.089
0.089	0.025	0.088	0.021	0.065	0.713	0.082	0.029
0.055	0.127	0.074	0.063	0.113	0.013	0.136	0.028
−0.406	0.234	−0.145	0.313	−0.590	0.531	0.138	0.740
−0.198	0.387	−0.117	0.455	—	—	−0.182	0.113
2.124	0.629	−0.809	0.343	−1.059	0.457	0.004	0.010
0.155	0.063	0.137	0.103	—	—	0.306	0.088
0.133	0.053	0.120	0.048	0.124	0.062	0.124	0.372
0.61		0.73		0.62		0.47	
0.60		0.72		0.60		0.45	
453		463		335		403	

Table B.10 Regression Coefficients and Standard Errors by Brand for High-Volume Stores for Medium Packages for Weeks 33–62

	Brand 1		Brand 2		Brand 3	
Variables	Reg. Coeff.	Std. Error	Reg. Coeff.	Std. Error	Reg. Coeff.	Std. Error
OSSB	−0.006	0.028	−0.040	0.017	0.303	0.184
KEYB(ALTB)*	−0.004	0.011	−0.011	0.015	−0.017	0.017
OSOB	−0.034	0.011	0.008	0.021	−0.025	0.021
AD0	—	—	−0.023	0.176	—	—
AD1	−0.090	0.173	0.072	0.341	—	—
AD2	−0.083	0.172	0.112	0.419	—	—
AD3	0.716	0.244	1.108	0.306	—	—
AD4	1.285	0.088	1.743	0.116	2.161	0.185
AD5	1.943	0.088	1.783	0.108	1.896	0.104
UAPZFM	0.085	0.018	0.085	0.023	0.073	0.017
UAPNFM	0.096	0.015	0.086	0.025	0.081	0.034
SPOPD	−0.200	0.077	−0.000	0.000	−0.367	0.257
SPORD	−0.186	0.108	—		0.185	0.506
SPOCD	—	—	4.080	1.000	4.860	0.926
CPE	0.113	0.082	0.156	0.068	0.143	0.165
CPM	0.128	0.256	0.125	0.251	0.133	0.080
R^2	0.65		0.64		0.68	
R_a^2†	0.64		0.62		0.66	
Number of Observations	446		445		267	

— Variable was zero over all observations.
*Variable is YR for all sizes of KEYB except for the KEYB results for which it is the YR for all sizes of ALTB.
†Adjusted for sample size.
‡Variable deleted because of collinearity

Brand 4		Brand 5		Brand 6		Brand 8	
Reg. Coeff.	Std. Error	Reg. Coeff.	Std. Error	Reg. Coeff.	Std. Error	Reg. Coeff.	Std. Error
0.019	0.062	−0.028	0.019	0.412	0.168	0.761	0.242
−0.025	0.019	−0.117	0.019	−0.015	0.015	−0.015	0.015
−0.023	0.017	—	—	−0.025	0.017	−0.034	0.013
—	—	—	—	0.274	0.354	—	—
0.302	0.577	0.257	0.551	0.319	0.349	0.408	0.336
—	—	0.144	0.311	1.031	0.229	−0.033	0.115
0.442	0.400	0.932	0.290	2.684	0.096	0.455	0.336
0.998	0.158	1.891	0.097	3.132	0.317	0.804	0.104
1.975	0.091	2.105	0.087	—	—	0.963	0.051
0.077	0.030	0.086	0.017	0.077	0.013	0.077	0.033
0.091	0.022	0.083	0.025	0.075	0.019	0.047	0.101
—	—	—		0.304	1.068	0.123	0.962
−0.322	0.526	−0.648	0.967	—	—	−0.811	0.122
1.269	0.654	−0.382	0.439	—	—	−0.176	0.101
0.181	0.047	0.125	0.752	‡	‡	0.064	0.018
0.128	0.384	0.129	0.194	−0.000	0.001	0.140	0.056
0.61		0.75		0.78		0.56	
0.60		0.74		0.77		0.54	
444		443		310		388	

Table B.11 Regression Coefficients and Standard Errors by Brand for High-Volume Stores for Large Packages for Weeks 2–32

	Brand 1		Brand 2		Brand 4		Brand 5	
Variables	Reg. Coeff.	Std. Error	Reg. Coeff.	Std. Error	Reg. Coeff.	Std. Error	Reg. Coeff.	Std. Error
OSSB	−0.028	0.028	−0.053	0.055	−0.134	0.233	−0.062	0.047
KEYB(ALTB)*	0.011	0.028	−0.108	0.047	−0.225	0.159	0.055	0.045
OSOB	0.017	0.015	−0.009	0.026	−0.038	0.112	0.051	0.028
AD0	–	–	–	–	–	–	–	–
AD1	0.268	0.119	1.189	0.465	–		0.260	0.302
AD2	0.282	0.214	–	–		–	–	–
AD3	1.638	0.191	1.001	0.304	–	–	‡	‡
AD4	–	–	2.166	0.436	2.734	0.442	–	–
AD5	–	–	3.325	0.426	–	–	–	–
UAPZFM	0.074	0.045	0.078	0.062	0.066	0.331	0.094	0.076
UAPNFM	0.049	0.018	0.085	0.031	0.081	0.027	0.071	0.065
SPOPD	−0.162	0.052	−0.266	0.121	−0.071	0.393	−0.313	0.115
SPORD	−0.042	0.017	−0.297	0.066	–	–	−0.058	0.033
SPOCD	–	–	–	–	–	–	–	–
CPE	–	–	0.186	0.061	0.053	0.046	0.138	0.246
CPM	0.128	0.384	0.129	0.323	0.077	0.033	0.116	0.073
R^2	0.31		0.47		0.38		0.11	
R_a^2†	0.28		0.43		0.31		0.05	
Number of Observations	278		243		95		165	

– Variable was zero over all observations.
*Variable is YR for all sizes of KEYB except for the KEYB results for which it is the YR for all sizes of ALTB.
†Adjusted for sample size.
‡Variable deleted because of collinearity.

Table B.12 Regression Coefficients and Standard Errors by Brand for High-Volume Stores for Large Packages for Weeks 33–62

	Brand 1		Brand 2		Brand 4		Brand 5	
Variables	Reg. Coeff.	Std. Error	Reg. Coeff.	Std. Error	Reg. Coeff.	Std. Error	Reg. Coeff.	Std. Error
OSSB	−0.061	0.157	−0.115	0.148	−0.110	0.057	−0.068	0.112
KEYB(ALTB)*	−0.042	0.038	0.026	0.042	−0.104	0.040	−0.159	0.051
OSOB	0.028	0.047	−0.087	0.053	−0.042	0.017	0.138	0.068
AD0	–	–	–	–	–	–	–	–
AD1	–	–	–	–	–	–	0.123	1.165
AD2	0.629	0.928	0.110	1.225	–	–	–	–
AD3	0.244	1.000	0.542	0.944	−0.455	0.219	–	–
AD4	–	–	1.206	0.675	–	–	–	–
AD5	3.347	0.240	1.896	0.270	4.083	0.363	4.077	0.303
UAPZFM	0.119	0.011	0.098	0.017	0.060	0.048	0.098	0.015
UAPNFM	0.096	0.019	0.085	0.105	0.060	0.048	0.151	0.022
SPOPD	−0.467	0.284	−0.413	0.307	–	–	−0.285	0.348
SPORD	−1.233	0.207	−0.785	0.211	0.307	1.086	−0.189	0.150
SPOCD	–	–	–	–	–	–	–	–
CPE	0.122	0.243	0.119	0.198	–	–	0.133	0.240
CPM	0.111	0.046	0.160	0.031	0.125	0.376	0.115	0.090
R^2	0.57		0.36		0.56		0.62	
R_a^2†	0.55		0.32		0.53		0.60	
Number of Observations	274		241		130		195	

– Variable was zero over all observations.
*Variable is YR for all sizes of KEYB except for the KEYB results for which it is the YR for all sizes of ALTB.
†Adjusted for sample size.

Table B.13 Regression Coefficients and Standard Errors by Brand for Low-Volume Stores for Small Packages for Weeks 2–32

	Brand 1		Brand 2		Brand 3	
Variables	Reg. Coeff.	Std. Error	Reg. Coeff.	Std. Error	Reg. Coeff.	Std. Error
OSSB	0.089	0.059	0.356	0.051	0.428	0.204
KEYB(ALTB)*	0.106	0.045	0.081	0.049	−0.036	0.100
OSOB	0.045	0.019	0.034	0.025	0.047	0.021
AD0	0.018	0.098	−0.005	0.014	−0.135	0.078
AD1	—	—	—	—	—	—
AD2	—	—	—	—	—	—
AD3	—	—	—	—		—
AD4	—	—	—	—		—
AD5	0.815	0.066	0.936	0.075	—	—
UAPZFM	0.042	0.028	0.038	0.026	—	—
UAPNFM	0.077	0.049	0.094	0.025	0.010	0.005
SPOPD	0.195	0.301	−0.396	0.177	—	—
SPORD	0.098	1.246	0.171	0.566	—	—
SPOCD	—	—	—	—	—	—
CPE	−0.001	0.000	0.214	0.129	—	—
CPM	0.119	0.079	0.129	0.323	0.150	0.150
R^2	0.31		0.41		0.26	
R_a^2†	0.29		0.39		0.16	
Number of Observations	403		393		59	

— Variable was zero over all observations.
*Variable is YR for all sizes of KEYB except for the KEYB results for which it is the YR for all sizes of ALTB.
†Adjusted for sample size.
‡Variable deleted, because of collinearity.

Brand 4		Brand 5		Brand 6		Brand 7		Brand 8	
Reg. Coeff.	Std. Error	Reg. Coeff.	Std. Error	Reg. Coeff.	Std. Error	Reg. Coeff.	Std. Error	Reg. Coeff.	Std. Error
−0.025	0.066	0.121	0.057	0.047	0.091	0.159	0.087	0.149	0.074
0.051	0.047	0.047	0.030	0.061	0.032	0.182	0.064	0.072	0.028
0.079	0.021	0.087	0.021	0.081	0.013	0.009	0.025	0.051	0.011
0.201	0.117	0.039	0.273	0.134	0.079	–	–	−0.022	0.046
−0.086	0.136	0.180	0.290	–	–	–	–	–	–
0.471	0.278	–	–	0.744	0.134	−0.039	0.073	0.073	0.286
–	–	–	–	–	–	–	–	–	–
–	–	–	–	–	–	–	–	–	
1.255	0.082	1.349	0.088	0.000	0.000	0.468	0.101	0.266	0.053
0.054	0.074	0.080	0.052	0.057	0.144	0.041	0.033	0.075	0.014
0.083	0.025	0.088	0.031	0.096	0.064	0.105	0.031	0.086	0.011
0.116	2.278	–	–	−0.803	0.256	−0.064	0.167	0.044	0.082
−0.366	0.207	0.196	0.471	0.347	0.228	0.387	0.213	0.251	0.201
–	–	–	–	–	–	–	–	–	–
0.033	0.009	‡	‡	–	–	−0.005	0.004	0.186	0.109
0.129	0.323	0.120	0.096	0.128	0.256	0.111	0.121	0.133	0.160
0.41		0.39		0.18		0.18		0.28	
0.38		0.37		0.16		0.13		0.25	
401		400		393		246		403	

Table B.14

Regression Coefficients and Standard Errors by Brand for Low-Volume Stores for Small Packages for Weeks 33–62

	Brand 1		Brand 2		Brand 3	
Variables	Reg. Coeff.	Std. Error	Reg. Coeff.	Std. Error	Reg. Coeff.	Std. Error
OSSB	0.182	0.049	0.195	0.042	−0.055	0.078
KEYB(ALTB)*	0.144	0.028	0.061	0.038	0.246	0.049
OSOB	0.093	0.015	0.127	0.019	−0.066	0.013
AD0	–	–	–	–	–	–
AD1	−0.106	0.107	−0.112	0.144	–	–
AD2	−0.040	0.037	−0.023	0.028	–	–
AD3	−0.050	0.038	0.019	0.118	–	–
AD4	–	–	0.081	0.241	–	–
AD5	0.298	0.090	0.503	0.066	−0.387	0.025
UAPZFM	0.046	0.008	0.048	0.011	0.034	0.002
UAPNFM	0.113	0.017	0.060	0.489	0.028	0.006
SPOPD	0.010	0.019	−0.107	0.300	–	–
SPORD	0.129	0.142	0.089	6.838	0.206	0.169
SPOCD	–	–	–	–	–	–
CPE	0.136	0.136	0.116	0.116	–	–
CPM	0.123	0.123	0.116	0.058	0.137	0.051
R^2	0.33		0.30		0.90	
R_a^2†	0.30		0.28		0.89	
Number of Observations	417		409		170	

– Variable was zero over all observations.
*Variable is YR for all sizes of KEYB except for the ALTB results for which it is the YR for all sizes of KEYB.
†Adjusted for sample size.

Brand 4		Brand 5		Brand 6		Brand 7		Brand 8	
Reg. Coeff.	Std. Error	Reg. Coeff.	Std. Error	Reg. Coeff.	Std. Error	Reg. Coeff.	Std. Error	Reg. Coeff.	Std. Error
0.051	0.021	0.095	0.025	0.272	0.085	−0.104	0.125	0.424	0.059
0.189	0.042	−0.023	0.021	0.053	0.028	0.202	0.076	0.038	0.023
0.096	0.015	0.085	0.011	0.025	0.013	0.125	0.019	0.021	0.011
—	—	—	—	0.110	0.122	—	—	—	—
0.290	0.173	0.047	0.335	—	—	—		—	—
0.066	0.135	0.008	0.017	0.080	0.159	—	—	−0.007	0.028
0.063	0.147	0.067	0.119	—	—		—	0.114	0.103
—	—	—	—	—	—	—	—	—	—
0.361	0.082	0.833	0.112	—	—	0.073	0.126	0.133	0.081
0.048	0.011	0.066	0.050	—	—	0.056	0.028	0.071	0.014
0.075	0.094	0.097	0.040	0.049	0.029	0.077	0.030	0.096	0.048
0.441	0.367	—	—	0.199	0.370	—	—	0.071	0.270
1.079	0.382	0.187	0.491	−0.087	0.145	0.460	0.153	−0.022	0.029
—	—	0.397	0.551	0.752	0.498	—	—	—	—
0.170	0.060	0.141	0.141	0.131	0.348	0.091	0.104	0.129	1.099
—	—	0.125	0.251	0.128	0.256	0.109	0.047	0.131	0.174
0.30		0.30		0.07		0.25		0.20	
0.28		0.28		0.04		0.22		0.17	
408		412		415		266		389	

Table B.15

Regression Coefficients and Standard Errors by Brand for Low-Volume Stores for Medium Packages for Weeks 2–32.

Variables	Brand 1 Reg. Coeff.	Brand 1 Std. Error	Brand 2 Reg. Coeff.	Brand 2 Std. Error	Brand 3 Reg. Coeff.	Brand 3 Std. Error
OSSB	**0.140**	**0.076**	**0.384**	**0.059**	**0.036**	**0.199**
KEYB(ALTB)*	**0.026**	**0.051**	**0.115**	**0.057**	**0.017**	**0.061**
OSOB	**0.002**	**0.021**	**0.059**	**0.026**	**0.057**	**0.026**
AD0	**0.085**	**0.438**	**−0.034**	**0.056**	–	–
AD1	–	–	–	–	–	–
AD2	1.412	0.281	0.231	0.156	–	–
AD3	0.881	0.053	0.962	0.069	0.330	0.186
AD4	0.634	0.090	1.971	0.141	1.928	0.173
AD5	–	–	–	–	–	–
UAPZFM	0.079	0.030	0.062	0.186	0.089	0.018
UAPNFM	0.060	0.136	0.071	0.045	0.065	0.519
SPOPD	0.316	0.198	−0.041	0.029	−0.203	0.089
SPORD	−0.024	0.012	−0.493	0.304	−0.137	0.035
SPOCD	−0.135	0.367	−1.272	0.327	–	–
CPE	‡	‡	0.125	0.502	–	–
CPM	0.000	0.001	–	–	0.124	0.124
R^2	0.50		0.56		0.49	
R_a^2†	0.48		0.54		0.46	
Number of Observations	400		398		212	

– Variable was zero over all observations.
*Variable is YR for all sizes of KEYB except for the KEYB results for which it is the YR for all sizes of ALTB.
†Adjusted for sample size.
‡Variable deleted because of collinearity.

Brand 4		Brand 5		Brand 6		Brand 7		Brand 8	
Reg. Coeff.	Std. Error	Reg. Coeff.	Std. Error	Reg. Coeff.	Std. Error	Reg. Coeff.	Std. Error	Reg. Coeff.	Std. Error
−0.011	0.074	0.174	0.061	0.076	0.132	0.339	0.098	0.148	0.112
0.064	0.049	0.096	0.032	0.083	0.049	0.074	0.064	0.114	0.038
0.076	0.021	0.042	0.023	0.045	0.019	0.051	0.025	0.076	0.015
0.289	0.212	0.090	0.146	–	–	–	–	–	–
–	–	–	–	–	–	–		–	–
–	–	0.608	0.137	–	–	–	–	–	–
0.820	0.068	0.661	0.058	–		0.238	0.120	−0.005	0.019
0.829	0.104	1.410	0.109	–	–	0.284	0.126	0.199	0.236
–	–	0.161	0.312	–	–	1.445	0.107	–	–
0.102	0.018	0.069	0.095	0.063	0.188	0.080	0.033	–	–
0.056	0.045	0.067	0.094	0.060	0.076	0.073	0.017	0.082	0.016
0.020	0.071	0.053	0.319	−0.456	0.158	−0.063	0.058	0.091	6.455
−0.109	0.116	−0.335	0.218	−0.224	0.156	−2.110	0.576	−0.131	0.099
0.083	3.051	0.386	0.336	–	–	−1.470	0.569	–	–
0.141	0.077	0.124	0.186	–	–	–	–	0.089	0.040
0.124	0.062	0.129	0.065	0.129	0.065	0.132	0.066	0.131	0.087
0.46		0.54		0.09		0.51		0.17	
0.44		0.52		0.06		0.48		0.14	
402		400		309		241		368	

Table B.16 Regression Coefficients and Standard Errors by Brand for Low-Volume Stores for Medium Packages for Weeks 33–62

	Brand 1		Brand 2		Brand 3	
Variables	Reg. Coeff.	Std. Error	Reg. Coeff.	Std. Error	Reg. Coeff.	Std. Error
OSSB	0.168	0.066	0.254	0.049	0.161	0.087
KEYB(ALTB)*	0.070	0.034	0.045	0.042	0.008	0.051
OSOB	0.032	0.017	−0.036	0.023	0.023	0.028
AD0	–	–	−0.178	0.137	–	–
AD1	0.108	0.118	0.113	0.100	–	
AD2	–	–	–	–	–	–
AD3	1.384	0.108	0.983	0.120		–
AD4	0.822	0.094	1.228	0.101		–
AD5	–	–	−0.237	0.142	–	–
UAPZFM	0.071	0.042	0.077	0.037	0.089	0.020
UAPNFM	–	–	–	–	0.060	0.095
SPOPD	−0.183	0.074	0.018	0.024	−0.714	0.272
SPORD	0.109	0.547	0.343	0.620	0.146	0.292
SPOCD	–	–	–	–	–	–
CPE	‡	‡	0.113	0.102	–	–
CPM	0.128	0.128	0.128	0.256	0.129	0.129
R^2	0.40		0.40		0.14	
R_2^a†	0.38		0.38		0.10	
Number of Observations	415		401		208	

– Variable was zero over all observations.
*Variable is YR for all sizes of KEYB except for the KEYB results for which it is the YR for all sizes of ALTB.
†Adjusted for sample size.
‡Variable deleted because of collinearity.

Brand 4		Brand 5		Brand 6		Brand 7		Brand 8	
Reg. Coeff.	Std. Error	Reg. Coeff.	Std. Error	Reg. Coeff.	Std. Error	Reg. Coeff.	Std. Error	Reg. Coeff	Std. Error
−0.036	0.028	0.070	0.042	0.407	0.151	0.064	0.070	1.086	0.144
0.059	0.042	0.068	0.032	0.172	0.049	0.098	0.045	0.057	0.034
0.008	0.019	0.047	0.019	0.030	0.017	0.030	0.013	0.023	0.017
0.202	0.190	—		0.070	0.161	—	—	—	—
0.145	0.086	0.062	0.128	—	—	—	—	−0.007	0.018
—	—	—	—		—	−0.130	0.095	—	—
1.578	0.206	0.718	0.091	—	—	0.249	0.097		—
1.042	0.058	0.945	0.051	—		−0.037	0.064	—	—
1.911	0.134	1.163	0.146	—	—	0.380	0.082	—	—
0.086	0.017	0.084	0.027	0.074	0.058	0.064	0.385	—	—
0.074	0.032	0.070	0.047	0.071	0.021	0.060	0.036	0.061	0.367
0.687	0.424	—	—	0.119	2.528	0.222	0.143	0.145	1.007
−0.053	0.158	0.073	1.283	0.220	0.520	—	—	0.305	0.493
—	—	—	—	—		—	—	—	—
0.109	0.047	‡	‡	0.122	0.243	—	—	—	—
0.129	0.065	0.125	0.125	0.125	0.125	0.124	0.124	0.123	0.082
0.64		0.13		0.55		0.19		0.18	
0.62		0.10		0.53		0.15		0.16	
409		303		414		264		343	

Table B.17 Regression Coefficients and Standard Errors by Brand for Low-Volume Stores for Large Packages for Weeks 2–32

	Brand 1		Brand 2		Brand 3		Brand 4		Brand 7	
Variables	Reg. Coeff.	Std. Error	Reg. Coeff.	Std. Error	Reg. Coeff.	Std. Error	Reg. Coeff.	Std. Error	Reg. Coeff.	Std. Error
OSSB	0.098	0.070	0.117	0.042	−0.208	0.144	0.167	0.255	−0.100	0.091
KEYB(ALTB)*	−0.002	0.072	−0.006	0.057	0.079	0.110	0.191	0.174	0.038	0.123
OSOB	0.100	0.025	0.078	0.025	0.144	0.055	0.068	0.045	0.087	0.028
AD0	–	–	0.039	1.006	–	–	–	–	–	–
AD1	–	–	0.132	0.162		–	–	–	–	–
AD2	–	–	–		–	–	–	–		–
AD3	–	–	–	–	–	–		–	–	–
AD4	–	–	2.034	0.203		–	–	–	–	–
AD5	–	–	–	–	–	–	–	–	0.082	0.193
UAPZFM	0.068	0.079	0.059	0.069	–	–	0.080	0.043	0.048	0.036
UAPNFM	0.065	0.389	0.071	0.019	–	–	0.064	1.154	0.060	0.036
SPOPD	0.028	0.047	−0.355	0.075		–	0.823	0.583	0.115	2.165
SPORD	0.047	0.061	−0.111	0.026	–	–	–	–	0.143	0.401
SPOCD	–	–	–	–	–	–		–	–	–
CPE	0.118	0.572	0.128	0.768	–	–	–	–	–	–
CPM	0.000	0.000	0.125	0.376	0.115	0.179	0.128	1.408	0.136	0.155
R^2	0.13		0.32		0.13		0.21		0.36	
R_a^2†	0.08		0.30		0.06		0.08		0.24	
Number of Observations	175		373		61		56		62	

– Variable was zero over all observations.
*Variable is YR for all sizes of KEYB except for the KEYB results for which it is the YR for all sizes of ALTB.
†Adjusted for sample size.

Table B.18 Regression Coefficients and Standard Errors by Brand for Low-Volume Stores for Large Packages for Weeks 33–62

	Brand 1		Brand 2		Brand 4		Brand 5		Brand 7	
Variables	Reg. Coeff.	Std. Error	Reg. Coeff.	Std. Error	Reg. Coeff.	Std. Error	Reg. Coeff.	Std. Error	Reg. Coeff.	Std. Error
OSSB	0.015	0.108	0.348	0.066	−0.127	0.096	0.339	0.624	0.157	0.114
KEYB(ALTB)*	0.074	0.062	0.006	0.047	‡	‡	−0.199	0.235	0.057	0.064
OSOB	0.049	0.021	0.044	0.025	0.110	0.036	−0.350	0.250	0.072	0.026
AD0	–	–	–	–	–	–	–	–	–	–
AD1	–	–	–	–	–	–	–	–	–	–
AD2	0.046	0.355	0.046	0.262	0.315	0.172	0.041	2.941	–	–
AD3	–	–	–	–	–	–	–	–	−0.101	0.102
AD4		–	–	–	1.433	0.166	−0.425	0.918	–	–
AD5	–	–	2.381	0.136	–	–	0.734	0.349	–	–
UAPZFM	0.062	0.062	0.062	0.062	0.069	0.026	0.057	0.044	0.056	0.011
UAPNFM	0.069	0.087	–	–	–	–	0.060	0.287	0.061	0.061
SPOPD	−0.072	0.072	−0.089	0.070	–	–	–	–	–	–
SPORD	0.127	0.377	‡	‡	–	–	−0.814	0.854	–	–
SPOCD	–	–	–	–	–	–	–	–	–	–
CPE	0.129	0.129	0.134	0.045	–	–	–	–	–	–
CPM	0.133	0.053	0.129	0.065	0.142	0.047	0.125	1.003	0.128	0.384
R_2	0.13		0.51		0.69		0.16		0.69	
$R_2{}^a$†	0.06		0.50		0.64		0.00		0.64	
Number of Observations	143		406		49		77		61	

– Variable was zero over all observations.
*Variable is YR for all sizes of KEYB except for the KEYB results for which it is the YR for all sizes of ALTB.
†Adjusted for sample size.
‡Variable deleted because of collinearity.

Bibliography

Bass, F. M. "A Simultaneous-Equation Regression Study of Advertising and Sales Analysis of Cigarette Data," Graduate School of Industrial Administration, Purdue University, June 1967.

Farley, John U. "Estimating Structural Parameters of Marketing Systems: Theory and Application," undated manuscript from the Graduate School of Industrial Administration, Carnegie-Mellon University, 1967.

Frank, Ronald E., and William F. Massy "Market Segmentation and the Effect of a Brand's Price and Dealing Policies," *Journal of Business*, 38 (April 1965): 186–200.

Frank, Ronald E., and William F. Massy. "Estimating the Effects of Short-Term Promotional Strategy on Selected Market Segments," in Patrick Robinson (Ed.), *Promotional Decisions Using Mathematical Models*. Boston: Allyn and Bacon, Inc., 1967.

Goldberger, Arthur S. *Econometric Theory*. New York: John Wiley & Sons, Inc., 1964.

Johnson, J. *Econometric Methods*. New York: McGraw-Hill Book Company, Inc., 1963.

Koyck, L. M. *Distributed Lags and Investment Analysis*. Amsterdam: The North-Holland Publishing Company, 1954.

Massy, William F. "Information and the Marketing Manager: A Systems Analysis," presented at the P. D. Converse Awards Symposium, University of Illinois, April 13–14, 1967.

Massy, William F., and Ronald E. Frank "Short-Term Price and Dealing Elasticities in Selected Market Segments," *Journal of Marketing Research*, 2 (May 1965): 171–185.

Massy, William F., and Ronald E. Frank "An Analysis of Retailer Advertising Behavior," *Journal of Marketing Research*, 3 (November 1966): 378–383.

Index

www.ingramcontent.com/pod-product-compliance
Lightning Source LLC
Chambersburg PA
CBHW061157220326
41599CB00025B/4518

* 9 7 8 0 2 6 2 5 6 1 8 9 1 *